Coteaching Reading Comprehension Strategies in Secondary School Libraries

Coteaching Reading Comprehension Strategies in Secondary School Libraries

Maximizing Your Impact

Judi Moreillon

American Library Association | Chicago 2012

Judi Moreillon is a literacies and libraries consultant and assistant professor in the School of Library and Information Studies at Texas Woman's University. She teaches courses in librarians as instructional partners, school library administration, multimedia resources, storytelling, and children's and young adult literature. Judi earned her master's degree in library science from the School of Information Resources and Library Science at the University of Arizona and a doctorate in education at the same university in the Department of Language, Reading, and Culture. During her thirteen-year tenure as a school librarian, she has collaborated with classroom teachers, specialists, and principals at the elementary, middle, and high school levels to integrate literature and information literacy into the classroom curriculum. Judi has also served as a district-level school librarian mentor, a literacy coach, a classroom teacher, and a preservice classroom teacher educator. She chaired the American Association of School Librarians (AASL) School Librarian's Role in Reading Task Force and served on the AASL Guidelines and Standards Implementation Task Force. Judi is currently researching the leadership and instructional partnership roles of school librarians and factors that influence preservice classroom teachers' understanding and practice of classroom-library collaboration.

Printed in the United States of America
16 15 14 13 12   5 4 3 2 1

Extensive effort has gone into ensuring the reliability of the information in this book; however, the publisher makes no warranty, express or implied, with respect to the material contained herein.

ISBNs: 978-0-8389-1088-7 (paper); 978-0-8389-9356-9 (PDF). For more information on digital formats, visit the ALA Store at alastore.ala.org and select eEditions.

Library of Congress Cataloging-in-Publication Data
Moreillon, Judi.
  Coteaching reading comprehension strategies in secondary school libraries : maximizing your impact / Judi Moreillon.
      p. cm.
  Includes bibliographical references and index.
  ISBN 978-0-8389-1088-7 (alk. paper)
  1. Reading comprehension—Study and teaching (Secondary) 2. Reading comprehension—Study and teaching (Middle school) 3. School librarian participation in curriculum planning. I. Title.
  LB1573.7.M66 2012
  375'.0010880278—dc23

                                                                    2011029708

Cover design by Kirstin Krutsch. Cover image © auremar/Shutterstock, Inc.
Interior design in St. Marie and Berkeley by Casey Bayer.

♾ This paper meets the requirements of ANSI/NISO Z39.48-1992 (Permanence of Paper).

To every educator who commits to helping students strive to become more engaged, effective, and critical readers

Contents

Supplemental materials, including lesson plan graphic organizers, available online as web extras.
See www.alaeditions.org/webextras/.

Acknowledgments

The lesson plans in this book represent my collaborative work with seventh- to twelfth-grade classroom teachers and school librarians too numerous to name here individually. I know I have been blessed to teach and learn in the company of my peers. Thank you all.

I am grateful for the trust of my editor, Stephanie Zvirin. My long-time friend and public librarian colleague, Mary Margaret Mercado, allowed me to pick her brain regularly and freely shared her professional advice on many aspects of this book. Thank you also to my school librarianship thinking partners, Debbie Abilock and Kristin Fontichiaro, for countless stimulating conversations.

Graduate assistant Liz Sikes and artist Jonathan Thompson breathed life into my script for the GoAnimate cartoon that presents the analogy between the car and the seven reading comprehension strategies. It was a wild ride to work with you! Editorial cartoonist David Fitzsimmons generously contributed his cartoon "Asterisk" for use in this book. Thank you also to artist Amy Stewart who created the comics for chapter 6, and to musician Sarah Alexander who composed "Take a Drive" expressly for the "slow side" of the "Fix-up Options: Read the Signs!" Animoto video. Qian Liu, Chinese Studies and South Asian Studies librarian at Arizona State University, graciously served as the cultural advisor for my retelling of "The Great Deed of Li Ji." Thank you for sharing your heritage knowledge and research.

A group of middle and high school librarians whom I called the Impact 10 Cadre inspired and urged me on as I developed lesson plans they could adapt for their own teaching environments. A special thank you to Sabrina Carnesi and Joan Reichel; you were especially pivotal in moving my work forward.

Finally, and most important, I am grateful for the love and encouragement of my husband, Nick Vitale, whose understanding helps make it possible for me to pursue my dreams.

Introduction

Teacher isolation is so deeply ingrained in the traditional fabric of schools that leaders cannot simply invite teachers to create a collaborative culture. They must identify and implement specific, strategic interventions that help teachers to work together rather than alone.

—Richard DuFour

The goal of *Coteaching Reading Comprehension Strategies in Secondary School Libraries: Maximizing Your Impact* is to help educators develop coteaching strategies to ensure student achievement, particularly in reading, a skill that impacts student success in every content area. It is founded on the belief that two heads—or more—are better than one. Coteaching improves practice for educators at the point of need, at the point of instruction. Research has shown a positive correlation between increased student achievement and school librarians and classroom teachers who engage in coplanning and coteaching (Achterman 2008).

In a study of principals who participated in an online course called "School Library Advocacy for Administrators," one administrator said: "We need to help the classroom teaching staff change their philosophy of what the school librarian can be in our building. I would like to see a shift toward collaboration and toward a new thinking about the librarian's role as an instructional partner" (Levitov 2009). Classroom-library collaboration for instruction is one strategic intervention that leaders can implement in order to build a collaborative culture in schools. Working together, school librarians, classroom teachers, specialists, administrators, and families can create dynamic learning communities in which what is best for student learning is at the heart of every decision. In these communities everyone is invested in everyone else's success. Through coteaching and sharing responsibility for all students in the school, educators can strengthen their academic programs, and school librarians can position the work of the school library program at the center of academic learning.

This book is about coteaching reading comprehension strategies. At the secondary level, content area textbooks, many trade books, classic literature, and other resources are particularly dense and can be challenging for many teen readers. These texts require educators to scaffold reading engagements by selecting shorter passages and modeling comprehension strategies using graphic organizers to support student learning. The online supplemental materials for this book facilitate modeling the strategies and include graphic organizing tools for students and completed teacher resources. When appropriate, sample writing pieces are available for reference. These web extra resources free up collaborators to focus on coteaching, monitoring, and assessing student learning. Once educators have read the strategy chapters, the web support makes these sample lessons ready to use on Monday morning. Find these supplements on the ALA Editions web extras site at www.alaeditions.org/webextras/.

While conducting research for this book and my previous book on this topic, which was targeted to an elementary and intermediate school readership, I have learned a great deal about literacy education that guides my teaching practices. The unfortunate, and somehow still surprising, aspect of this research is that the work of school librarians and the role of school library programs are rarely, if ever, mentioned outside of our own publications. National literacy research and initiatives such as *Reading Next—A Vision for Action and Research in Middle and High School Literacy: A Report to the Carnegie Corporation of New York* (Biancarosa and Snow 2006) do not address school library programs, resources, or professional staff. Educational publishers release new books that share case studies of how educators are using new texts and addressing new literacies—and school librarians are not mentioned. It is as though we are invisible to others. Sadly, this may be part of the reason many schools have eliminated professional school librarians from their indispensable list of faculty positions. How can we reverse this trend?

One way is to improve the practice of school librarians and maximize the impact of school library programs on student achievement. I wrote this book to support the collaborative work of middle and high school librarians who want to develop their understanding of teaching reading comprehension strategies. I wrote it for educators who want to increase their expertise in using currently recognized best practices in instruction. School librarians with whom I hope to share this work understand that, in order to make an impact on student achievement, they must teach what really matters in their schools. The most effective way to do that is to teach standards-based lessons every day in collaboration with classroom teacher and specialist colleagues. "Fundamentally, the school librarian's effectiveness as a literacy leader depends on a commitment to ongoing learning about literacy education" (Achterman 2010, 41). Through coteaching and other forms of professional development, school librarians can achieve a leadership role on their literacy teams.

I have targeted preservice school librarians as a readership for this book. As students in school librarianship prepare for their careers, I hope they embrace the mission of the school library program as a hub of learning. The coteaching strategies offered in this book can help them make their instructional partnership role a top priority. This book can help preservice librarians learn the vocabulary and practices that guide the work of their classroom teacher colleagues. This can help them be better prepared to enter the profession, ready to create partnerships that will impact student learning.

Preservice classroom teachers are another readership for this book. All elementary education majors at Emporia State University were required to successfully complete a course titled "The Elementary Teacher and the Library Media Specialist: Partners in Teaching Literature Appreciation and Information Literacy." For four semesters from fall 2008 through spring 2010 and in all five sections of the course, preservice teachers read my previous book, *Collaborative Strategies for Teaching Reading Comprehension: Maximizing Your Impact* (Moreillon 2007). The goal of the course was to teach future elementary teachers the roles and responsibilities of the school librarian in teaching reading comprehension skills, as well as the responsibility to seek out classroom-library collaboration for reading and information literacy instruction (Dow 2010). In "Library Materials for Children," a Texas Woman's University course for undergraduate preservice classroom teachers, I use that book to illuminate the invaluable instructional partnerships that classroom teachers and school librarians can build.

I hope classroom teachers, literacy coaches, specialists, and principals find this book useful in their work. The collaborative strategies presented in this book can be applied in many coteaching situations. The book can support lesson study, professional reading study groups, and site-level or district-level staff development efforts. School librarians can share this book with their administrators and colleagues as a seed that can contribute to growing a culture of collaboration in their schools.

From my experience as a teacher educator, I learned that beginning classroom teachers need help locating appropriate and effective resources. They need a great deal of support to learn curriculum design. They need to know how to integrate performance objectives from more than one content area into each of their lessons. They benefit from explicit modeling and from specific feedback about their teaching. With more novices entering the profession, there is a real need to provide support for new teachers so they can be successful—so they are motivated to remain in the profession and continue to develop as educators.

From my experience as a school librarian, most recently in a seventh- to twelfth-grade combined middle and high school facility, veteran teachers also want and need instructional partnerships. They need coteachers who will take risks with them in learning and integrating new technology tools. They need partners who will help them step outside of the comfort zone of the units they have taught in the past, from lessons that have grown stale and generate little enthusiasm from students. They want to be lifelong learners in the company of their peers. School librarians, whose schedules are variable, who have developed effective interpersonal skills, and who create a welcoming, rigorous learning environment in the library are positioned to serve as instructional partners with each and every member of the school learning community.

This book is my way of sharing the "library story" from my own experience as a practitioner. "The most powerful forms of professional learning are embedded in teachers' daily work, address the core tasks of teaching, and support teachers in forming productive relationships with colleagues and students" (Sparks 2007, 169). The strategies presented in this book describe the high-level coteaching exemplified in the most effective school library programs. The complexity of 21st-century literacy learning requires educators to collaborate to ensure that all students, regardless of their background and prior achievement, develop 21st-century skills for success.

With members of an undergraduate teacher preparation cohort, I conducted a longitudinal study titled "Two Heads Are Better Than One: The Factors Influencing the Understanding and Practice of Classroom-Library Collaboration" (Moreillon 2008). This is a summary of what I learned. When these K–8 preservice teachers stepped into the building where they conducted their student teaching experience or first year of classroom teaching, little of what we had done in the university classroom made a significant difference. If their cooperating teacher or colleagues had a value for classroom-library collaboration and worked with the school librarian, so did the student teacher or first-year teacher. If the school librarian was someone who reached out to support the work of new educators in the building, then the student teacher or new teacher collaborated with the library program. If there was a paraprofessional or an incompetent school librarian serving in the library, or if a rigid library schedule did not provide opportunities for classroom teachers to have their curriculum needs met, then new educators did not collaborate with the library staff. If the library staff was unwelcoming, these teachers and the students in their care simply did not use the library at all.

The bottom line is this: Our profession is only as strong as each individual who serves in the role of school librarian. Each school librarian is the representative of the profession for the stakeholders in her school community. School librarians must take responsibility for developing the necessary skills and professional dispositions required for teaching in

21st-century libraries (Fontichiaro, Moreillon, and Abilock 2009). This book will provide you with background knowledge in literacy instruction based on research and writing in the fields of education and librarianship and sample lessons to adapt with educators with whom you serve for the students in your collective care. Will you apply this information to make a ripple or to make a wave in the literacy program in your school? It's up to you.

Finally, I have used the term *school librarian* in this book because it was adopted in 2010 by the American Association of School Librarians as the official term for professionals who serve in this role. I personally prefer the term *teacher-librarian* and have used that term to describe myself during the twenty years I have served in the profession. However, because school librarians in some states are not required to have classroom teacher preparation, certification, or experience, teacher-librarian is not appropriate for everyone practicing our profession. Just as I believe that all educators who call themselves school librarians should have graduate-level library science education and be state certified, I would suggest that people who lack teacher preparation and certification not call themselves teacher-librarians. I believe that preparation and certification really do matter.

Collaborative Teaching in the Age of Accountability

People learn by watching one another, seeing various ways to solve a single problem, sharing their different "takes" on a concept or struggle, and developing a common language with which to talk about their goals, their work, and their ways of monitoring their progress or diagnosing their difficulties. When teachers publicly display what they are thinking, they learn from one another, but they also learn through articulating their ideas, justifying their views, and making valid arguments.

—Alison Zmuda and Violet H. Harada

Today's young adults need increasingly sophisticated literacy skills in order to be successful students, effective workers, and involved citizens. In our knowledge-based society, 21st-century youth will read and write and use technology tools more than any other generation in human history. They will engage with and produce texts in more formats than most of their grandparents can imagine. As the literacy bar is being raised for all of us, too many young people are not adequately prepared to participate in this complex new world. "In October 2005, approximately 3.5 million 16- through 24-year-olds were not enrolled in high school and had not earned a high school diploma or alternative credential such as a GED" (Laird, Kienzl, DeBell, and Chapman 2007, 6). This is approaching 10 percent of all youth in that age bracket. But dropouts are not the only challenge today. Both dropouts and high school graduates are demonstrating less proficient reading skills than they did ten years ago (NCES 2005). As life becomes more complex, too many young adults are underprepared to be informed, productive members of our nation and the global society.

In this environment, the demands on middle and high school educators are at an all-time peak. Although there are many variables that affect student achievement, including socioeconomic factors, motivation, curriculum relevance, quality and quantity of print and digital resources, and quality of instruction, society has primarily focused on teacher proficiency as the target for improvement. The pressure on individual educators to measure learning in terms of student achievement on standardized tests has never been more intense and competitive.

Fortunately, many leaders and decision makers within the education community have come to value the potential impact of *teaching partnerships* for improving instruction and student learning. While complying with government regulations such as Response to Intervention or engaging in site-based initiatives such as professional learning communities and lesson study, individual schools and entire districts are raising the bar for collaboration among faculty members. Working within collaborative structures, curriculum planning, joint lesson design, coteaching, and coassessment are becoming more valued, more widely practiced—and more effective. In this culture of collaboration, coteaching among classroom teachers, reading and literacy specialists, special education teachers, and school librarians can contribute to improvements in educator proficiency and student learning.

How can school librarians maximize the potential of this trend? Will serving on teaching teams as essential educators have an impact on student achievement, particularly in literacy instruction? The American Association of School Librarians (AASL) adopted a Position Statement on the School Librarian's Role in Reading (AASL 2009b). The rationale for the statement also appears in *Empowering Learners: Guidelines for School Library Media Programs* (AASL 2009a). These are some of the reasons why and how school librarians can be key contributors to achievement in reading in their schools:

1. Reading is a foundational skill for 21st-century learners.

2. Guiding learners to become engaged and effective users of ideas and information and to appreciate literature requires that they develop as strategic readers who can comprehend, analyze, and evaluate text in both print and digital formats.

3. The extent to which young people use information depends on their ability to under-

stand what they read, to integrate that understanding with what they already know, and to form their unanswered questions.

4. Twenty-first-century learners must become adept at determining authority and accuracy of information and analyzing and evaluating that information to synthesize new knowledge from multiple resources.

5. The school librarian has a key role in supporting print and online reading comprehension strategy instruction in collaboration with classroom teachers and reading specialists.

6. School librarians codesign, coimplement, and coevaluate interdisciplinary lessons and units of instruction that result in increased student learning (AASL 2009a, 22–23).

As the position statement notes: "School librarians are in a critical and unique position to partner with other educators to elevate the reading development of our nation's youth" (AASL 2009a, 22).

This statement appears in the *Standards for the 21st-Century Learner* under the common belief related to reading: "The degree to which students can read and understand text in all formats (e.g., picture, video, print) and in all contexts is a key indicator of success in school and in life" (AASL 2007). In short, students must be proficient readers in order to become information literate, but far too many are not. In fact, at the secondary level where reading classic literature and difficult textbooks in the content areas requires sophisticated vocabulary and content-specific reading strategies, all adolescents are challenged to a greater or lesser extent to comprehend these texts and to master the expected content area knowledge (Brozo and Simpson 2007). It is important to note that the Common Core Standards (http://corestandards.org) emphasize reading in social studies and science classes as well as language arts. This presents a timely opportunity for school librarians to support content area teachers through coteaching reading strategies using subject-specific texts.

The most recent report of the Carnegie Council on Advancing Adolescent Literacy, "Time to Act: An

Agenda for Advancing Adolescent Literacy for College and Career Success" (2010), posits that adolescent literacy should be a national priority and the overarching focus of school reform efforts. According to the report, successful adolescent literacy initiatives focus on professional development for teachers and the effective use of data. Unfortunately for our profession, the words *librarian* and *school library* do not appear anywhere in this report. (Students conducting research in libraries is mentioned once; classroom libraries is mentioned twice.) Still, secondary school libraries with their wide array of resources and effective programs headed by professional school librarians are positioned to serve as hubs for adolescent literacy initiatives within school learning communities.

Biancarosa and Snow (2006) suggest fifteen key elements of effective adolescent literacy programs. Figure 1-1 aligns AASL's *Position Statement on the School Librarian's Role in Reading* with most of these key elements.

There are several elements of effective adolescent literacy programs such as strategic tutoring and intensive writing that are not addressed in AASL's position statement. However, several other elements not noted above can be implied as components of effective instruction, namely, extended time for literacy and ongoing formative assessment of students and ongoing summative assessment of students and programs. All types of assessments are aspects of the evidence-based practice included in AASL's position statement.

SCHOOL LIBRARIANS AS LITERACY LEADERS

In *Empowering Learners: Guidelines for School Library Media Programs* (AASL 2009a), the critical role of "leader" has been added to the school librarian's roles of instructional partner, information specialist, teacher, and program administrator. These new guidelines charge school librarians with positioning the library at the center of the academic program and taking a leadership position in order to impact teaching and learning throughout the school community. With access to a variety of resources in every discipline and

in various formats at a wide range of reading levels, what is the best way for school librarians to maximize their influence as coleaders in adolescent literacy initiatives? School librarians must effectively integrate literacy instruction into library instruction.

Although research has consistently shown that ready access to a wide variety of reading materials increases the chances that students will become readers and choose to read (Krashen 2004), serving as recreational reading motivators and nurturers is not enough. If all educators are literacy teachers as "Time to Act" (2010) asserts, then school librarians must join with teachers in every content area to support student achievement in reading through systematic instruction. Forming partnerships with classroom teachers and specialists to teach students how to employ their decoding skills and make meaning from text is natural work for school librarians and school library programs.

Classroom-library collaborative instruction can include how-to reading comprehension strategy lessons in order to reach all students while they are engaged with library resources and content across disciplines. These lessons and units of instruction can become the "assured" learning experiences in which every student in the school participates during a particular course or at a specific grade level. Some possible examples include a health and wellness unit in which all eighth-grade students engage, a junior research paper in history, or a senior project in science and technology. The school librarian can play a key role in codeveloping these units, coteaching to the targeted learning objectives, and coassessing students' mastery of literacy skills and the effectiveness of instruction. Librarians can participate in collecting data, analyzing it, reporting on it, and modifying instruction in order to ensure that students are learning through these assured experiences.

The practices put forward in this book move school librarians up the taxonomy to the highest instructional design levels, where they serve as full partners with classroom teachers in coteaching lessons supported by the resources of the school library and beyond (Loertscher 2000). In the age of accountability, this level of involvement in the school's academic

Fig. 1-1 Alignment of Selected Bullet Points from the *Position Statement on the School Librarian's Role in Reading* (AASL 2009b) and the Fifteen Key Elements for Effective Adolescent Literacy Programs (Biancarosa and Snow 2006)

*Position Statement on the School Librarian's Role in Reading**	Selections from the Fifteen Key Elements for Effective Adolescent Literacy Programs
Library media centers provide students, staff, and families with open, nonrestricted access to a varied high-quality collection of reading materials in multiple formats that reflect academic needs and personal interests.	• Diverse texts • A technology component
School librarians practice responsive collection development and support print-rich environments that reflect the curriculum and diverse learning needs of the school community.	• Diverse texts
School librarians take a leadership role in organizing and promoting literacy projects and events that engage learners and motivate them to become lifelong readers.	• Motivation and self-directed learning
Classroom teachers, reading specialists, and school librarians select materials, promote the curricular and independent use of resources (including traditional and alternative materials), and plan learning experiences that offer whole classes, small groups, and individual learners an interdisciplinary approach to literacy learning.	• Effective instructional principles embedded in content • A technology component • Teacher teams
Classroom and library collaborative instruction is evidence-based, using research in librarianship, reading, English-language arts, and educational technology in order to maximize student learning. School librarians partner with classroom teachers, specialists, and other literacy colleagues to make decisions about reading initiatives and reading comprehension instruction, and to develop all learners' curiosity in and intellectual access to appropriate resources in all formats and media.	• Direct, explicit comprehension instruction • Text-based collaborative learning • Motivation and self-directed learning • Teacher teams • A comprehensive and coordinated literacy program
When learners follow an inquiry process they assess and use reading comprehension strategies. The skills identified in the *Standards for the 21st-Century Learner* align with the reading process.	• Direct, explicit comprehension instruction
Opportunities for planned and spontaneous library use best serve learners as they identify, analyze, and synthesize ideas and information by using a wide range of materials in a variety of formats and media. Availability of library resources and professional staff at point of need encourages intellectual behaviors that transfer to future academic pursuits and lifelong academic and public library use.	• Motivation and self-directed learning • Diverse texts • A technology component
Along with classroom and reading specialist colleagues, school librarians provide and participate in continual professional development in reading that reflects current research in the area of reading instruction and promotion.	• Professional development • Teacher teams • Leadership • A comprehensive and coordinated literacy program

program is a necessity. Students, classroom teacher and specialist colleagues, and administrators should understand through firsthand experience and be able to cite examples of the central role of the school librarian in the school's literacy program. Throughout the school day, school librarians serve in various capacities, depending on the needs of students, classroom teachers, and specialists, but the goal should always be to spend the majority of time and energy at the top of the taxonomy, as full-fledged collaborating members of their school's instructional teams.

STRATEGIES FOR COLLABORATIVE TEACHING

What does it mean to collaborate? Friend and Cook explain interpersonal collaboration as "a style for direct interaction between at least two coequal parties voluntarily engaged in shared decision making as they work toward a common goal" (2010, 7). Collaboration describes *how* people work together rather than *what* they do. It is a dynamic, interactive process between equal partners who strive together to reach excellence.

Collaborative teaching involves an ongoing, engaging relationship. On the other hand, coteaching can occur in limited form with minimal collaboration. Although the title of the book contains the word *coteaching*, the goal of team teaching the sample lesson plans is to plant seeds from which coteaching can blossom into true collaborative instructional partnerships.

Collaboration can happen in the planning, implementation, and assessment stages of teaching. Ideally, it happens at all three. In the planning process, educators establish shared goals and specific learning outcomes for students as well as codevelop assessment tools to evaluate student outcomes. They discuss students' background knowledge, prior learning experiences, and skill development, and determine what resources will best meet learners' needs (see www .alaeditions.org/webextras/ for sample Collaborative Planning Forms).

Educators decide on one or more coteaching approaches, assign responsibilities for particular aspects of the lesson, and schedule teaching time based on the needs of students and the requirements of the learning tasks. Figure 1-2 shows possible coteaching configurations (Friend and Cook 2010, 120–28). Depending on the lesson, students' prior knowledge and skill development, areas of expertise of educators, and the level of trust with one another, collaborators can assume one or more of these roles during a lesson or unit of instruction.

Of these five approaches, team teaching requires the most collaboration and is the approach needed to most effectively teach the sample lessons offered in this book. Team teaching requires careful planning, respect for each educator's style, and ultimately a shared belief in the value that this level of risk taking can offer students and educators. Collaborative work can be supported or hindered by school culture. In order to be most effective, principals must set expectations and educators must welcome coteaching and use shared planning time for collaborative work. They must value the investment in time and effort. A shared spirit of experimentation and the commitment to developing trust are essential when adult learners form instructional partnerships. Respect for each other's areas of expertise and willingness by all to continue learning are critical to successful collaboration. School librarians, working within a supportive learning community, must develop interpersonal skills as well as teaching expertise that can allow team teaching to flourish.

After coplanning and coimplementing lessons and units of instruction, it is logical that evaluating student learning products is part of a shared responsibility for coteaching. Checklists, rating scales, rubrics, and self-reflections, developed with colleagues or with students in advance of the lesson or early in the unit, establish the criteria for formative assessments during the lesson or summative assessment at the end of a unit. Students should use these tools to guide, revise, and self-assess their work. Educators can use the same criteria to inform their teaching and to assess students' learning processes and their final products.

Educators may decide to divide assessment on the basis of components of the lesson for which each one took primary responsibility. For example, school librarians may take the lead in teaching notemaking skills and may then take responsibility for assessing students' notes with a rubric. Joint assessment can happen before designing a lesson when educators administer pretests to determine the students' level of skill development or prior knowledge of a particular topic or concept. Even if they did not coteach a lesson, educators might ask one another to provide another set of eyes to evaluate the effectiveness of instruction based on students' learning products. In *Assessing Learning: Librarians and Teachers as Partners*, Harada and Yoshina (2005) provide a comprehensive guide to best practices in assessment.

Coassessing the lesson or unit of instruction is too often overlooked. After coplanning, coteaching, and coassessing students' work, instructional partners must make time to debrief in order to determine which aspects of the lesson helped students meet the learning objectives and which components need revision. If educators are team teaching, then some of this evaluation occurs as they share responsibility for monitoring learning and adjusting teaching while the lesson or unit is in progress. Returning to diagnostic data, such as a content-specific pretest or information literacy pretest like TRAILS: Tool for Real-time Assessment of Information Literacy Skills (www.trails-9.org), provides educators with information they need to analyze summative achievement data. Evaluating these data and reflecting on the lesson or unit after it has been taught are important for instructional improvement and for educators' professional growth. These best practices help educators clearly articulate the relationships between their goals and objectives for student learning and student outcomes. Reflective practitioners focus on students' learning to improve their own practice and revise instruction.

COLLABORATION AND SCHOOL REFORM

Why is collaboration necessary in our schools? What could happen if classroom teachers and school

---

Fig. 1-2   Coteaching Approaches

One Teaching, One Supporting	One educator is responsible for teaching the lesson while the other observes the lesson, monitors particular students, and/or provides assistance as needed.
Station or Center Teaching	After determining curriculum content for multiple learning stations, each educator takes responsibility for facilitating one or more learning centers while in other centers students work independently of adult support.
Parallel Teaching	After collaborative planning, each educator works with half the class to teach the same or similar content. Groups may switch and/or reconvene as a whole class to share, debrief, and/or reflect.
Alternative Teaching	One educator preteaches or reteaches concepts to a small group while the other educator teaches a different lesson to the larger group. (Preteaching vocabulary or other lesson components can be especially valuable for English-language learners or special needs students.)
Team Teaching	Educators teach together by assuming different roles during instruction, such as reader or recorder or questioner and responder, modeling partner work, role-playing or debating, and more.

Adapted from Friend and Cook (2010)

librarians combined their expertise and talents to share responsibility for teaching students? Barth observes that collegial relationships in schools are both "highly prized" and "highly elusive" preconditions for school reform, and in a collegial school he would expect to see educators

- talking about practice,
- sharing craft knowledge,
- observing one another while they are engaged in practice, and
- rooting for one another's success (2006, 11).

Classroom-library collaboration meets all four of these criteria. When educators coplan, coimplement, and coassess lessons and units of instruction, they cannot help but talk about practice, share craft knowledge, observe one another teaching, and root for one another's success. Through coteaching, educators develop a common language, a common set of practices, and channels for communication that can increase student learning and help the entire school community better serve the academic and social needs of students and families.

In *What Works in Schools: Translating Research into Action,* Marzano (2003) shares thirty-five years of research related to improving student achievement as measured by standardized tests. He delineates school-level, teacher-level, and student-level factors that affect student achievement. At the school level, a guaranteed and viable curriculum, challenging goals and feedback, parent and community involvement, a safe and orderly environment, and collegiality and professionalism all had positive impacts on student outcomes. At the teacher level, instructional strategies, classroom management, and classroom curriculum design improved student achievement. At the student level, the home atmosphere, learned intelligence and background knowledge, and motivation all affected students' learning. Many of these factors including collegiality, instructional strategies, and curriculum design are directly addressed in this book.

Students come to school with varying background knowledge, learning styles, linguistic and cultural heritages, values and beliefs about learning, and prior experiences with schooling. The resulting diversity among students requires that schools continuously adapt and step up to meet each individual learner's needs. Today's school reform movements are based in large part on the challenge of making sure all students have the opportunities they need to reach their potential. Collaborative teaching between classroom teachers, specialists, and school librarians using the strategies suggested in this book benefits students because it puts the focus on learning outcomes. Coteaching also positively impacts adult learning as well. Figure 1-3 outlines the benefits of collaborative teaching to both students and educators.

In school restructuring, teacher isolation is a powerful impediment to reform. "Teachers must become 21st century learners themselves, learning from inquiry, design, and collaborative approaches that build a strong community of professional educators" (Trilling and Fadel 2009, 124). Just as learning is social for students, it is also social for adults. Innovations in teaching cannot spread throughout a learning community if educators remain isolated, separated in their classrooms or libraries. As figure 1-3 clearly shows, educators who teach collaboratively not only improve student learning but also create learning opportunities for themselves and for each other. This model for practicing job-embedded professional development should be of interest to school site and district-level administrators.

PROFESSIONAL DEVELOPMENT AT THE POINT OF PRACTICE

Adult learning in schools is best implemented at the point of practice. My experience as both a literacy coach and a school librarian confirms Zmuda and Harada's assertion: "Informal leaders are better suited to coaching the work at the classroom level based on identified learning principles and practices, whereas formal leaders are better suited to the enforcement of such principles and practices" (2008, 31). School librarians, who wisely create a shared professional development space in the library and

Fig. 1-3   Benefits of Classroom-Library Collaboration Based on Coteaching

For Students . . .	For Educators . . .
More individualized attention	More opportunities to work one-on-one with students
Better designed lessons	Clarification of goals and objectives through joint planning; coassessment of lesson effectiveness
Increased opportunity for differentiated instruction	Improved facilitation of differentiated instruction
Access to information at the point of need	Literature and information literacy skills integrated in a meaningful way into the classroom curriculum
Access to multiple resources, including technology	Shared responsibility for gathering engaging, effective resources
More engagement due to fewer distractions	Fewer classroom management issues
More material or deeper investigations into concepts and topics	More teaching time (due to fewer management issues and scheduling to achieve student learning objectives)
Expanded opportunities for creativity	Expanded opportunities for creativity
Acquiring of skills for lifelong learning	Personal and professional growth opportunities through coteaching and coassessment of student learning
Integrated learning	Integrated teaching

its accompanying computer labs, offer colleagues an opportunity to model and practice lifelong learning alongside them in a nonthreatening environment. Some have called this model the "Information Commons," where student learning and curriculum and professional development are focused in the physical and virtual space of the school library (Loertscher, Koechlin, and Zwaan 2008).

Rather than being a formal one-day or separate event, effective professional development should be more informal, a regular part of an educator's everyday work. It should occur in real time, with real students and real curriculum, and within the real support and constraints in which students learn and teachers teach. Ongoing, continuous improvement in teaching practices is necessary if educators are to ensure that diverse learners have the maximum opportunity for achievement. Classroom-library collaboration for instruction can succeed if educators approach this model as reciprocal mentorship between two coequal

partners whose goal is to engage students in learning and to improve their own teaching practices.

"The single most effective way in which principals can function as staff development leaders is providing a school context that fosters job-embedded professional development" (DuFour 2001, 14–15). School principals are central figures in building a culture of collaboration within the school learning community. They must provide educators with time to coplan during contract hours. They can support coteaching by endorsing collaborative teaching for performance evaluations and by spotlighting effective collaborative teaching in faculty meetings and in newsletters to families. As instructional leaders, principals are pivotal in establishing value for collaborative teaching.

Using resources as an entrée, school librarians have natural opportunities to begin curriculum conversations. These conversations provide doors through which school librarians can invite and initiate classroom-library collaboration for instruction.

The model for collaborative teaching offered in this book is founded on parity and shared risk taking. The resulting coteaching fosters job-embedded professional development for classroom teachers, specialists, and school librarians that will impact the literacy learning in their schools.

If educators hope to prepare young people for living and working in the 21st century, and they target 21st-century skill objectives in their lessons, then they should be mindful of the ways they do or do not model these behaviors for students. What is the covert curriculum in our schools? What attitudes and behaviors are educators modeling as they teach a standards-based curriculum? *Empowering Learners: Guidelines for School Library Media Programs* (AASL 2009a) and organizations such as the Partnership for 21st Century Skills (P21 2006) charge educators with teaching learning and thinking skills such as critical thinking, problem solving, collaboration, communication, and information and media literacy. Coteaching is one way for educators to model and practice these behaviors. "The idea of making classrooms into learning communities for students will remain more rhetoric than real unless schools become learning communities for teachers, too" (Wald and Castleberry 2000, 136).

The organic nature of the classroom-library collaboration model offers on-site, job-embedded professional development integrated into the daily practice of educators. Through shared responsibility, collaborators create opportunities for reciprocal mentoring and ongoing shared reflection. Collaboration for instruction lowers student-to-teacher ratios. More students have opportunities for individualized attention, and groups of students can be better supported as they learn essential skills and content in different ways. Two or more educators can monitor and adjust teaching and assess students' learning processes and products as well as evaluate the lessons themselves. The opportunity to learn alongside a colleague as an equal improves teaching practices for novice as well as veteran educators.

School librarians' effectiveness as educators may hinge on being considered a peer by classroom teacher colleagues and coequals with classroom teachers by administrators. As Zmuda and Harada attest: "Effective partnerships help teachers to meet their existing priorities, which include the implementation of a standards-based curriculum" (2008, 38). With the current emphasis on accountability, school librarians must meet the imperative to foster student achievement through effective instruction. But until school librarians serve as full members of instructional teams, their true value as educators cannot be measured.

2

Maximizing Your Impact

No subject of study is more important than reading.... All other intellectual powers depend on it.

—Jacques Barzun

Literacy is a foundational tool; it is also a lifelong process. In the 21st century, there is universal agreement on the goal of developing the higher-order thinking capabilities of our nation's youth. This ability is founded on literacy. Comprehension, critical thinking, reasoning, and problem solving are top priorities (Fullan 2003). In order to achieve this level of excellence and equity in education, educators must be fully engaged and empowered to create, develop, and monitor the conditions for success for all students. That means educators and students must take the literacy learning journey together.

At the middle and high school levels, educators can set the expectation that each of us, youth and adults, is engaged in an ongoing process of *becoming* literate as we interact with increasingly diverse texts using an array of ever-changing tools and devices. Taking a stance of learning *with* adolescents creates opportunities for openness, experimentation, and democracy in classrooms and libraries. The dynamic context of living and working in this time and place requires that we be so engaged.

However, "[s]ome 70 percent of older readers require some form of remediation. Very few of these older struggling readers need help to read the words on the page; their most common problem is that they are not able to comprehend what they read" (Biancarosa and Snow 2006, 3). If a solid majority of secondary students can benefit from reading comprehension instruction, what does providing "intellectual access" mean for school library programs today? Embedding reading comprehension strategies in content area curriculum lessons is one way to ensure that students have opportunities to develop these strategies (Alger 2009) and achieve a "higher level of competence" in reading (RAND Reading Study Group 2002).

Many practitioners and scholars alike who write about literacy teaching in secondary schools affirm that students can improve reading proficiency with regular, direct instruction in reading comprehension strategies. An interdisciplinary team-oriented approach that includes ongoing professional development and involves content area teachers as well as specialists has a greater chance of improving students' literacy levels (Biancarosa and Snow 2006). School librarians must be literacy leaders and members of these interdisciplinary teams.

Reading comprehension strategies are tools that proficient readers use to solve the comprehension problems they encounter in texts. Learning and practicing these strategies does not end at elementary school. Secondary students must continue to develop and practice strategies with different genres and text formats in different content areas for different purposes. The sociocultural context of reading at the secondary level often includes higher expectations for comprehension and the ability to use texts in socially appropriate ways as determined by school-based expectations. For example, students are often assigned reading as homework. This can involve them in reading more difficult texts within shorter periods of time isolated from the support of peers and teachers.

In this book, I define seven reading comprehension strategies. Readers who learn and employ these strategies have tools they can use to solve comprehension problems:

1. Activating or building background knowledge

2. Using sensory images

3. Questioning

4. Making predictions and drawing inferences

5. Determining main ideas

6. Using fix-up options

7. Synthesizing

Each of the following chapters defines one of these reading comprehension strategies, discusses considerations for teaching it, offers young adult literature resources, and presents three sample how-to strategy lessons that will help students use the strategies to make meaning from text. The lessons are intended as models for educators to modify to meet the needs of the learners in their care and to adapt for the content of their school curricula. The lessons include before, during, and after reading strategies that help students develop as readers who understand their own thinking processes, who practice metacognition.

The seven strategies discussed in this book also align with those needed to successfully answer standardized test questions. "State reading assessments are increasingly dominated by skills such as the ability to infer; to identify an author's bias or persuasive techniques; to support interpretations or main ideas with evidence from the text; and to summarize, synthesize, analyze, and evaluate" (Schmoker 2006, 40). As students matriculate through the grades, standardized tests are also based more heavily on informational texts, particularly essays, speeches, biographies, and autobiographies. The lessons offered in this book use all genres, but informational texts make up the majority of mentor texts in the sample lessons.

Although the lessons offered in this book can be taught by individual educators, they are designed to maximize opportunities for coteaching and lowering the student-to-teacher ratio during instruction through classroom-library collaboration. The lessons allow educators to work with smaller groups and with individuals because flexible groupings are best facilitated with two or more educators in the same room at the same time. These lessons can also be taught effectively by school librarians in collaboration with classroom and special education teachers, reading and literacy coaches, and curriculum and other specialists.

"Building comprehension must account for many traditional literacy skills but also include strategies to help students read their worlds, include the worlds made of diverse disciplines and filled with media-rich texts" (Sipe 2009, 20). The study of online reading comprehension is relatively new. Online comprehension appears to be related to factors on which most middle and high school librarians currently focus much of their teaching: effective online searching, including the relative importance of search engine hits; determining the authority of website authors; and evaluating the currency, accuracy, and bias of online information (Leu et al. 2005). Integrating texts in various formats and technology tools into the learning process and student products are ways to address student motivation and engagement, which are critical factors in discussions of 21st-century adolescent literacy (Guthrie and Wigfield 2000). Lessons must stimulate teen readers' curiosity and help them make connections and find relevance between school-based and community-based literacy.

FOUNDATIONS AND BEST PRACTICES FOR TEACHING READING COMPREHENSION STRATEGIES

The how-to lessons presented in this book provide models that can guide educators as they help students learn, practice, and master reading strategies. The strategies define what is taught; however, how the lessons were designed and how they are intended to be taught are equally important. These lessons are based on five foundational best practices in instruction and school librarianship: evidence-based practice, backward planning, aligning and integrating information literacy standards with classroom curricula, using research-based instructional strategies, and modeling metacognition with think-alouds.

School librarians can confidently build collaborative practices on the firm foundation of the findings of the School Library Impact Studies conducted at the time of this writing in twenty states and one province (www.lrs.org/impact.php). Assuming adequate library staffing and a well-funded collection, these studies and others show positive correlations between the instructional role of the school librarian and student achievement. Planning with teachers, coteaching, teaching ICT (information and communication technologies), and providing in-services to teachers are among the library predictors of students' academic achievement on standardized tests, particularly in reading and language arts (Achterman 2008, 62–65).

Research aside, practitioners in the field must continually demonstrate to school administrators, classroom colleagues, students, parents and caregivers, and the public at large that their daily practice results in improved student learning. School librarians must understand that everyone is from Missouri, the show-me state, and needs to have proof that school library programs make a difference. Using the sample lessons offered in this book and collecting data from formative assessments, school librarians can advance local academic goals that connect with what matters in most secondary schools today—achievement in reading as a foundational skill for learning in all content areas, including STEM (science, technology, engineering, and math). While coteaching reading comprehension strategies alongside classroom teachers, school librarians gather evidence that shows classroom-library instruction makes a difference in student outcomes.

According to Wiggins and McTighe (2005), effective instructional design begins with determining student learning outcomes. Understanding by design, commonly called backward planning, is a conceptual framework that requires educators to first identify student learning objectives (based on curriculum standards). With its focus on outcomes, the backward design framework is ideal for evidence-based classroom-library collaborative instruction. Learning objectives should be based on pretests, student inventories and reporting, teacher observation, or other data. Standardized assessments also provide data on which to base instruction. Once the intended learning outcomes are identified, educators codevelop assessments to measure student learning.

Standards for the 21st-Century Learner (AASL 2007) are addressed in these strategy lessons. Keywords in the AASL standards are not always readily found in state-level core subject curriculum standards. For example, a reading standard that requires students to "synthesize and make logical connections between ideas within a text and across two or three texts" is aligned with AASL Indicator 1.1.7: "Make sense of information gathered from diverse sources by identifying misconceptions, main and supporting ideas, conflicting information, and point of view or bias." Many states and districts have aligned state and local standards with the AASL standards. For school librarians working in locations that have not done so it is especially important that they be proficient at identifying the terms used in the content area standards that relate to the *Standards for the 21st-Century Learner* and align these and other standards accordingly.

Figure 2-1 shows the alignment between the seven strategies presented in this book and selected AASL standards indicators. Within each state's standards, librarians will find many additional points of alignment. School librarians will also want to consider additional standards initiatives privileged at their school sites, such as the Common Core Standards (http://corestandards.org), the skills outlined by the Partnership for 21st Century Skills (www.p21.org), or the NETS, the International Society for Technology in Education Standards for Students (www.iste .org/Content/NavigationMenu/NETS/ForStudents/ NETS_for_Students.htm).

In *Classroom Instruction That Works: Research-based Strategies for Increasing Student Achievement,* Marzano, Pickering, and Pollock (2001) offer a summary of a meta-analysis of studies conducted by researchers at Mid-continent Research for Education and Learning. These studies analyzed the effectiveness of specific components of instruction. The authors identified nine instructional strategies that have a strong effect on student achievement; six of these are used as support for the how-to lessons in this book. Figure 2-2 identifies the strategies selected for the lessons and the related percentile gains for student achievement on standardized tests.

The gain figures in figure 2-2 are based on an average student being exposed to a particular strategy compared with a student who was not instructed in the strategy. The authors used a statistical conversion table to transform study effect sizes into student percentile gains. For example, if a student learns to employ the similarities and differences strategy, then her score on achievement tests may increase by as much as 45 percentage points. The instructional strategies integrated into the sample lesson plans in this book were selected based on their appropriateness for supporting the learning objectives and their potential to positively impact student learning.

Several forms of identifying similarities and differences are used in the lessons: comparing using Venn diagrams, classifying using category matrices and webs, creating metaphors (or similes), and creating analogies. Summarizing is used in many lessons, including the main ideas strategy lessons and reflective paragraphs in lessons in other chapters.

Notemaking is used throughout the lessons. While note taking implies that learners have "taken" notes from texts, *notemaking* implies that learners record connections, information, and questions in their own words. Notemaking is an essential skill that helps students practice and achieve AASL Indicator 2.1.2: "Organize knowledge so that it is useful."

In these lessons, educators model cooperative learning strategies, and students engage in cooperative group work. Setting objectives and providing feedback are essential components of every sample lesson. In several lessons, cues, questions, and advance organizers help students set a purpose for reading and thus activate or build their prior knowledge and prepare them for the learning tasks.

Finally, using think-aloud strategies during modeling is a common thread throughout the how-to lessons. Educators can view think-alouds as providing learners with reading apprenticeships. This best practice in reading instruction makes the invisible cognitive processes of reading "visible" to students. Providing models for striving readers, proficient readers use

Fig. 2-1   Alignment Matrix for Reading Comprehension Strategies and
Indicators from *Standards for the 21st-Century Learner*

Reading Comprehension Strategies	Selected Indicators from AASL *Standards for the 21st-Century Learner*
Activating or Building Background Knowledge	• Use prior and background knowledge as context for new learning. (1.1.2) • Read widely and fluently to make connections with self, the world, and previous reading. (4.1.2) • Connect ideas to own interests and previous knowledge and experience. (4.1.5) • Recognize how to focus efforts in personal learning. (4.4.3)
Using Sensory Images	• Read, view, and listen for information presented in any format (e.g., textual, visual, media, digital) in order to make inferences and gather meaning. (1.1.6) • Read, view, and listen for pleasure and personal growth. (4.1.1)
Questioning	• Develop and refine a range of questions to frame the search for new understanding. (1.1.3) • Find, evaluate, and select appropriate sources to answer questions. (1.1.4) • Display initiative and engagement by posing questions and investigating the answers beyond the collection of superficial facts. (1.2.1)
Making Predictions and Drawing Inferences	• Read, view, and listen for information presented in any format (e.g., textual, visual, media, digital) in order to make inferences and gather meaning. (1.1.6)
Determining Main Ideas	• Organize knowledge so that it is useful. (2.1.2)
Using Fix-up Options	• Monitor own information-seeking processes for effectiveness and progress, and adapt as necessary. (1.4.1)
Synthesizing	• Make sense of information gathered from diverse sources by identifying misconceptions, main and supporting ideas, conflicting information, and point of view or bias. (1.1.7) • Continue an inquiry-based research process by applying critical-thinking skills (analysis, synthesis, evaluation, organization) to information and knowledge in order to construct new understandings, draw conclusions, and create new knowledge. (2.1.1) • Use strategies to draw conclusions from information and apply knowledge to curricular areas, real-world situations, and further investigations. (2.1.3)
All Reading Comprehension Strategies	• Read, view, and listen for information presented in any format (e.g., textual, visual, media, digital) in order to make inferences and gather meaning. (1.1.6) • Respond to literature and creative expressions of ideas in various formats and genres. (4.1.3)

Excerpted from *Standards for the 21st-Century Learner* by the American Association of School Librarians, a division of the American Library Association, ©2007 American Library Association. Available for download at www.ala.org/aasl/standards/.

think-alouds while reading a text in order to share how they solve comprehension problems.

The goal of integrating all of these best practices into the how-to strategy lessons is to help educators gain experience using these practices. This also gives collaborating educators a common vocabulary and set of practices that can be applied across contexts and content areas—in the classroom and in the library. See www.alaeditions.org/webextras/ for a glossary of terms.

Fig. 2-2 Selected Categories of Instructional Strategies That Affect Student Achievement on Standardized Tests

Category	Percentile Gain
Identifying similarities and differences	45
Summarizing and note taking (notemaking)	34
Nonlinguistic representations	27
Cooperative learning	27
Setting objectives and providing feedback	23
Questions, cues, and advance organizers	22

Selected from Marzano, Pickering, and Pollock (2001)

THE ANALOGY OF DRIVING A CAR AT NIGHT

Whether they live in an urban environment and use public transportation or anticipate inheriting an older sibling's car to commute from home to a suburban school or after-school job, many young adults consider driving a rite of passage. For this book, I have created an analogy to relate the seven reading comprehension strategies to the way particular car parts function for a driver setting out at night. Constructing analogies is one of the research-based instructional strategies that increases student achievement (Marzano, Pickering, and Pollock 2001).

Analogies serve as handy shorthand for students and educators to communicate about the meaning of the comprehension strategies. The GoAnimate cartoon and the Analogy of the Car presentation slides available on the web extra site share these strategies in terms of the functions of car parts for successful driving. A bookmark that can be reproduced and used to remind students of these connections is also available online. The parts of the car and the analogous reading comprehension strategies are listed on one side of the bookmark. The sixteen fix-up options are listed on the reverse side. The fix-up options are also the subject of two Animoto videos (see chapter 8).

Educators and students could be deceived by perceiving each reading comprehension strategy as able to stand alone or isolated from the others. In truth, all of these strategies use aspects of the others. When applying background knowledge, readers recall sensory images. Inferences are based on background knowledge, on what readers know from life experiences or remember from reading other texts. Identifying main ideas and synthesizing are common aspects of our thinking processes in all of these comprehension strategies. Many of the fix-up options are based on the strategies themselves: try to visualize, ask a new question, draw an inference, and so on. Active readers utilize multiple comprehension strategies as they engage with texts. The ultimate goal is for readers to utilize combinations of strategies when they are appropriate to different types of texts, purposes for reading, and comprehension challenges. (The order of the chapters in this book reflects one possible sequence for building students' comprehension strategy repertoires. Educators may elect to teach only a few of these strategies or determine another order depending on students' needs.)

SAMPLE LESSONS AND LESSON FORMAT

This book offers sample lesson plans at three levels of reading development: advancing, advanced, and challenging. These levels of literacy development are not related to specific grade levels; rather, the lessons in each chapter are relatively difficult compared to each other. A lesson that may be appropriate for eighth-grade students in one school may be equally effective for tenth-grade students in another school. After assessing students' level of proficiency, it is up to educators to determine which lesson level or levels are appropriate.

Figure 2-3 shows the lesson format for the how-to strategy lessons. The planning section extends from the reading comprehension strategy through the standards, and the lesson implementation or process follows. All of the lessons assume that educators have determined in advance that students will benefit from learning the target reading comprehension strategy. Learning and practicing the strategy are the overarching objectives for the lesson. The lesson format lists the level of reading development, followed by the research-based instructional strategies selected to support this lesson. The lesson plan length is an average. One "session" is about fifty minutes of instructional time. Depending on the learners' characteristics, educators may need to revise the lesson length. When a plan calls for four or more lessons, it is considered a unit of instruction. It is assumed that lessons are taught in whatever location is best suited for the students, educators, and content being engaged, whether in the library, computer lab, or classroom.

The purpose for the lesson is directly related to the students' need and readiness for the instruction. The objectives use terms taken from performance objectives found in the Texas state standards. Other state standards are likely to use similar terms. If necessary for local documentation, educators can conduct electronic searches of standards documents to locate keywords found in the objectives for these lessons. In this book, the term *text* refers to a work in its totality,

that is, words and illustrations. The term *print* refers to the words only, and the term *illustration* refers to artwork, charts, graphs, or a variety of other graphic features.

In the list of tween and young adult literature at the end of some chapters, the starred titles indicate books used in the lessons. At the time of this writing, all of the literature chosen for the lessons was available for purchase. Educators are not limited to using these

---

Fig. 2-3 Sample How-to Strategy Lesson Format: Planning and Implementation

Planning
- Reading Comprehension Strategy
- Reading Development Level
- Instructional Strategies
- Lesson Length
- Purpose
- Objectives
- Resources, Materials, and Equipment
  - Tween and young adult literature
  - Websites
  - Graphic organizers
  - Materials
  - Equipment
- Collaboration
- Assessment
- Standards
  - Reading and/or writing
  - Listening and speaking
  - Other content areas
  - Educational technology
  - AASL indicators

Implementation
- Process
  - Motivation
  - Student-friendly objectives
  - Presentation
  - Student participation procedures or
  - Student practice procedures
  - Guided practice
  - Closure
  - Reflection
- Extensions

particular books but are advised to choose substitute texts that have similar characteristics. Only websites with relative permanence are included in this book. I will maintain Internet Pathfinders to ensure that lesson plan websites are functional. A complete set of graphic organizers and rubrics is available as part of the web support for this book. Required materials are listed, as is equipment. When the term *project* appears in the lesson plan, educators can use document cameras, data or overhead projectors, or interactive whiteboards to share documents with students. The resources and materials for each lesson were carefully selected to support the instructional objectives.

In the collaboration section, strategies for coteaching the lessons are described. These strategies can and should be adapted to fit the needs of students, educators, and the particular learning environment. In making adjustments, educators should remember that the lessons were designed to lower the student-to-teacher ratio, especially during the presentation (modeling) or guided practice components of the lessons. The sources for assessment of student outcomes are given in the assessment section. It is critical that educators share the assessment criteria with students in advance of the guided practice and that they model using the rubrics and other assessment tools.

The curriculum standards are listed as keywords and phrases. Like the terms used in the lesson objectives, educators can search standards documents for these keywords. The curriculum standards suggested are not exclusive, and educators should add to them as they see fit. The lessons are interdisciplinary in order to maximize students' ability to transfer their learning and to make connections across content areas that will strengthen the impact of the learning experience (Wolfe 2001).

When students write about what they read in social studies, science, and language arts, their comprehension improves (Graham and Hebert 2010). All lessons include writing components, such as responding to, analyzing, or interpreting texts; notemaking; composing summaries; or posing and answering questions. If resources are available, educators and students can use electronic webbing, notemaking, citation makers,

and other thinking and information organizing tools when appropriate. As new Web 2.0 tools appear every day, librarians should adjust the technology tools suggested in the lessons as necessary or when more appropriate tools are available.

The implementation or process section of the lesson plans is guided by the essential elements of instruction, also known as the Madeline Hunter model (Hunter 1994), a process recommended for today's students by Schmoker (2011, 57). The lessons begin by offering motivation for participating in the learning engagement. This section is critical and should be adapted as needed to engage students' attention, curiosity, or emotions. Student-friendly objectives, which set the purpose of the lesson, are listed next and should be posted for students and educators to refer to during the lesson. The presentation components of the lesson are what educators model to prepare students to practice the reading strategy. Through think-alouds and modeling during the presentation phase, educators reinforce the purpose for the lesson and make their thinking evident to students. These are essential elements of effective instruction. If the presentation includes opportunities for student participation, a list of student participation procedures is provided; these too can be posted for students' and educators' reference. If the lesson moves from presentation to guided practice, there is a list of student practice procedures that should be posted.

The guided practice provides students with opportunities to practice with their peers and under the guidance of educators. This section specifies what educators pay attention to as they monitor students' work and check for understanding. (Educators should stop at strategic points throughout the lesson to check for understanding and adjust their teaching accordingly.) The lesson closure includes student sharing or a review of the strategy and an assessment. The reflection is offered in the form of questions that can be posted and responded to orally or in writing. Possible extensions to the lesson conclude the format.

These lesson plans do not constitute a reading program, but rather are examples of lessons that can be cotaught in order to teach, practice, and apply reading comprehension strategies in authentic learning situations. The ultimate goal of all the how-to lessons is for students to apply strategies as needed in various combinations in their independent interactions with texts. Because all lesson plans are guides rather than prescriptions, educators are advised to modify and adapt lesson procedures to fit the needs of students, local curricula, available resources, and their own teaching styles.

CONSIDERATIONS FOR ENGLISH-LANGUAGE LEARNERS

As schools welcome more and more English-language learners (ELLs), school librarians and classroom teachers must consider these students' needs as they carefully plan and implement instruction. Across the United States, school districts, state departments of education, and colleges of education are recognizing the necessity of providing practicing and preservice educators with tools that help their students acquire and learn English. The sheltered instruction approach is one model that has gained widespread use (Echevarria, Vogt, and Short 2008). If ELLs are members of the classroom community, then ELL language arts standards must be integrated into each lesson as well. As educators learn to articulate and plan language objectives clearly, they are advised to collaborate with colleagues who are trained in sheltered instruction or other English-language teaching and learning approaches.

All of the reading comprehension strategies highlighted in this book are specified in the sheltered English instruction approach. ELLs especially benefit from lessons based on published standards, with content and language objectives clearly stated orally and in writing and posted participation and practice procedures. Teaching strategies that use think-alouds and modeling explicitly are cornerstones of the sheltered approach. Because ELLs must simultaneously learn language and content, graphic organizers offer essential instructional scaffolds that help them organize information. Educators can modify the provided graphic organizers to meet the needs of ELLs by embedding concept definitions or elaborations that further explain the content. These strategies and methods are important for all learners, but they are imperative for ELLs. And perhaps most of all, ELLs and striving readers alike need time on a daily basis to read shared and self-selected texts of all kinds.

MAXIMIZING YOUR IMPACT

There is no better way to promote the instructional partner role of the school librarian and the school library program than to document how classroom-library collaboration impacts student outcomes *and* improves educator proficiency. Coteaching the how-to lessons in this book is one place to begin. Collecting and sharing results from pre- and post-lesson data, documenting students' learning processes, gathering and assessing student outcomes, and disseminating testimonials from collaborating colleagues can inform library stakeholders about the impact of collaboration on student learning.

Coteaching reading comprehension strategies is job-embedded professional development. It helps educators develop a shared vocabulary and understanding of these processes in order to facilitate their students' intellectual access to ideas and information across content areas and with a wide variety of texts. Through purposefully designed lessons using think-alouds and modeling, educators make these internal processes evident to students. And these strategies give learners the tools they need to be proficient readers and independent learners so they can effectively find and use ideas and interact with information that lead to knowledge.

3

Reading Comprehension Strategy One
Activating or Building Background Knowledge

How much a reader already knows about the subject is probably the best predictor of reading comprehension.

—Douglas Fisher and Nancy Frey

Why do teen readers (and adult readers for that matter) stand in lines waiting for the library or bookstore doors to open so they can be first to buy a copy of a long-anticipated next title in a popular series? Why do youthful moviegoers flock to see the release of the film made from the book they loved and read three times last year? Why do youth arrange their weekly social schedules around the shows they all watch and talk about or record religiously so as not to miss a single episode? It's just possible that the knowledge of characters, settings, themes, and even plots in familiar texts encourage readers to connect and have a satisfying experience with the next book, the next film, or the next episode in a TV series.

When we meet new literacy events with the necessary background knowledge, we are confident and anticipate a pleasurable and familiar experience. Our brains seek out patterns, our thinking involves making connections. Understanding the importance of background knowledge to comprehension is critical because we connect new information with prior knowledge before we integrate and organize that new information. "Learning always proceeds from the known to the new. Good teaching will recognize and build on this connection" (Wilhelm, Baker, and Dube 2001, 18). Just as a driver should always check the rearview mirror first and frequently, a reader should always assess and activate background knowledge and experience before journeying with a new text. When we look in the rearview mirror, we see our prior knowledge backing up comprehension as we move forward with new texts.

Researchers who study reading comprehension believe that assessing, building, and activating background knowledge are fundamental tasks for readers and for educators (Fisher and Frey 2009). As we go through life meeting and revisiting ideas and information, we organize our understandings into schemas. We assess our background knowledge by examining our schema for that concept or subject matter. According to McGee and Richgels, a schema is a "mental structure in which we store all the information we know about people, places, objects, or activities" (1996, 5). If we have no schema for a particular topic, we begin that encounter with new ideas or information with an immediate struggle for comprehension.

How can educators model and help students activate personal background knowledge or prior experience and relevant schema before and during reading? How can we model the need for background knowledge and then help students build knowledge related to vocabulary, concepts, and contexts before and during reading? Before introducing a new topic, the educator's goal is to determine what students already know, or think they know. Do students have accurate schema on which to build new information? Or do they have misconceptions, oversimplifications, or overgeneralizations that will impede their comprehension? If so, how can educators bring these to light or correct them before students enter into the new learning event? And what if students lack relevant background knowledge for meeting a new text? Then it is educators' responsibility to give them the opportunity to build that knowledge before engaging with the new information.

Educators must model how readers activate relevant background knowledge to make sense of text. Through think-alouds, educators share their thought processes with developing readers in order to demonstrate the importance of considering what they already know about a topic, genre, author, and more before they read, view, or listen to a new text. Whether it is reading the next title in a trilogy, the next section of the social studies textbook, conducting a science experiment, or calculating a math problem, activating what learners already know is critical to their success.

Rosenblatt (1978) developed a theory of reading as a transaction between the reader, the text, and the intention of the author. She posited that each reader brings his own feelings, personality, and experiences to the text and that each reader is different each time he revisits a particular text. Background knowledge is what the reader brings to the reading event. Each reader's interpretation and each reading of the text are potentially unique. This theory helps explain our individual responses to literature, art, and music and can be applied more broadly to our generalized responses in all areas of learning.

For proficient readers, this process is automatic. Many readers who have read widely and proficiently and have rich and varied life experiences may be able to connect more easily to academic topics. However, less proficient readers with incomplete or inaccurate prior understandings or little background knowledge may lack the necessary foundation on which to build when they encounter denser or more sophisticated texts such as science and social studies textbooks or classic literature.

Introducing lessons and units of study with brainstorms and questions about students' prior ideas and information on particular topics is an essential component of lesson design. In order to find a firm starting point for student learning, educators often utilize K-W-L charts (or some variation of this tool) to help the class or individual students assess their background knowledge. If students have the necessary schemas, they have support for confidently leaping into the learning experience. If they do not yet have a schema, then it is up to educators to help them build background knowledge. Extending the K-W-L chart allows for the possibility that educators will need to help students build background knowledge before identifying what they already know and want to learn:

- What background knowledge do we need to *build*?
- What do we already *know*?
- What do we *wonder* about?

- What did we *learn*?
- What are our new *questions*?

This B-K-W-L-Q chart, based on the work of Janet Allen (2004), also acknowledges that in many cases background knowledge must be built and that inquiry is a dynamic process and can generate as many questions as it answers.

"Researchers argue that prior knowledge—what a person already knows—may be the most important variable for understanding" (Buehl 2009, 4). That said, many educators have learned not to make assumptions about students' prior understandings. Instead, they develop engaging ways to assess, build, or activate students' background knowledge. In his song "We Didn't Start the Fire," singer-composer-lyricist Billy Joel strings together a chronological list of people and events that shaped the years and decades between 1949 (the year he was born) and 1989 (the year the song was released). Using Joel's song as a framework, educators teaching late 20th-century history, politics, government, film, or other subjects have used these lyrics as an anchor around which to develop resources to fill in students' background knowledge. "Mrs. Oz," a high school geography, history, and film teacher, created a resource that includes a YouTube video, a music video, and a pathfinder of resources to help students assess, build, and activate background knowledge of the people and events listed in Joel's song (www.teacheroz.com/fire.htm). Wikipedia has an excellent article on the song, and YouTube videos abound on this and any related subjects. Educators can capitalize on students' affinity for popular culture as well as their preference to learn from multimedia resources to assess, build, or activate students' prior knowledge.

The National Research Council's report on how people learn attests that knowledge must be organized, conditionalized, and transferable in order to be useful in school-based learning (2000). The concept of organized knowledge is related to the schema theory discussed previously. Two strategies educators can use to support learners in organizing information are graphic organizers and notemaking. Both of these tools model the types of mind maps that learners need in order to organize information. When knowledge is conditionalized, the learner knows where, when, and why to apply it. Educators who effectively use think-alouds share their schema for making sense of texts. When think-alouds are applied to teaching reading comprehension strategies, educators help students conditionalize these processes by verbally sharing where, when, and why they apply these strategies.

Knowledge must also be transferrable. Rather than memorize a sequence, learners must understand the concepts that underlie these tasks so they can apply them more broadly. By explicitly modeling and practicing prior knowledge assessment, educators can help students develop their own procedures for assessing their background knowledge before they begin explorations into new learning territories. If students determine that they need more prior knowledge, educators should give them time to build it before encountering a new concept. When school librarians bring reading comprehension strategies into their collaborative lessons with educators in all content areas, students can learn that these processes are applicable in multiple contexts.

HOW TO TEACH THE STRATEGY

Educators have long known the benefits of teaching through storytelling. We store memories and much of our learning in story format because the brain functions narratively. In addition to research to back up his claims regarding the impact of storytelling on comprehension and writing skills, Haven (2007) shares anecdotes about how several middle and secondary educators used story to help students connect with and remember content. When a middle school librarian noticed that students repeatedly confused almanacs and atlases on standardized tests, she told them the story of Atlas, how he is depicted holding up the Earth but actually was punished by holding up the sky. Students remembered the story, and that year none of them missed the test questions about atlases. After a high school music teacher created and told a story about the life of Italian composer Vivaldi, he noticed his students' practice logs showed they were playing this composer's music more than previous classes had. When the music teacher asked why this was the case, they replied Vivaldi is "cool." A high school biology teacher dressed in costume to share a first-person story of the life and work of Charles Darwin. When he noted that students did better on test questions related to Darwin's work, he repeated this technique for three additional scientists with the same result. In all of these cases, building background knowledge to make connections as well as the story format may have had a hand in assisting students in learning content.

With think-alouds, educators let students know that ideas come into their minds before beginning to read a book or article, view a video or piece of art, or listen to music. Sharing background knowledge during reading requires that educators stop and reflect, reinforcing for students that reading is an active, complex, nonlinear process that goes beyond the literal denotations of words on a page or images on a screen. After reading, sharing connections helps students access the messages and themes suggested by the text. Talking about how these connections support comprehension is an important part of learning to activate and use relevant background knowledge. Educators must be specific in sharing how their background knowledge helped them comprehend the text and encourage their students to be specific as well. Figure 3-1 shows a sample of how to model making connections before, during, and after reading a text.

Librarians and classroom teachers could use this example as a model for students to conduct the same exercise with the school's student code of conduct or the district's acceptable use policy. Educators can guide students as they think aloud with partners or in small groups and as they make connections while reading these texts.

CONNECTION TYPES

Readers can use each of these frames to identify the source of their prior knowledge connections. If a single student or an entire class lacks background knowledge,

educators help them by "front-loading" the lesson, by building background and jump-starting readers' ability to make connections before reading. "The most powerful time to support reading is before students begin to read" (Wilhelm, Baker, and Dube 2001, 96).

These frames also provide ways to think and talk about ideas and information and help readers connect with and build schemas before, during, and after reading. As with all the strategies, readers should ultimately internalize these "thinking about thinking" questions and utilize them as a means of exploring the ways they are connecting to what they read, hear, and view. Metacognition gives readers control of their learning. Making connections helps readers make sense of what they read, it helps them remember what they read, and it also gives meaning and value to the literacy events in which they engage. Building connections not only supports comprehension, it also enriches readers' literate lives by giving deeper significance to literacy experiences.

TEXT-TO-SELF CONNECTIONS

Text-to-self connections require that educators know the students in their classrooms and be familiar with students' out-of-school lives. Classroom teachers often bring a deeper knowledge of individual students to classroom-library collaboration. School librarians often bring a broader knowledge of the resources available in the school library in print or electronic format, through interlibrary loan, and by way of the Web. Through collaboration, classroom teachers and school librarians can connect students' background knowledge with a rich array of tween and young adult literature and resources, thereby providing them with opportunities for making connections based on shared, familiar experiences of the students themselves.

When modeling text-to-self connections, educators use think-aloud questioning to share their thinking processes. These sample questions center on three areas of text-to-self connection: feelings, experiences, and ideas.

- Have you ever felt like the character(s) in this story? Describe what happened and how you felt.

Fig. 3-1 Making Text-to-Self, Text-to-Text, and Text-to-World Connections

Text: *Access for Children and Young Adults to Nonprint Materials: An Interpretation of the Library Bill of Rights*, by the American Library Association

Making Connections	How Connections Support Comprehension
Before Reading	
I am a librarian whose job it is to ensure that our library has the materials students need to be successful. This statement is important to me because it relates to my job. I think about and act on this topic every day. (Text-to-self)	The fact that this statement is important to my work will increase its relevance for me. It will have more meaning. The text-to-self connection increases my motivation to read and understand the document.
The subtitle of this statement includes the phrase "bill of rights." I am very familiar with the Bill of Rights in the U.S. Constitution. This includes ten amendments that specify rights of individuals. This document is also related to another document; it is an interpretation of the "Library Bill of Rights." (Text-to-text)	These text-to-text connections help me predict this document is about the rights of students. I'm thinking it might be important for me to read the "Library Bill of Rights" first to put this document in the context of the work of the author, the American Library Association.
During Reading	
The phrases "not be denied or abridged," "free access," and "unrestricted use" are important. These sound like terms I have read in legal documents. (Text-to-text)	The fact that this document uses legal-sounding terms makes me take it seriously.
I am a parent so the section about only parents having the right to restrict access has meaning for me. There were things my daughter's friends did that I did not allow her to do. As a parent, I want to maintain the right to guide my child. (Text-to-self)	The sections about parents' rights are personally meaningful. In the context of this statement, I want to be sure to understand my role both as a parent and as a school librarian who must respect the rights of parents and of students.
The library should neither mark out ratings nor add ratings to materials that are not already rated. This puts this statement in the larger context of the issue of censorship. (Text-to-world)	The connection between access and censorship is important because I believe in the concept of intellectual freedom for authors and for everyone who uses our library. Making this broad connection helps me see how this statement fits with what I already know and do as a librarian.
After Reading	
This interpretation of the "Library Bill of Rights" is important information for all librarians, particularly for me as a school librarian because children and youth use our library every school day. (Text-to-self)	These connections make me understand this document in terms of the performance of my job. I am a professional who wants to uphold the principles of my profession. If and when there is a challenge to students having access to particular materials through our school library, I want to be able to explain this document to others.
The last sentence jumped out at me because it relates to other texts and statements I read in my education as a school librarian: "Librarians have a responsibility to ensure young people's access to materials and services that reflect diversity of content and format sufficient to meet their needs." (Text-to-text)	This reminds me that this document reflects larger issues related to the open access to information in our democratic society. (Text-to-world)

Text available at www.ala.org/ala/issuesadvocacy/intfreedom/librarybill/interpretations/accesschildren.cfm.

- Have you had a similar experience? Compare your experience to that of the character(s).
- Have you heard or read information on this topic before? What does this information mean to you?
- How does connecting a story or information to your own life experiences or to other things you've read or viewed help you better understand it?

TEXT-TO-TEXT CONNECTIONS

In addition to making connections to their own background knowledge and experiences, learners can be guided to make connections *between* texts. In a broad sense, a text can be any communication from which a person makes meaning. This includes all forms of paper-based documents as well as oral communication and music, visual images, and electronic resources. This view of a text offers learners a wider range of possible sources for making connections. When youth begin to notice commonalities between texts situated both inside and outside of school, they may begin to find more relevance in their school-based learning experiences too.

The following sample questions center on making text-to-text connections. They can be used to guide educators' and students' thinking as they model and practice this strategy.

- In what other types of texts have you read about this topic? Did one resource help you better understand another?
- How does making connections between different types of texts help you better understand the topic?
- Have you read another book or seen a movie or play in which the characters have feelings or experiences similar to the ones in this story? Describe how they are the same or different.
- Have you read another book or seen a movie or play in which a story element (setting, plot, conflict, theme, or style) is similar to the one in this story? Describe how they are the same.

- Have you read another book or seen a movie or play in which the writer used language or text structure similar to that in this story? Describe how these texts are similar.
- How does making connections to familiar texts help you comprehend the new text?

TEXT-TO-WORLD CONNECTIONS

With text-to-world connections, readers stretch their thinking beyond the particulars of what they read, hear, and view to connect story themes or information with larger life issues or concepts that apply more broadly in the world. These topics often include social and political problems related to historical or current events.

For instance, when studying earth science topics such as hurricanes or tsunamis, educators can share a current newspaper article or video news clip about the actual effects of these weather events on the physical features of the earth as well as the sociopolitical structures in the places where they are occurring or have occurred. Students can use the study of actual events to build the background knowledge they need to help them understand the facts as presented in the textbook. Alternatively, they can use information in a textbook as a starting place and then compare the facts as presented to the physical impact of a current disaster and the experiences of people in a current events article or newscast.

When students make broader connections such as these, they begin to explore using literacy as a tool for forming opinions about social and political issues. Readers come to understand that authors and illustrators of print and electronic texts include messages or perspectives on world events in their work. The author's intention, which is usually inferred, is one aspect of the meaning readers make (Rosenblatt 1978).

These are some questions that can be used to guide educators' or students' thinking as they practice making text-to-world connections.

- What do you think the author's message or purpose was in writing this story or presenting this information?

- Did the author suggest a message that connects with bigger ideas about the way things are in the world? What do you already know about these issues?
- What do you think was the author's opinion or perspective on the big ideas in this text? Do you agree? Why or why not?
- How does making connections to larger issues help you comprehend this text?

Figure 3-2 shows a category matrix based on subtopics in the "education" category on the TakingIT Global website (www.tigweb.org). A category matrix such as this one can be projected on an interactive whiteboard and can be completed by small groups of students assigned to build text-to-world background knowledge related to education. Using one of the subtopics, the school librarian and classroom teacher can model completing one or more resource categories based on the resources found on this site. For example, in the literacy subtopic, educators can use think-alouds to note the number of literacy organizations listed. Then collaboratively they negotiate and choose one, for example, "Women's Organization to Combat Illiteracy," which is concerned with literacy among Jordanian women. They can make notes about this organization in the appropriate cell on the category matrix (literacy/organizations). Individuals, partners, or small groups of students can continue this work by contributing entries in self-selected or assigned categories. The completed matrix, generated by the entire class, provides a rich resource to support learners as they select an inquiry project topic or develop a research question.

MAKING LITERATURE AND OTHER RESOURCE CONNECTIONS

Books of all genres that relate to students' interests and life experiences provide fertile soil for background knowledge strategy lessons. Students can quickly learn to make connections to books and resources whose topics, story elements, authors, or illustrators are familiar to them. They find relevance in texts on topics in which they have an interest or about which they are familiar. Adolescents are particularly drawn to characters that are just a few years older than they are, because this allows them to try on various paths for their future. In these texts, characters, settings, and plots may be particularly strong aspects of readers' connections.

However, at the middle and high school levels, the greater challenge is that many students lack

Fig. 3-2 Category Matrix: Topic—Education

Education Subtopics	Organizations	Publications	Blogs	Policies	Statistics	News
Educational Technology						
Global Education						
Informal/ Experiential Learning						
Literacy						

Education subtopics and Resource Categories from TakingITGlobal (www.tigweb.org).

accessible background knowledge on which they can draw to make connections of any kind. Text sets developed by classroom teachers and school librarians and organized around topics, themes, genres, story elements, structural patterns, story variants, and author-illustrator studies are a powerful support for students who are learning to build background knowledge and make connections. Text sets at the secondary level most often include both print and electronic resources. Figure 3-3 shows a variety of possible frameworks around which educators can build text sets.

Using educator-selected text sets, educators can guide students as they make connections—with the ultimate goal of supporting learners in creating their own text sets based on self-selected topics, text types, and themes. The Sample Thematic Text Set available at www.alaeditions.org/webextras/ is an annotated text set built on the theme "When cultures meet, people have choices about how they respond." It includes both picture books and novels from a wide variety of genres, including biography, historical and realistic fiction, informational books, and poetry, and it also includes a website. Developed through classroom-library collaboration and by students themselves, text sets of all types provide rich resources for background knowledge strategy lessons.

LESSON PLANS

In the following how-to lessons, classroom teachers and school librarians use think-aloud strategies to demonstrate how and why they are assessing and building their background knowledge and how they are using it to comprehend new texts before, during, and after the reading. The lesson plans are constructed for students at three levels of development. Readers at all levels can benefit from how-to lessons until these reading strategies are integrated into their repertoires as reading skills. The organization of instruction in the lessons maximizes the benefit of two equal-partner collaborators by lowering the student-teacher ratio.

Each lesson plan utilizes a different type of connection to demonstrate this strategy: text-to-self, text-to-text, and text-to-world. Although it is recommended that strategy lessons focus on one connection framework at a time, readers should not be limited in making a particular type of connection; these examples simply share one dominant connection framework. Whether the text is assigned or read by the student independently of an assignment, the ultimate goal of these lessons is for readers at all levels of development to learn to notice when they need to connect or to build background knowledge before, during, or after reading in order to support comprehension.

Fig. 3-3 Sample Conceptual Frameworks for Organizing Text Sets in Secondary Libraries

Concept	Examples
Topics	Content area topics such as physical forces that affect climate (earth science), various decades (U.S. history), important legislation or legal decisions (government), discoveries made by scientists or mathematicians (sciences or mathematics)
Text Features	Informational books with topical chapters, chapters with subheadings, images with captions, charts, graphs, glossaries, time lines, bibliographies
Genres	Biographies, essays, speeches, poetry, science fiction
Story Elements	Similar settings, characters, plots and conflicts, themes, cultural features, illustration media or styles
Story Structures	Legends, fables, myths
Story Variants	Fairy tale and folktale variants such as Cinderella stories
Author and Illustrator Studies	Multiple works by the same author or illustrator

LESSON PLAN 3.1

Reading Comprehension Strategy One
Building Background Knowledge

Reading Development Level: Advancing

Instructional Strategies
Cues and Questions, Classifying, Notemaking and Summarizing

Lesson Length
1 or 2 sessions (depending on the length of the mentor text)

Purpose
The purpose of this lesson plan is to make notes and build background knowledge, to make text-to-self connections, and to apply new knowledge to further reading, research, or inquiry. This lesson can be preparation for reading and retelling a piece of traditional literature for a drama, speech, or language arts class, reading a historical or contemporary short story or novel set in another culture, or inquiring about a historical time period. In the application of this lesson, students use multiple sources in multiple formats to build background knowledge. This lesson can also stand alone.

Objectives
At the end of these lessons, students will be able to
  1. Describe the culture under investigation.
  2. Make notes, cite sources, and organize information.
  3. Make comparisons between the character's culture and students' own cultures.
  4. Self-assess using an exit slip.
  5. Application: Use multiple sources in multiple formats to continue to build background knowledge and apply this knowledge to another text based in the culture or time period under investigation.

Resources, Materials, and Equipment
Mentor texts (traditional literature, picture books, or short stories): The 3.1 Mentor Text Example is based on a traditional folktale from China, "The Great Deed of Li Ji," retold by Judi Moreillon
Application: Select additional culture-specific texts or use the selected, suggested folklore titles at http://ls5633.wikispaces.com/Bibliographies
Graphic organizers: 3.1 Category Matrix, 3.1 Teacher Resource—Completed Category Matrix, 3.1 Exit Slip, 3.1 Teacher Resource—Completed Exit Slip; Works Cited Graphic Organizer
Internet access and data projector, overhead, or interactive whiteboard, CD player, or document camera if available

Collaboration

The educators demonstrate the importance of background knowledge in understanding culture. They model locating information and making notes from the mentor text. This lesson can be cotaught with classroom teachers in any content area. In the application of this lesson, educators model using multiple sources in multiple formats and monitor students' research processes, or the school librarian may take responsibility for supporting student research in library center rotations. Educators share responsibility for guiding and assessing students' graphic organizers and application of this strategy.

Assessments

The students' category matrices and exit slip show the process and results of their learning.

Standards

Reading keywords: Analyze stylistic elements in traditional literature; extract information and use graphic organizers to comprehend text; connect information and events in text-to-self connections.

Social studies keywords: Define the concept of culture; identify traits of specific cultures; analyze similarities and differences between cultures.

History, mathematics, science, speech, and drama keywords: Use secondary source materials to study people and events from the past.

AASL STANDARDS INDICATORS*

- Use prior and background knowledge as context for new learning. (1.1.2)
- Organize knowledge so that it is useful. (2.1.2)
- Consider diverse and global perspectives in drawing conclusions. (2.3.2)
- Interpret new information based on cultural and social context. (4.4.4)

Determine additional standards and indicators for the application and extensions.

PROCESS

This is an outline rather than a detailed procedure. I have chosen a folktale to demonstrate this lesson. Use this text or choose a mentor text that supports the application of this lesson to the content under study.

MOTIVATION

Each educator shares an example of experiencing empathy for another's embarrassment, anxiety, fear, or suffering. Examples could include feeling the embarrassment of a mother shopping with four young children when one throws a tantrum or the suffering of a homeless person who lives in the park where you walk.

Discuss the idea of empathy for another's experiences. Being able to put one's self in the shoes of another can involve knowing something about that person's culture as well as their day-to-day life. Use students' own family experiences and community norms to develop a list of categories that encapsulate their culture. Project the 3.1 Category Matrix and use it to fill in aspects of culture that students may not have included in their definitions.

Students read a folktale in order to identify cultural features of the main character's life. They make text-to-self connections by recording how their own culture is the same or different from the main character's culture. If students will be applying this strategy to further study, suggest how this lesson prepares them for the next lessons.

STUDENT-FRIENDLY OBJECTIVES
1. Define culture.
2. Identify cultural information in a short folktale and connect that information to the student's own culture.
3. Record information on a graphic organizer.

PRESENTATION
Ask students to share some ideas of what life in ancient China could have been like for a young person their own age. Record these ideas of the board.

Distribute the 3.1 Mentor Text Example, "The Great Deed of Li Ji," and the 3.1 Category Matrix. Educators read the entire story aloud without interruption, or students read it with a partner orally or silently to themselves. Focus on expression and fluency. Read the author's notes about the cultural context of this folktale.

One educator rereads the beginning of the story. Pause the reading to identify a cultural feature and make a personal cultural connection. The other educator records the culture feature in the appropriate cell on a projected 3.1 Category Matrix. Using think-alouds, educators model recording text-to-self connections with different colors that show what is similar and what is different between the character and each educators' cultures (see 3.1 Teacher Resource—Completed Category Matrix). Students record their own text-to-self cultural connections on the graphic organizer using one color for cultural aspects that are the same and another for aspects that are different.

After initial modeling, students participate with educators. Depending on the sophistication of the mentor text and students' proficiency, educators can continue this process as a whole class to the end of the story or can stop at an appropriate point and give students the opportunity to finish the reading and complete the graphic organizer as individuals, in pairs, or in small groups.

STUDENT PARTICIPATION PROCEDURES
1. Raise hand to pause the reading to make a cultural connection.
2. Note the cultural information on the graphic organizer.
3. Record connections to one's own individual culture.

GUIDED PRACTICE
Monitor students' recording of text-to-self connections on the 3.1 Category Matrix, or after modeling educators can monitor individual, pairs, or small group work.

CLOSURE
Students sit in small groups to share their cultural connections with the main character in the story. What are the similarities and differences between that character's culture and students' own cultures?

Distribute the 3.1 Exit Slip. After students complete it, use it to conduct the reflection. Use the 3.1 Teacher Resource—Completed Exit Slip for reference.

REFLECTION
How does learning about a character's culture help the reader understand the character's actions?
How does making text-to-self connections help the reader reach a deeper meaning of the story?

APPLICATION
Students browse and choose titles from the application text set. Distribute the 3.1 Category Matrix to each student. Educators model using resources beyond the mentor text in order to learn more about the culture or time period presented in the book. Link source numbers on the 3.1 Category Matrix with source numbers on a bibliography graphic organizer.

EXTENSIONS

Students who made a deeper connection to a folktale or other piece of traditional literature can use this work as a text for oral or digital storytelling or composing a retelling by bringing the story into the 21st century and their own cultural context.

Continue to use the text-to-self category matrix, especially when students are interacting with texts that have a pronounced cultural or historical context different from their own.

LESSON PLAN 3.2

Reading Comprehension Strategy One
Building Background Knowledge

Reading Development Level: Advanced

Instructional Strategies
Classifying, Notemaking and Summarizing

Lesson Length
2 or 3 sessions

Purpose
The purpose of this lesson plan is to make notes and build background knowledge from resources in multiple formats, to make text-to-text connections, and to determine which types of texts best provide a variety of types of information. This lesson can be preparation for an inquiry into this topic (ocean currents) or any other topic in any content area for which educators identify multiple texts that satisfy content knowledge needs. The lesson can be taught before, during, or after students have read the information in a textbook.

Objectives
At the end of these lessons, students will be able to
1. Define scientific terms and concepts related to ocean currents.
2. Make notes, cite sources, and organize information.
3. Make text-to-text connections and comparisons to determine the relative value of texts based on the information need and the learner's preference.

Resources, Materials, and Equipment
   Mentor texts: Earth science textbook, science database (such as *Science Resource Center*), library reference section print texts, or online sources such as an atlas, dictionary, regular or subject-specific encyclopedias, and subject-specific science reference resources
   Graphic organizers: 3.2 Category Matrix, 3.2 Teacher Resource—Completed Category Matrix, Cornell Notemaking Graphic Organizer, 3.2 Teacher Resource—Completed Cornell Notemaking Graphic Organizer (with Works Consulted)
   Internet access and data projector, overhead, or interactive whiteboard, or document camera if available

Collaboration
The educators demonstrate the importance of background knowledge in understanding science vocabulary by making text-to-text connections. They model locating information from multiple sources in many formats and making notes from texts. This lesson can be cotaught with classroom teachers in any content area. Educators share responsibility for guiding and assessing students' graphic organizers.

Assessments

The students' text-to-text category matrices and notemaking graphic organizers with citations show the process and results of their learning.

Standards

Reading keywords: Locate appropriate print and nonprint information using text and technical resources; organize and record new information in systematic ways such as notes, charts, and graphic organizers.

Science keywords: Identify influences on climate; interrelationships between ocean currents, climates, and geologic features; and interactions and interdependent cycles.

AASL STANDARDS INDICATORS*

- Read, view, and listen for information presented in any format (e.g., textual, visual, media, digital) in order to make inferences and gather meaning. (1.1.6)
- Organize knowledge so that it is useful. (2.1.2)
- Use technology and other information tools to analyze and organize information. (2.1.4)
- Demonstrate flexibility in the use of resources by adapting information strategies to each specific resource and by seeking additional resources when clear conclusions cannot be drawn. (2.2.1)

PROCESS

This is an outline rather than a detailed procedure. I have chosen ocean currents to demonstrate this lesson. Use these texts or choose other mentor texts that support the topic under study. Students can work individually, in pairs, or in small groups to complete the text-to-text category matrix.

MOTIVATION

Search YouTube for surfing videos such as "GoPro HD Hero Camera: Kalani Robb—Slow Motion Pipeline." Ask students if they have ever surfed. What does a surfer need to know about ocean currents? Show a video related to oil spills such as "Oil in the Ocean." If there is a recent oil spill disaster, make a connection to current events. What does a scientist studying an oil spill need to know about ocean currents? Educators respond to these questions or extend students' responses with further questions.

Students build background knowledge about ocean currents by searching for definitions related to this topic from a variety of sources in multiple formats. They determine and describe which resource was most helpful in learning the term.

STUDENT-FRIENDLY OBJECTIVES

1. Define scientific terms and concepts related to ocean currents.
2. Make notes, cite sources, and organize information on a graphic organizer.
3. Make comparisons between texts and determine the relative value of texts based on the information need.

PRESENTATION

In order to help build background knowledge about ocean currents, determine some of the key concepts. Learners can use their science textbook chapter on "Movements of the Ocean: Ocean Currents" to do this. Another way is to conduct a Google search for "ocean currents" (no quotation marks). Under "All results,"

---

* Excerpted from *Standards for the 21st-Century Learner* by the American Association of School Librarians, a division of the American Library Association, copyright © 2007 American Library Association. Available for download at www.ala.org/aasl/standards. Used with permission.

use the "Wonder wheel" feature. Display the 3.2 Category Matrix. Read the introduction to the graphic organizer and show the list of vocabulary terms (derived from the Wonder wheel). Students define these terms using resources in multiple formats.

Distribute the Cornell Notemaking Graphic Organizer. Educators use think-alouds to determine one term to use as a model. (The 3.2 Teacher Resource—Completed Category Matrix is for the "Coriolis effect.") Read through the choices for various resources and move left to right to show an example of searching and reading for information in each category. Make notes on the Cornell Notemaking Graphic Organizer. Students also individually record notes on their own notemaking graphic organizers. If appropriate, review the Notemaking Chart. Note how references to resources are abbreviated. Students contribute to notes.

While reading different resources, keep a list of citations at the end of the table under the heading "Works Consulted." Use the citation feature in databases; use an electronic citation maker for other sources.

STUDENT PARTICIPATION PROCEDURES
1. Raise hand to pause the reading or viewing.
2. Describe the new information and suggest a note.
3. Record the note on the graphic organizer.

When educators have read information from all of the different types of sources and recorded notes, use think-alouds while one educator summarizes information from each resource and the other records notes in the appropriate cell on the 3.2 Category Matrix. Discuss which resource was the most helpful in understanding the term, place a star beside it, and record a reason in the "Why Best Resource?" column. Discuss how making connections between texts helped build background knowledge.

Students can continue researching the terms individually, in pairs, or in small groups. If appropriate, educators can use a jigsaw strategy and give specific students or teams responsibility for one or more terms rather than researching all of them.

GUIDED PRACTICE
Educators monitor students' searching and recording notes and engage students in conversations about why a particular resource was best.

CLOSURE
Students sit with a different partner or in small groups to share their text-to-text comparisons and conduct oral reflection with partner(s).

REFLECTION
Are all resources equally helpful in learning new vocabulary and concepts? Why is it important to consult more than one text if you are unsure or do not comprehend a particular word or concept? How does making connections between texts help build background knowledge?

EXTENSIONS
Use this background knowledge to begin an inquiry into the impact of ocean currents and other natural phenomena or the human impact on global warming.

Continue to use text-to-text category matrix graphic organizers to research vocabulary and concepts in science or other content areas in which students lack background information.

LESSON PLAN 3.3

Reading Comprehension Strategy One
Building Background Knowledge

Reading Development Level: Challenging

Instructional Strategies
Classifying, Notemaking and Summarizing

Lesson Length
3 or 4 sessions

Purpose
The purpose of this unit is to make notes and build text-to-world background knowledge from resources in multiple formats in order to better comprehend the context of a document. This series of lessons can be preparation for a deeper inquiry into this topic ("children's rights") or any other topic in any content area for which educators identify multiple resources; that is, resources that originate in various countries/cultures, provide a global perspective, satisfy content knowledge needs, and provide social action projects.

Objectives
At the end of this unit, students will be able to
1. Identify resources for youth social action projects.
2. Make notes, cite sources, and organize information.
3. Make text-to-world connections and comparisons to situate social issues in a global context.

Resources, Materials, and Equipment
Mentor texts: Photo essays: "The Rights of the Child, 1" and "The Rights of the Child, 2" (www.unicef.org/crc/); "Convention on the Rights of the Child" (www2.ohchr.org/english/law/crc.htm) or a version in kid-friendly language (www.unicef.org/rightsite/files/uncrcchilldfriendlylanguage.pdf); and TakingITGlobal (www.tigweb.org)

Graphic organizers: 3.3 Category Matrix, 3.3 Teacher Resource—Completed Category Matrix, 3.3 Summary Graphic Organizer, 3.3 Teacher Resource—Completed Summary Graphic Organizer, 3.3 Teacher Resource—Sample Synthesis Essay, 3.3 Synthesis Essay Rubric

Internet access and data projector, overhead, or interactive whiteboard, or document camera if available

Collaboration
The educators demonstrate the importance of building background knowledge through making text-to-world connections. They model locating information from multiple, predominantly non-U.S.-based web resources in many formats and making brief notes from texts. Similar lessons can be cotaught with

classroom teachers in any content area. Educators share responsibility for guiding and assessing students' graphic organizers and essays.

Assessments

The students' text-to-world category matrices, synthesis essays, and rubrics show the process and results of their learning.

Standards

Reading keywords: Locate appropriate print and nonprint information using text and technical resources; organize and record new information in systematic ways such as notes, charts, and graphic organizers.

Social studies and government keywords: Identify examples of political, economic, and social oppression and violations of human rights; investigate the impact of globalization of economics, law, and social life; assess the degree to which human rights and democratic ideals and practices have been advanced throughout the world.

AASL Standards Indicators*

- Read, view, and listen for information presented in any format (e.g., textual, visual, media, digital) in order to make inferences and gather meaning. (1.1.6)
- Display persistence by continuing to pursue information to gain a broad perspective. (1.2.7)
- Seek divergent perspectives during information gathering and assessment. (1.3.2)
- Organize knowledge so that it is useful. (2.1.2)
- Use technology and other information tools to analyze and organize information. (2.1.4)
- Consider diverse and global perspectives in drawing conclusions. (2.3.2)

PROCESS

This is an outline rather than a detailed procedure. For this lesson, I have chosen the United Nations "Convention on the Rights of the Child" (CRC) as the document for which students need background information. Use this topic and these resources, select another topic and resources found at TakingIT Global, or choose other mentor texts that support the topic under study. Students work individually, in pairs, or in small groups to complete the text-to-world category matrix.

Days 1 and 2

Motivation

Project the United Nations CRC and ask why there needs to be a document called "Convention on the Rights of the Child." While one educator leads students in a discussion, the other records students' initial ideas about the problems and issues in the world about which children and youth need protection, such as food, water, health, physical safety, work, legal rights, and more.

Show the photo essays on the UNICEF website: "The Rights of the Child, 1" and "The Rights of the Child, 2" (www.unicef.org/crc/). Ask students to pay attention to the images only. After viewing, ask them to "think-pair-share" their initial responses to these images. What is the status of children around the world? Do these problems only apply in countries other than the United States?

Read the "Preamble" to the CRC. Note the legalistic language. Is it easy to understand? What might help readers comprehend this document? The CRC addresses an international need. Rather than making text-to-self or text-to-text connections, it may be important to connect to larger, more global issues in order to understand this document. Students build background knowledge and make text-to-world connections using U.S. and non-U.S.-based web resources in order to summarize articles found in this UN document.

STUDENT-FRIENDLY OBJECTIVES
1. Determine a keyword and use it as a search term.
2. Locate and read resources developed in the United States and other countries.
3. Make notes, cite URLs, and organize information on a graphic organizer.
4. Use information gathered to compose a synthesis essay and construct a Works Consulted.

PRESENTATION
In order to help build background knowledge about children's rights in the global context, determine some of the key concepts. Link to TakingITGlobal (TIG) (www.tigweb.org). Educators demonstrate using think-alouds as they skim and scan the "About Us" page to learn about this organization. Show the broad categories at TIG, such as health, human rights, education, and globalization, and the subtopics under several topics.

As a model, educators use think-alouds to determine the key concept from one article from the CRC (see 3.3 Teacher Resource—Completed Category Matrix for Article 32). Project Article 32 and circle keywords. Demonstrate how to connect an overarching keyword such as "economic exploitation" to the broad topics and subtopics on the TIG. Let students know they follow the same procedure in order to learn more about what is happening related to children's rights in countries around the world.

Read through the choices for various topics, subtopics, and resources. Using think-alouds, one educator locates information in the resources and the other records notes on the 3.3 Category Matrix. Involve students in determining which links to pursue and why. Read the TIG information on the home page for the topic. Provide one or two examples of notemaking from subtopic resources. When students have had sufficient demonstration, show them the completed graphic organizer for one article and one subtopic.

STUDENT PARTICIPATION PROCEDURES
1. Raise hand to choose a link.
2. Describe the resource (title, country of origin, and URL) and determine where it belongs on the graphic organizer.
3. Suggest a note.

While one educator facilitates students' contributions, the other records information on the graphic organizer. Discuss how making text-to-world connections helps build background knowledge for understanding the CRC.

Students can continue building text-to-world connections individually, in pairs, or in small groups. Students choose or educators assign one or more articles from the CRC; articles 6 through 40 are most appropriate for this research. Distribute the 3.3 Category Matrix electronically in order to facilitate keeping a record of URLs.

GUIDED PRACTICE
Educators monitor students' determining keywords, searching and recording on the category matrix. Engage students in conversations about particular resources.

CLOSURE

Students sit with (different) partners or in small groups to share one or more of their text-to-world resources. What information did students learn? How did it help them understand the article from the CRC?

DAY 3 OR 4

PRESENTATION

Educators model completing the 3.3 Summary Graphic Organizer. Students use it as prewriting for drafting a synthesis essay. Use the 3.3 Teacher Resource—Completed Summary Graphic Organizer and 3.3 Teacher Resource—Sample Synthesis Essay to guide this demonstration. Also project the 3.3 Synthesis Essay Rubric and use it to assess the sample essay.

Educators demonstrate how to use the URLs from the resources they consulted for their summary and the "Autocite" feature of an online citation maker, such as Easybib.com, in order to construct a Works Consulted.

GUIDED PRACTICE

Educators monitor students' individual summary graphic organizers and essays and support students in constructing a Works Consulted.

CLOSURE

Students lead a discussion about the need for a document such as the CRC. Replay the photo essays that launched this investigation. What text-to-world connections can students make now that they have background knowledge?

Students use the 3.3 Synthesis Essay Rubric to self-assess their work before turning it in for educators' assessment.

REFLECTION

How do we know when to seek out and build background information? How do we know when we should look for text-to-world connections to make sense of texts?

EXTENSIONS

Using the photo essays as models, students create multimedia presentations to share their summaries with the class or a web audience. They can also use this text-to-world background knowledge to begin an inquiry into global human rights issues. Students' inquiries can culminate with persuasive writing or presentations based on information from global resources. They may participate in social action in the local, state, national, or global community related to these issues.

Continue to use text-to-world category matrix graphic organizers to locate resources and information related to broad or global topics in which students lack sufficient or accurate background information.

4

Reading Comprehension Strategy Two

Using Sensory Images

Comprehension involves breathing life experiences into the abstract language of written texts. Proficient readers use visual, auditory, and other sensory connections to create mental images of an author's message.

—Doug Buehl

COLLABORATIVE TEACHING IN THE AGE OF ACCOUNTABILITY

MAXIMIZING YOUR IMPACT

» **Strategy One:** *Activating or Building Background Knowledge*

» **Strategy Two:** *Using Sensory Images*

» Strategy Three: *Questioning*

» Strategy Four: *Making Predictions and Drawing Inferences*

» Strategy Five: *Determining Main Ideas*

» Strategy Six: *Using Fix-up Options*

» Strategy Seven: *Synthesizing*

Just as the network of associations that readers build through prior knowledge helps them learn and remember new material, so do sensory images help readers retain information. Sensory experiences are a significant aspect of our background knowledge. Sensory imagery is an important part of our schemas. When we think about our sensory experiences, we are creating representations of those experiences in our memories (Marzano 2004, 35). In fact, our most powerful memories are attached to sensory experiences. A smell or a taste can trigger a long-cherished recollection—bread baking in the oven in grandma's kitchen or the damp earth that signals rebirth in nature each spring. The analogy of a car's headlights as a necessity for illuminating a dark road reminds us that we can and should tap into sight and all of our senses as we read. When we bring our sensory knowledge to the reading of a text, we can have a "lived through" experience with all genres of literature. Buehl (2009) describes this as "breathing life" into abstract language. We are the directors of the movies that play inside our heads as we read, and our literacy experiences are richer and more memorable if they include a variety of sensory details.

Some students may effectively use visualization as they read fictional texts but may not apply this strategy to their reading of informational texts. They may easily envision a scene from a novel, play, or short story but have difficulty or lack experience in creating mental representations of information such as a scientific process like cell mitosis.

41

In addition to increasing enjoyment, mental images also help readers more effectively retain and recall information. Foer (2006) studied people who have a high capacity to remember. He found that being able to associate sensory details with information, particularly with factual information, enhanced memory. In middle and high schools where students are expected to master and recall a great deal of content knowledge, they can benefit from developing the ability to use sensory details in both the service of reading for enjoyment and reading for information.

Does the bombardment of visual information in 21st-century technological society actually diminish students' ability to imagine? Sousa (2005) notes that technology provides many images for students, so many that it makes visualization more difficult for them. Like underused muscles, students' ability to use their imaginations is being reduced by the lack of opportunity. When novels, textbooks, and other information resources lack illustrations, readers can learn to create mental pictures and sensory images for characters, settings, and plots as well as information presented in texts.

One of the research-based instructional strategies recommended by Marzano, Pickering, and Pollock (2001) is nonlinguistic representation. Generating mental pictures and composing visual images to represent a concept or process and engaging in kinesthetic activities are brain-compatible strategies. As support for linguistic representations, they help learners connect both hemispheres of the brain. In *Action Strategies for Deepening Comprehension: Role Plays, Text Structure Tableaux, Talking Statues, and Other Enrichment Techniques That Engage Students with Text,* Wilhelm (2002) provides strategies that require students to involve their bodies, voices, and minds in the service of comprehension. Although all of these strategies rely on the effective use of the senses in making meaning, tableaux in particular relates directly to using sensory imagery because it requires students to use their bodies and gestures to express meaning.

Gardner's (1993) theory of multiple intelligences reminds us that some learners have diverse and strongly developed pathways for learning that emphasize one or more of their senses. Students with visual-spatial, musical, and body-kinesthetic intelligences may utilize their senses of sight, hearing, or touch spontaneously as they make meaning with text. Educators can capitalize on these preferences and invite these young people to share their gifts with classmates. Classroom teachers and school librarians themselves may be talented in utilizing one or more of their senses. Art, music, and physical education teachers can contribute their expertise and talents in coteaching and learning focused on developing sensory knowledge and the ability to use it in the service of reading comprehension. Spotlighting one particular sense can hone readers' ability to create or focus on individual senses (see lesson 4.2). For the most part, however, when readers become sophisticated at utilizing their senses, sensory imagery involves a variety of senses that work together to enhance understanding and enjoyment of text.

HOW TO TEACH THE STRATEGY

Teaching the concept of using sensory images to make meaning with middle school and high school students can require risk taking on the part of educators. Some students may resist educators' efforts to construct learning experiences that invite students to create their own mental images. Some students may feel threatened or vulnerable when asked to close their eyes, to visualize, or to use their bodies to learn or demonstrate comprehension. Educators' willingness to model these strategies and to value all student approximations of the tasks is necessary for effective sensory image strategy lessons.

One way to involve many young adult readers in exploring sensory imagery is to appeal to their own preference for audio or visual images. There are many less proficient readers of printed text who can recall details, share interpretations, and evaluate ideas and information that are presented to them auditorily or visually. Interacting with film, audiobooks, and other multimedia may be most effective for these learners. Helping students deepen their transactions with these formats and transfer their success with these media to the printed page is essential for their success (see *Knowledge Quest:* "Visual Literacy" [Abilock 2008] for articles, lessons, and projects).

Graphic organizers are one strategy that can help. When educators develop graphic organizers, they show learners ways to organize and represent information. These tools can serve as mind maps that show readers how they can organize and link information in their own mental images. Providing learners with opportunities to use electronic mind-mapping tools to create their own organizational structures can reinforce the idea of creating mental images as a valuable aspect of reading comprehension. One goal of using graphic organizers and mind maps is to help readers successfully use mental images to transfer understandings in one domain to another.

MAKING LITERATURE CONNECTIONS

Published writers use language effectively to bring to life the worlds within texts. Educators structure engagements with texts that will prompt readers to recognize the writer's craft in order to deepen their aesthetic reading experience. Many tween and young adult literature authors offer powerful sensory imagery to draw teen readers into a particular time period, landscape, culture, or emotion. Writers use literary devices such as similes, metaphors, and analogies to help shape readers' sensory experience of text and make connections between their senses and language. Understanding and creating metaphors and analogies are research-based instructional strategies highlighted in this book.

Students who recognize authors' powerful uses of language can employ their senses in the service of reading comprehension. Educators can support students in developing this ability by pointing out and using think-alouds to ponder rich language. They can model by reading selected passages expressively and inviting students to close their eyes and visualize the imagery in the text. Working together, school librarians and classroom teachers can collect resources,

such as those spotlighted in the figures that follow, for lessons focused on using sensory images as a reading comprehension strategy.

Educators often think of poetry first when they search for literature resources to support students in practicing this strategy. Lessons that engage students in drawing mental pictures while reciting, listening to, or composing poetry are effective. "Found Poetry" is one lesson that involves students in skimming and scanning for themes developed through imagery (see lesson 4.2). Each time I have cotaught this lesson, I have noticed that students gravitate first to the rhyming poetry they enjoyed as elementary students. Poems by Shel Silverstein and Jack Prelutsky are fun, perennial favorites. Figure 4-1 shows a collection of Jack Prelutsky's poems from *The New Kid on the Block.* Each of these poems appeals to a particular sense. The poet's lively language helps listeners and readers imagine the characters, settings, and events presented in these poems.

Coteaching with art and music teachers can be an effective way to privilege sensory learning and teach this reading comprehension strategy. Combining hands-on art experiences and poetry writing is a powerful way to connect the senses to meaning making. Interdisciplinary units such as "Behind the Masks: Exploring Culture and Self through Art and Poetry" (Moreillon 2004) can be especially effective. Collaborating with music teachers also provides opportunities for students to practice using their senses to construct meaning (see lesson 9.2).

Novels written in verse offer a bridge between fiction and poetry. These books combine a narrative frame with the poetry format, a combination that often appears less daunting to many striving readers. With the constraint of having fewer words to express ideas, information, and emotion, many novels written in verse are particularly strong in sensory imagery. Authors such as Jen Bryant, Margarita Engle, and Sonya Sones frequently write in this format and provide readers with rich sensory experiences.

Young adult novels are likewise sources for the exemplary use of language to communicate imagery. Figure 4-2 offers sensory-rich passages from young

Fig. 4-1   Sensory Poetry Classification Matrix

Poems from *The New Kid on the Block*, by Jack Prelutsky

Sight	Hearing	Taste	Smell	Touch
"My Dog, He Is an Ugly Dog"	"Louder Than a Clap of Thunder!"	"Jellyfish Stew"	"Drumpp the Grump"	"I've Got an Itch" "Super-Goopy Glue"
"The Zoosher"	"I've Got an Incredible Headache"	"Yubbazubbies"	"Be Glad Your Nose Is on Your Face"	"Suzanna Socked Me Sunday"
"Baloney Belly Billy"	"Floradora Doe"	"Gussie's Greasy Spoon"		
"Forty Performing Bananas"	"Happy Birthday, Dear Dragon"	"When Tillie Ate the Chili"		
		"I'd Never Eat a Beet"		
		"I'd Never Dine on Dinosaurs"		

adult novels that show how authors use images to help draw readers into their stories.

Many informational trade books, especially those published in the past decade, engage readers with vivid language as well as high-interest visuals (see figure 4-3). Marc Aronson, Susan Campbell Bartoletti, Russell Freedman, Jim Murphy, and Sally M. Walker use rich descriptions and dramatic action in their biographies and trade books on social studies and science topics, most of which are written with a narrative frame and are highly illustrated with photographs, drawings, maps, charts, and more. School librarians can support the curriculum and the use of sensory imagery, in particular through selecting and integrating such high-quality informational texts as well as fiction resources.

Inviting students into sensory experiences prompted by literacy engagements helps them deepen their comprehension as well as appreciate and learn the writer's craft of using language to involve the senses in the reading process. Educators must model this process by sharing their own experience of using their senses before, during, and after reading. The think-aloud strategy in figure 4-4 describes how a classroom teacher and school librarian can collaborate to demonstrate the effective use of sensory images to achieve comprehension.

EVER-EXPANDING DEFINITIONS OF LITERACY

"Teachers can still include the old 'basics' in their programs, but they must be part of the new 'basics' of multimodal texts, multiliteracies, technologies, collaboration, new ways of knowing, innovation, problem solving, and creativity" (Ryan 2008, 200). One of the challenges for middle and high school readers is the dominance of textbooks in content area curricula. Not only are many textbooks written beyond the proficient reading level of the students who are expected to learn from them, but the information found in textbooks does not follow the narrative frame with which many readers are most familiar and skilled. The print in these types of texts does not include the sensory imagery that has been found to help students connect with and recall information (Foer 2006). In addition, in a textbook-centric class, students are often asked to assume a passive role answering questions found at the end of the chapter rather than take the active role reading comprehension strategy lessons require.

Fortunately, more and more educators are embracing an inquiry-based process that includes textbooks as just one of many types of resources that can be used for student-directed learning. In these classrooms and libraries, students can use other types of informational texts, including trade books, websites, and multimedia, to practice using sensory imagery as

---

Fig. 4-2   Passages from Tween and Young Adult Novels That Capitalize on Sensory Imagery

Sight

"Moonlight misted over the rough floors and made the sparse room glow silver, the goldfish bowl looking like a second moon. The shabby walls and worn stones seemed to shimmer as if a translucent silk veil covered them, muting any flaws and transforming the house into a dwelling of luminous lights and delicate shadows. Minli had never seen her home look so beautiful" (265). *Where the Mountain Meets the Moon*, by Grace Lin

Taste

"It [chocolate] was so dark it was almost black and it melted on her tongue into an ancient flavor of seed pod, earth, shade, and sunlight, its bitterness casting a shadow of sweet. It tasted…fine, so subtle and strange it made her feel like a novitiate into some arcanum of spice" (51). *Lips Touch: Three Times*, by Laini Taylor

Touch/Taste

"Her lips were not like rose petals, not like silk and velvet, not like the tender colors of dawn over the desert, or like the breath of the evening wind. Her lips were rough as her hands, rough from the desert sand. Lips like the storm that blinds you among the dunes, like the desert's unbearable heat, like the trunks of palm trees in the oases, like the blazing sun at noon, like the sky just before it darkens with the rain that so seldom comes. Raka did not withdraw. Latlit tasted all the colors of India in her mouth" (302). *Tiger Moon*, by Antonia Michaelis

Smell

"The man Jack sniffed the air. He ignored the scents that had come into the room with him, dismissed the scents that he could safely ignore, honed in on the smell of the thing he had come to find. He could smell the child: a milky smell, like chocolate chip cookies, and the sour tang of a wet, disposable, nighttime diaper. He could smell the baby shampoo in its hair, and something small and rubbery—a *toy*, he thought, and then, *no something to suck*—that the child had been carrying" (9). *The Graveyard Book*, by Neil Gaiman

Hearing

"The silence seemed unbreakable. As I closed the door, the soft click of the latch exploded in the air. Mama jumped as if it had been a gunshot. The knife slid to the ground with a sharp ping against the tile" (115). *The Rock and the River*, by Kekla Magoon

All

"She takes my hand. We walk to the place where the seeds were just planted. The soil is wet and black. A spade has turned it upside down, so the buried earth meets the sky and the sky brings its breath underground. It feels like I could fall right into that deep, rich place. I crouch, pick up a handful of dirt, and rub it between my fingers. I breathe in the mineral smell of leaves rotting to make a bed for the new. The smell of change" (19). *Radiant Darkness*, by Emily Whitman

"Something hit him. The impact was so jarring, so unexpected that there was barely time to register what was happening. It was Charlie—he'd rammed a rock-hard shoulder into Marcus's sternum and dropped him where he stood. The ball squirted loose, but Marcus wasn't even aware of it. He lay like a stone on the grass, ears roaring, trying to keep from throwing up his breakfast" (5). *Pop*, by Gordon Korman

a reading comprehension strategy in which they are active rather than passive in the meaning making and information-seeking processes.

In their daily lives, students engage with a complex set of information and communication technologies (ICTs) that appeal to their various senses. Cope and

---

Fig. 4-3 Passages from Tween and Young Adult Informational Trade Books That Capitalize on Sensory Imagery

Sight

"The night air felt brisk as the wintry wind swept down the street. From balconies and windows above the streets, colorful flags napped crisply. Most flags were red and white with think black swastikas, the symbol of the Nazi Party. On some hastily homemade banners, the swastikas had been sewn on backward. But it didn't matter: Their good intentions fluttered like dark birds above the city streets" (16). *Hitler Youth: Growing Up in Hitler's Shadow*, by Susan Campbell Bartoletti

"At the moment Hamilton released the towrope, the wave was in full bloom, thick and long. He sped down the face, carved back into its fullness and danced within the curl that was forming over his head. He charged full speed down the center of the wave as it began to surround him, fully covering his body" (26). *Extreme Sports*, by Ron Horton

Touch

"You are floating in a tank of water the exact same temperature as your body. Where does your body end and the water begin? A full over-the-head mast with air holes to breathe through is used with some subjects. But drips of water creeping in could be distracting, and the air line sometimes leaks. You opt for foam pillows around your neck and waist to help keep you afloat." (23). *Almost Astronauts: 13 Women Who Dared to Dream*, by Tanya Lee Stone

Hearing

"There was, though, an ominous feeling, a deep-in-the-gut sensation that something powerful and painful was unfolding. From across the street at the Stock Exchange came a weird and relentless roar that could be heard clearly by the crowd. Steady and high-pitched, it was the combined voices of more than a thousand men inside trying to hold on to the last shreds of the greatest financial boom ever" (15). *Six Days in October: The Stock Market Crash of 1929*, by Karen Blumenthal

All

"The garden in our courtyard was my favorite place, with flowers taking turns to blossom even in late fall. Our golden daffodils—or water fairies, as Lao Lao [grandmother] called them—proudly announce the coming of spring. In the summer, pale jasmine opened up at night, filling our *siheyuan* [courtyard surrounded by buildings] with its fragrance. Lao Lao encouraged the jasmine's nimble vines to climb freely up and around our bamboo fence, forming a blooming wall that separated the garden from the rest of the yard. Hardy chrysanthemum—in pink, yellow, and white—flowered from season to season. It was in this garden, I was told, that I took my first steps, surrounded by aunts and uncles, their arms reaching out to catch me if I fell" (4). *Snow Falling in Spring: Coming of Age in China during the Cultural Revolution*, by Moying Li

"Everything is clothed in moss. The moss is studded with ferns. The ferns are dotted with lichens, liverworts, and fungi. They come in every color, shape, and texture you can imagine. Light green fungi feel like the rubbery ears of a grandfather. Here lichens come in red, and moss can be yellow. Mushrooms look like little umbrellas, or lace, or the icing piped on a birthday cake" (37). *Quest for the Tree Kangaroo: An Expedition to the Cloud Forest of New Guinea*, by Sy Montgomery

Fig. 4-4   Sensory Imagery Literacy Engagement

Based on Dr. Martin Luther King, Jr.'s "I Have a Dream" speech.

Before Reading: Connecting to Prior Sensory Knowledge

Note the date of Dr. King's speech: August 28, 1963. Using as many sensory images as possible, educators discuss what they know about the event surrounding the speech. Who was in Washington, D.C., at the Lincoln Memorial that day? Why were they there? Show the photograph of more than 250,000 people who were part of the March on Washington for Jobs and Freedom (http://en.wikipedia.org/wiki/File:View_of_Crowd_at_1963_March_on_Washington.jpg). What is the weather like in D.C. in August? How do people feel when they are marching for a cause in which they believe? It was hot and humid that day. Marchers felt tired and were chatting with one another as they waited anxiously to hear Dr. King's speech. They might have noticed a hush come over the crowd as Dr. King came to the podium and began to speak.

During Reading: Activating Sensory Images

One educator reads; one closes her eyes. Students are also invited to close their eyes during the reading.

The reader asks listeners to imagine the sound of 250,000 people clapping. The listening educator shares her images and connections with students. For example: "I am sure the sound of 250,000 people clapping inspired Dr. King. The marchers were exhausted, but hearing the applause reenergized their spirits. They were excited to hear what their great leader had to say."

In reference to the Emancipation Proclamation, Dr. King uses the phrase "great beacon light of hope." The listening educator shares her connections to the symbolism of a beacon of light. "I imagine the news of their freedom was to slaves like a lighthouse is to sailors lost in a storm. They could see a future for themselves, and in the case of the slaves, for their children as well. Picturing this light as 'hope' gives me a sense of how important it was for Dr. King to make his 'dream' speech at that event, the March on Washington for Jobs and Freedom, and at that place, the Lincoln Memorial."

But Dr. King goes on to say that the "manacles of segregation and the chains of discrimination" keep African Americans from achieving equality. The listening educator shares her mental images of people as bound prisoners who cannot fully participate in society. "I can see people who are denied access to an equal education, economic equality, and full participation in society as prisoners of prejudice. I imagine them behind bars able to see what they are denied, but unable to reach it."

Dr. King's speech is rich with figurative language that provides listeners with sensory images on which they can build their comprehension of the meaning, the themes, he conveyed to the audience that day. Continue reading the speech and pause to share sensory and mental images. Involve students as appropriate.

After Reading: Reflection

The listening educator shares her images and connections with the students. For example:

> "I think Dr. King effectively used figurative language throughout the 'I Have a Dream' speech in order to touch the hearts and minds of his listeners and the readers he may have imagined would later read this speech. His imagery is so vivid that almost fifty years later, we can understand the themes of his speech and can still imagine what it was like to hear him speak that day. His reference to his own children is one of the most-quoted passages from this speech. I am a mother who wants her children to be judged, not on the basis of their physical appearance, but on the 'content of their character.' At this point in the speech, I could picture Dr. King's children, my own children and students I have known, and all the children that have been born since that day. I know what it is like to have dreams for better lives for our nation's youth. His final images of U.S. geography and references to people of different races and with different religious beliefs made me see a U.S. map in my mind's eye. These images strengthened my belief that Dr. King was sharing a dream that was truly for everyone, everywhere in our country."

Text of "I Have a Dream" available at www.mlkonline.net/dream.html.

Kalantzis identify multiple formats for 21st-century literacy: linguistic, visual, audio, gestural, and spatial (1999). These formats are combined in various ways to create multimodal texts. An ever-expanding aspect of literacy in this century involves understanding the meaning these texts—with or without linguistic features—intend to communicate and the meaning readers make from them. It is, then, natural and wise to integrate texts in multiple formats when teaching the sensory images reading comprehension strategy. For linguistic-focused educators, unpacking the meaning in other formats can be challenging. Educators who understand the value of multiple literacies and are willing to learn alongside students will have the greatest success integrating these texts into their curricula.

That said, beginning with visualizing is a basic technique used for activating sensory imagery. After modeling this practice, educators can invite students to close their eyes and imagine the information as these texts are read aloud and then ask listeners to share their mental images. Guided visualizations like "Rock to Rock" in *Keepers of the Earth: Native American Stories and Environmental Activities for Children* (Caduto and Bruchac/Fadden and Wood) invites students to visualize the rock cycle and provides an effective model for teaching this strategy. Combining this short narrative with music such as the *Grand Canyon Suite* (Grofé) is a way to deepen students' sensory experiences with the information. Taking this one step further, ask students to focus on other science curriculum concepts and use that information to compose narratives with sensory imagery. Educators can challenge students to extend their narratives with sound or music or compose music of their own to enhance readers' visualization of the scientific processes being described.

Along with this practice, it is important to anchor students' comprehension by exploring the impact of visual information on meaning making. Middle and high school classroom teachers and school librarians should take full advantage of the richness and sophistication of illustration in picture books by focusing on the visual information and aesthetic experiences these titles provide. Picture books can and should be used in the secondary curriculum. *The Power of Picture Books: Using Content Area Literature in Middle School* (Fresch and Harkins 2009) is an excellent resource for connecting picture books with content area curriculum. Conducting illustrator studies or studies based on the media used in a selection of texts can focus students' attention on the visual feast offered by these books. There are a number of author-illustrators whose highly sophisticated work deals with themes that are most appropriate for middle and high school readers (see figure 6-4).

Graphic novels are another example of print and illustration that are gaining acceptance in school-based literacy learning. In recent years, authors and illustrators have created graphic novel versions of some of the classic literature that comprises the foundational texts in many middle and high school English-language arts classrooms. Readers and educators can find multiple graphic novel versions of titles originally penned by Dickens, Brontë, Shakespeare, Shelley, and more.

In addition to popular graphic novel series such as Amulet (Kibuishi), Bone (Smith), and Sandman (Gaiman), other titles in this format on nearly every imaginable topic hold promise for many formerly aliterate students. Classics such as the Maus series about the Holocaust by Art Spiegelman and new classics such as Larry Gonick's cartoon guide and history books on topics from genetics and statistics to the United States and the universe appeal to many teen readers and provide them with comprehensible visual images for abstract and difficult concepts. Other titles that use the graphic novel style, such as *Inside Out: Portrait of an Eating Disorder* (Shivack), may reach and support readers who gravitate to books that provide information as well as visual stimulation. Educators can help graphic novel readers "see" how the images on the pages help them make meaning and then help readers build a bridge to creating their own mental images when illustrations are not available in a text.

When readers compare movie versions of tween and young adult novels to the original printed or audiobook, they can focus on the similarities and differences between the film visuals compared with the mental images they formed while reading the book.

They can discuss how these images affected their comprehension and responses to the themes and story elements. They may also question the movie director's choices when a reader feels tension or discrepancies between two formats. For an excellent resource on using film in school, see *Knowledge Quest:* "Film in Education: Visual Literacy with Moving Images" (Abilock 2010). These learning engagements give readers input for making comparisons based on visualization through their sense of sight as well as from the narration, script, and other elements.

Although our eyes contain 70 percent of the body's sensory receptors and we take in more information visually than through any of the other senses (Wolfe 2001), educators can challenge students to use all of their senses in the service of meaning making. For example, visual imagery alone provides an incomplete picture of a Civil War soldier's experience in battle. When readers can also imagine the taste of fear in the soldier's mouth, hear the anguished cries of fallen comrades and horses, feel the trembling of his fingers on a Springfield musket, and smell acrid gunpowder, they have achieved a "lived-through" experience. They no longer stand outside the text but have entered into it and participated in the action along with the characters. When they can create mental images that include all of the senses while reading expository information in a textbook that lacks sensory details, then they have achieved the ultimate goal of this strategy. They can deeply comprehend the text by making their own mental images and meaning from the print on the page.

Engaging with digital storytelling, which combines print, narration, still and video images, sound, or music, is another effective way to maximize the role of the senses in comprehension. The University of Houston maintains an extraordinary collection of digital storytelling examples in many disciplines (http://digitalstorytelling.coe.uh.edu). Educators can use these resources in various content areas, and students can view them as well as use these examples as inspiration for their own digital storytelling projects. The challenging lesson in this chapter provides an example.

TWEEN, YOUNG ADULT, AND ADULT LITERATURE CITED

Starred titles are used in the lesson plans.

Almost Astronauts: 13 Women Who Dared to Dream, by Tanya Lee Stone

Amulet, by Kazu Kibuishi

*The Atlantic Slave Trade, by Johannes Postma

Bone, by Jeff Smith

*The Book of Qualities, by J. Ruth Gendler

The Cartoon Guide to Genetics, by Larry Gonick

Extreme Sports, by Ron Horton

The Graveyard Book, by Neil Gaiman

Hitler Youth: Growing Up in Hitler's Shadow, by Susan Campbell Bartoletti

*I Never Metaphor I Didn't Like: A Comprehensive Compilation of History's Greatest Analogies, Metaphors, and Similes, by Dr. Mardy Grothe

Inside Out: Portrait of an Eating Disorder, by Nadia Shivack

Keepers of the Earth: Native American Stories and Environmental Activities for Children, by Michael J. Caduto and Joseph Bruchac, illustrated by John Kahionhes Fadden and Carol Wood

Lips Touch: Three Times, by Laini Taylor

*A Mango-Shaped Space, by Wendy Mass

Maus: A Survivor's Tale, by Art Spiegelman

*The Middle Passage: White Ships/Black Cargo, by Tom Feelings

The New Kid on the Block, by Jack Prelutsky

Pop, by Gordon Korman

Quest for the Tree Kangaroo: An Expedition to the Cloud Forest of New Guinea, by Sy Montgomery

Radiant Darkness, by Emily Whitman

The Rock and the River, by Kekla Magoon

Sandman, by Neil Gaiman

Six Days in October: The Stock Market Crash of 1929, by Karen Blumenthal

Snow Falling in Spring: Coming of Age in China during the Cultural Revolution, by Moying Li

Tiger Moon, by Antonia Michaelis

Where the Mountain Meets the Moon, by Grace Lin

Lesson Plans

In the following how-to lesson plans, classroom teachers and school librarians use think-alouds to demonstrate how and why they are using sensory imagery to comprehend texts before, during, and after reading. The lessons are constructed for students at three levels of development. Readers at all levels can benefit from how-to lessons until these reading strategies are integrated into their repertoires as reading skills. The organization of instruction in the lessons maximizes the benefit of two equal-partner collaborators by lowering the student-teacher ratio.

The mentor texts for each lesson are rich in sensory images to provide learners with models: a wordless book in the advancing lesson, excerpts from a novel in the advanced lesson, and metaphors and personifications rich with sensory images and literary devices in the challenging lesson. In each of these lessons, students compose texts that communicate concepts and emotions through sensory imagery.

These lesson plans reinforce the importance of practicing and assessing reading comprehension strategy outcomes through student-generated writing. Improved reading proficiency can improve writing and vice versa. Reading and writing are two sides of the same coin.

LESSON PLAN 4.1

Reading Comprehension Strategy Two
Using Sensory Images

Reading Development Level: Advancing

Instructional Strategies
Cues and Questions, Classifying, Notemaking and Summarizing

Lesson Length
6 or 7 sessions

Purpose
The purpose of this unit is to use sensory images to deepen students' comprehension. They engage with multimodal primary and secondary resources, make and categorize notes, and make text-to-text connections to build background knowledge. This lesson is designed as preparation for inquiry into the slave trade from the perspective of an artifact or person who took part in this business. The unit continues as outlined below resulting in students' final product, original blues poem stanzas based on the information and sensory images generated and inferred from their research. The first lesson or the first and second lessons can also stand alone as elaboration for social studies textbook information about the slave trade.

Objectives
At the end of this unit, students will be able to
1. Use their senses to begin to comprehend the impact of the slave trade on all stakeholders.
2. Distinguish primary and secondary source materials.
3. Make and categorize notes, cite sources, and organize information.
4. Self-assess their notes and Works Consulted using a rubric.
5. Compose and perform a group four-line stanza written from the point of view of their topic of study.

Resources, Materials, and Equipment
Mentor texts: *The Middle Passage: White Ships/Black Cargo,* by Tom Feelings, and *The Atlantic Slave Trade,* by Johannes Postma; 4.1 Teacher Resource—Primary Source Excerpts (from *The Atlantic Slave Trade*)

Slave Trade Text Set and Internet Pathfinder: www.storytrail.com/impact12/slave.htm

Graphic organizers: Notemaking Graphic Organizer, 4.1 Teacher Resource—Completed Notemaking Graphic Organizer (for Olaudah Equiano), 4.1 List/Group/Label Graphic Organizer, 4.1 Teacher Resource—Completed List/Group/Label Graphic Organizer, 4.1 Notemaking and Works Consulted Rubric, 4.1 Blues Poem Assignment Sheet and Rubric

Blues music or call-and-response African-American spiritual music

Rhyming dictionaries (or use online resource found on Internet Pathfinder)

Internet access and data projector, overhead, or interactive whiteboard, or document camera if available

Collaboration

Educators demonstrate the importance of connecting with sensory images in understanding historical events. They model responding to sensory input, locating information, and making notes from the mentor texts. The educators model distinguishing primary and secondary source material and making notes from multiple sources in multiple formats. They monitor students' research processes. The school librarian may take responsibility for supporting student research in library center rotations. Educators share responsibility for guiding and assessing students' notemaking, Works Consulted, and blues poem final product.

Assessments

The students' graphic organizers, notes and responses, blues poem stanzas, and rubrics show the process and results of their learning. Students self-assess; student reviewers assess each other's work as well.

Standards

Reading keywords: Extract information and use graphic organizers to comprehend literary and nonfiction text; analyze passages; use comprehension skills to analyze words, images, graphics, and sounds; make inferences and draw conclusions from research.

History keywords: Differentiate primary and secondary source materials in multiple formats; use multiple sources to study people and events from the past; understand various patterns of economic activity.

AASL STANDARDS INDICATORS*

- Develop and refine a range of questions to frame the search for new understanding. (1.1.3)
- Find, evaluate, and select appropriate sources to answer questions. (1.1.4)
- Read, view, and listen for information presented in any format (e.g., textual, visual, media, digital) in order to make inferences and gather meaning. (1.1.6)
- Follow ethical and legal guidelines in gathering and using information. (1.3.3)
- Organize knowledge so that it is useful. (2.1.2)
- Demonstrate teamwork by working productively with others. (3.2.3)
- Assess the quality and effectiveness of the learning product. (3.4.2)
- Interpret new information based on cultural and social context. (4.4.4)

PROCESS

Although this unit focuses on the slave trade, educators can use these lessons as a guide to design similar learning engagements in which students use sensory images to comprehend human experience in historical contexts.

MOTIVATION

Cues: Share the title page illustration from Tom Feelings's *The Middle Passage: White Ships, Black Cargo* (just over halfway through this unpaged book). To which senses does this image appeal?

Show the illustration of Africans packed tightly on a slave ship (the previous double-page spread). Ask for volunteers to simulate the arrangement of people in the slaver hold (six or seven square feet, two to three feet of head room, ankles shackled with neighbor). Ask students to respond to this tableau with a "think-pair-share" with a partner, then with the class. Pose the questions: "How do we know what it was like on slave ships?" "How can we use all of our senses to increase our ability to comprehend this horrific experience?" The purpose of this learning experience is to use sensory images to comprehend as closely as possible the experience of enslaved Africans.

STUDENT-FRIENDLY OBJECTIVES
1. Name and list sensory words to describe illustrations.
2. Group and label the terms by sense.

PRESENTATION
One educator takes the students on a bookwalk through *The Middle Passage*. The other educator records the sensory words students use to describe the images in the book. Create three columns on the board: one for words related to the enslaved Africans' experience, one for the conquerors' experience (both white and African), and one for inanimate objects such as the ship itself.

Model the participation procedures. Using think-alouds, educators take turns. The recording educator puts suggestions on the list on the whiteboard.

STUDENT PARTICIPATION PROCEDURES
1. Raise hand to suggest a word or short phrase.
2. Tell in which of the three columns it belongs.

Continue until the book is read. Record only words or phrases that evoke sensory images such as terrifying scream, trembling hands, moaning, bulging biceps, acrid sweat, and so on. After the book is completed, divide the class into three groups, one for each column.

STUDENT PRACTICE PROCEDURES
1. Work with partner(s) to group the words or phrases in the assigned column.
2. Label each group by sense.

GUIDED PRACTICE
Monitor students' negotiations and understanding of how words or phrases relate to sensory images.

CLOSURE
Ask for volunteers to share their column heading examples from one group and the label they assigned to it. Record questions if students have them at this point.

REFLECTION
To which senses did these images most appeal? Would another medium elicit other senses? Describe it.

DAYS 2 AND 3

MOTIVATION
Pose the question: "Was Tom Feelings actually present in Africa at the time of the slave trade?" "Are his illustrations primary or secondary sources?" "How might the actual words or actual drawings of someone who was involved in the slave trade evoke sensory images?"

PRESENTATION

Students read firsthand testimonials from an enslaved African or other stakeholder in the slave trade. Name these primary source document authors: kidnapped African, slave trader, and slaver (ship) captain. One group may also study the ship itself.

Pose these questions: "What if the words aren't as descriptive as Feelings's illustrations?" "How can readers use sensory images to visualize and deepen their experience of primary source documents?"

Project the 4.1 List/Group/Label Graphic Organizer. Using Olaudah Equiano's piece (Document 1 on the 4.1 Teacher Resource—Primary Source Excerpts), educators model reading using think-alouds and stopping to record sensory images on the graphic organizer. Use the 4.1 Teacher Resource—Completed List/Group/Label Graphic Organizer as a guide. Include an example of interpretation such as scratchy and dark for "put in a sack." Give examples for which students practice visualizing using all of their senses. After a few entries on the graphic organizer, involve students more fully while one educator reads and the other records students' and educators' ideas.

STUDENT PARTICIPATION PROCEDURES
1. Raise hand to pause the reading.
2. Suggest a word or short phrase that evokes sensory images.
3. Interpret the text to elaborate on sensory imagery.

Continue until the excerpts have been read. Using different color markers, group the items on the list and label them by sense. Educators model a think-aloud in which they share the emotional feelings that these sensory images evoke. Record a brief emotional response using sensory images (see the 4.1 Teacher Resource—Completed List/Group/Label Graphic Organizer).

Divide the students into pairs or small groups. Distribute the primary source documents from *The Atlantic Slave Trade* and the 4.1 List/Group/Label Graphic Organizer. Students may compose individual, partner, or small group brief emotional responses.

STUDENT PRACTICE PROCEDURES
1. Complete the top portion of the graphic organizer.
2. Work with partner(s) to identify sensory words or phrases.
3. Record on the graphic organizer.
4. Group the words or phrases and label each group by sense.
5. Compose a brief emotional response based on sensory images.

GUIDED PRACTICE

Educators monitor students' negotiations and understanding of how the text evokes sensory images. Educators provide writing conference support for responses if necessary.

CLOSURE

Divide the class into two groups. Ask for volunteers to share: identify the stakeholder, provide a brief description of the person or object (the ship), and give brief emotional responses. Record questions if students have them at this point.

REFLECTION

What were the similarities and differences in the sensory images that Feelings's illustrations and the first-person, primary source documents evoke? How did using sensory images increase your understanding of the person's (or ship's) experience?

DAYS 4 AND 5

MOTIVATION

Educators conduct a think-aloud about Document 1. Considering the circumstances of his capture and his age at the time, does Olaudah Equiano's testimony seem relatively calm? How frightened was this eleven-year-old boy? (Remind students that Olaudah Equiano wrote this document thirty-five years after his kidnapping in Nigeria.) Are there secondary sources we can use to get more information about the experience of participants in the slave trade?

PRESENTATION

Define secondary sources. Students interact with secondary source documents in center rotations that involve a print text set, an Internet Pathfinder, and a video, if available and appropriate. (Preview the video to determine which parts relate best to collecting information for particular slave trade stakeholders.)

Project the Notemaking Graphic Organizer. Review notemaking formats if necessary (see the Notemaking Chart). Educators use one secondary source related to a kidnapped African to model notemaking (see the 4.1 Teacher Resource—Completed Notemaking Graphic Organizer).

Emphasize citing the secondary source designation after each note from this document. Return to the information collected on the 4.1 List/Group/Label Graphic Organizer and to *The Middle Passage* bookwalk experience and add a few notations to the notemaking sheet. Emphasize citing the primary or secondary source designation after each note. Show the sample Works Consulted at the bottom of the 4.1 Teacher Resource—Completed Notemaking Graphic Organizer.

STUDENT PRACTICE PROCEDURES

1. Rotate through centers.
2. Record notes on graphic organizer.
3. Label notes with "P" or "S."
4. Keep a record of sources used.

GUIDED PRACTICE

Educators monitor students' notemaking and bibliographic records.

CLOSURE

Return to the sample notes. Discuss and circle or highlight the most captivating and researched ideas, sensory words, and vivid word choice. Students do the same with their own notes.

DAY 6

MOTIVATION

Play blues music or call-and-response spirituals. Pose the question: "How does this music reflect the misery of Africans who became slaves in the American colonies and early nation?"

PRESENTATION

Project the 4.1 Blues Poem Assignment Sheet and Rubric. Share the sample blues poem about Olaudah Equiano. Use the self-assessment section to note areas of strength and weakness in the poem. Use the rubric to assess it. Review links on the Internet Pathfinder for blues poem support. Students work individually, with partners, or in small groups to compose poems based on their research.

STUDENT PRACTICE PROCEDURES

1. Use notes to identify sensory images, possible word choice, and specific information.
2. Brainstorm end-of-line rhyming words.
3. Compose three-line blues poem stanzas.
4. Self-assess by stanza using the rubric.

GUIDED PRACTICE

Educators monitor students' adherence to the blues poem format, including end-of-line rhyming words.

CLOSURE

Ask for student volunteers to share their poems-in-progress with the class. Remind the students to self-assess using the rubric and revise their poems as necessary. Complete poems as homework.

DAY 7

PRESENTATIONS

Students practice, then perform their blues poems. Educators ask for a volunteer and model using the rubric to review a poem, including citing one example for each stanza. Emphasize the importance of specific and positive feedback.

STUDENT PRACTICE PROCEDURES

1. Complete the top portion of the rubric self-assessment, including one example for each stanza.
2. Exchange poems with someone else.
3. Use another color writing implement to add your name to the reviewer's line.
4. Add to the rubric assessment by noting one example for each stanza.

GUIDED PRACTICE

Educators monitor for specific and positive feedback.

CLOSURE

Educators lead half-class or whole group discussions about using sensory images to build understanding of the experiences of other people, times, events, and places. Discuss how some texts contained more or fewer sensory images.

REFLECTION

How did a focus on sensory images help readers comprehend the mentor texts and text set selections? When should readers use sensory images to gain or regain comprehension?

EXTENSIONS

Continue a study into the economic impact of slavery in the United States in the years leading up to the Civil War. Compare the sensory images offered for this topic in the social studies textbook with those generated in this unit of study.

Continue to use sensory images to visualize other people, places, or historical events. Use visualization in other content areas such as science. Ask students to share examples of when they use visualization to improve their comprehension of text.

LESSON PLAN 4.2

Reading Comprehension Strategy Two
Using Sensory Images

Reading Development Level: Advanced

Instructional Strategies
Classifying

Lesson Length
5 sessions

Purpose
The purpose of this unit is to increase students' awareness of how sensory images deepen their comprehension and engagements with texts. Students engage in skimming and scanning for keywords while reading poetry and quotations. They construct a "found poem" focused on one single sense, introduce it with a quotation, and give it an original title. Students use parenthetical citations, create a Works Cited page, and present their poems in a multisensory mode.

Objectives
At the end of this unit, students will be able to
1. Skim and scan poetry and quotation texts for sensory images and keywords.
2. Construct a found poem organized around a single sense.
3. Cite poetry and quotation sources.
4. Create a multisensory poem presentation.
5. Self-assess the poem and Works Cited page using a rubric.

Resources, Materials, and Equipment
Mentor text: *A Mango-Shaped Space,* by Wendy Mass (passages on pages 3, 17, 41, 47–48, and 124–25)

Synesthesia image: http://en.wikipedia.org/wiki/File:Synesthesia.svg

Poetry and Quotations Text Set

Poetry Pathfinder and Quotation Resources: www.storytrail.com/impact12/poetry.htm

Graphic organizers: 4.2 Found Poetry Assignment Sheet, 4.2 Teacher Resource—Sample Found Poem and Works Cited, 4.2 Found Poem, Works Cited, and Presentation Rubric

Materials: Sticky notes

Internet access and data projector, overhead, or interactive whiteboard, or document camera if available

Collaboration

Educators demonstrate the importance of connecting with sensory images in understanding text. They model responding to sensory input and describe their multisensory visualizations. The educators model skimming and scanning for sensory images and for keywords in poetry texts and locating quotations by topic in print and online sources. They monitor students' poem construction and Works Cited and jointly assess students' final products.

Assessments

The found poems, Works Cited, multisensory poem presentations, and rubrics show the process and results of students' learning. Students self-assess their work.

Standards

Reading keywords: Use strategies such as skimming and scanning; use comprehension skills to analyze words, images, graphics, and sounds; make inferences about how sensory language creates imagery, mood, or tone; follow a style manual such as the *MLA Handbook;* and accurately cite sources.

AASL STANDARDS INDICATORS*

- Read, view, and listen for information presented in any format (e.g., textual, visual, media, digital) in order to make inferences and gather meaning. (1.1.6)
- Follow ethical and legal guidelines in gathering and using information. (1.3.3)
- Assess the quality and effectiveness of the learning product. (3.4.2)
- Respond to literature and creative expressions of ideas in various formats and genres. (4.1.3)
- Use creative and artistic formats to express personal learning. (4.1.8)

PROCESS

Although this lesson focuses on using poetry as the source for found poems, any type of text can be used including street signs, newspaper articles, websites, lists, advertisements, phone books, novels, or any genre of writing from textbooks to engaging lines from published poems.

MOTIVATION

Project the synesthesia image. Talk about how some people's senses function differently than others' senses do. In this example, letters and numbers are shown with colors that a synesthete would perceive involuntarily and simultaneously. In other words, the letter *S* and the number 8 would always be purple. Think-pair-share about how this might affect a synesthete's daily life.

While one educator reads a passage from *A Mango-Shaped Space* (Mass), the other closes her eyes. After reading, think-pair-share sensory responses to the passage. Then ask students to close their eyes. Read additional examples and ask students to imagine the colors Mia Winchell sees when she perceives certain letters, numbers, and sounds. Think-pair-share after reading each passage.

Perceiving or consciously creating sensory images are ways people deepen their experiences of life and with texts. Our mental visualizations should include all our senses. Students skim and scan poetry for sensory images in order to create a "found poem" that they present creatively in a multisensory mode.

* Excerpted from *Standards for the 21st-Century Learner* by the American Association of School Librarians, a division of the American Library Association, copyright © 2007 American Library Association. Available for download at www.ala.org/aasl/standards. Used with permission.

STUDENT-FRIENDLY OBJECTIVES
1. Define "found poetry."
2. Skim and scan for sensory images and keywords.

PRESENTATION
Project the 4.2 Teacher Resource—Sample Found Poem and Works Cited. Educators read the poem aloud and then reread it. They model skimming for sensory images. Determine a dominant sense in each selection. Model scanning for keywords related to the dominant sense in the entire poem. Reread the poem and ask students to close their eyes and use the dominant sense to better visualize the poem.

STUDENT PARTICIPATION PROCEDURES
1. Raise hand to share the dominant sense.
2. Share a sensory image elicited by the poem.
3. Identify two consecutive lines that are exceptional in eliciting sensory images.

Educators choose additional poems with strong sensory images. Continue modeling and eliciting students' participation until they have had sufficient modeling in skimming, scanning, and determining the main sense.

Project the 4.2 Teacher Resource—Sample Found Poem and Works Cited. Read the title, quotation, and poem. Discuss how the poem was constructed around one sense—hearing—and note how the lines came from consecutive lines from published poems found online and in print sources. Note the parenthetical citations. Mention the quotation to introduce the poem and the original title.

STUDENT PRACTICE PROCEDURES
1. Skim and scan poems from text set.
2. Softly read aloud poems that elicit sensory images.
3. Write name and period on sticky notes and place them next to exceptional consecutive lines.

GUIDED PRACTICE
Educators monitor for understanding of found poem two-consecutive-lines rule.

CLOSURE
Ask for volunteers to share exceptional consecutive lines. Ask other students to identify the dominant sense and share the mental image the lines evoke.

DAYS 2 AND 3

MOTIVATION
Share the final product, the 4.2 Teacher Resource—Sample Found Poem and Works Cited, including Wordle and cricket sounds. Discuss the found poet's choices of color, image, and sound.

PRESENTATION—DAY 2
Project and review the 4.2 Found Poetry Assignment Sheet. Demonstrate how to search one of the resources on the Poetry Pathfinder. Teach or review parenthetical citations and Works Cited page format. Discuss the various types of poem citations and demonstrate using an electronic citation maker to create poetry citations.

PRESENTATION–DAY 3

Project the 4.2 Teacher Resource—Sample Found Poem and Works Cited. Discuss the mood and tone of the poem. (The mood is the feeling the reader or viewer gets when reading a piece of literature or watching a film or play. The tone of a piece is reflected in the emotional state of the narrative voice.) Note the sensory keywords and make connections to the quotation and the original title.

Project the index of a quotations reference book. Demonstrate how to use it to locate quotations within the book. Do the same for an online quotations website. Demonstrate how to cite a quotation from a print source and from an online source.

STUDENT PRACTICE PROCEDURES

1. Continue to skim and scan and locate exceptional lines in print and online resources.
2. Use sticky notes or record lines and URLs for online sources.
3. Determine a dominant sense and compose a poem around that sense.
4. Determine a theme.
5. Locate and add a quotation related to the theme.
6. Compose an original title.
7. Create a Works Cited page.

GUIDED PRACTICE

Educators monitor for found poem rules, correct use of parenthetical citations, and correct Works Cited formatting.

CLOSURE

Ask for volunteers to share poems and the sensory keywords from their poems. Brainstorm possible multisensory methods for sharing one or two poems.

REFLECTION

How do poets and writers use sensory images to draw the reader into the text? How do readers use sensory images to deepen their engagement with texts?

DAY 4

MOTIVATION

Demonstrate how to create a Wordle from the keywords in the poem. Show variation examples and discuss how colors, font type, and layout can suggest different senses, moods, and tones.

PRESENTATION

Project the 4.2 Teacher Resource—Sample Found Poem and Works Cited. As a class, assess the entire assignment (poem, Works Cited, and presentation) using the rubric.

STUDENT PRACTICE PROCEDURES

1. Identify sensory keywords.
2. Create a Wordle and use it to introduce the poem.
3. Create a final poem and Works Cited.
4. Self-assess with the rubric.
5. Brainstorm multisensory presentation ideas with a partner or small group.

GUIDED PRACTICE

Monitor students' poems, use of media, and self-assessments.

CLOSURE

Educators model a found poem presentation. The poem is on one side of the presentation; the Works Cited on the other (see the 4.2 Teacher Resource—Sample Found Poem and Works Cited). One shows the Works Cited side of the presentation while reading the found poem (on the other side). Share the multisensory aspect of the presentation. Students share their poem presentations at the next class meeting.

DAY 5

PRESENTATION

Educators repeat presentation. One identifies the dominant sense and shares the sensory images she visualized. The listening educator provides positive feedback.

Divide the class in half or form small groups and take turns sharing found poem presentations and providing others with feedback.

STUDENT PRACTICE PROCEDURES

1. Take turns sharing poem presentations.
2. Ask for feedback from each listener beginning clockwise from the presenter.

GUIDED PRACTICE

Educators monitor students' sharing and providing positive feedback.

CLOSURE

Conduct the reflection with partners. Students turn in their self-assessment using the 4.2 Found Poem, Works Cited, and Presentation Rubric.

REFLECTION

How did a focus on sensory images deepen readers' comprehension of the poems and prose passages? When should readers use sensory images to gain or regain comprehension? When should writers use sensory images to support readers' comprehension?

EXTENSIONS

Display students' poetry presentations in the library and classroom. Invite other classes or students' families to view and respond to the presentations. Encourage students to continue to collect vivid sensory images passages from all of the texts they read and to incorporate sensory imagery into their writing. Create found poems from other types of text or from multiple types of text. Continue to use sensory images to support comprehension in all genres and content areas.

Reading Comprehension Strategy Two
Using Sensory Images

Reading Development Level: Challenging

Instructional Strategies
Category Web, Metaphors/Analogies

Lesson Length
6 sessions

Purpose
The purpose of this unit is to increase students' awareness of how sensory images and figurative language deepen their comprehension and engagement with texts. Students brainstorm sensory images and construct a personification extended metaphor focused on a single vocabulary word or concept. Students use a Web 2.0 tool to present their work in digital storytelling format with narration and cite the sources of the images or sounds they use.

Objectives
At the end of this unit, students will be able to
1. Define poetic devices, tropes, and schemes and use them to develop a personification extended metaphor.
2. Brainstorm sensory images and keywords.
3. Construct a digital storytelling presentation.
4. Cite the images used in the presentation.
5. Self-assess writing and presentation using rubrics.

Resources, Materials, and Equipment
Mentor texts: *I Never Metaphor I Didn't Like: A Comprehensive Compilation of History's Greatest Analogies, Metaphors, and Similes,* by Dr. Mardy Grothe, and *The Book of Qualities,* by J. Ruth Gendler

Web resources: Literary devices, tropes, and schemes: www.storytrail.com/impact12/literary_devices.htm; Mind-mapping tools, Web 2.0 presentation tools, sources for copyright-free images, sounds, and music: www.storytrail.com/impact12/web2.0_tools.htm

Graphic organizers: 4.3 Category Web, 4.3 Teacher Resource—Completed Category Web, 4.3 Personification Extended Metaphor Assignment Sheet and Rubric, 4.3 Teacher Resource—Personification Extended Metaphor Completed Rubric, 4.3 Sample Personification Extended Metaphor, 4.3 Teacher Resource—Sample Personification Extended Metaphor with Coding, 4.3 Group Work and Multimedia Product Rubric

Sample storyboard using Wallwisher: www.wallwisher.com/wall/digital-story-wonder

Sample digital story using VoiceThread: http://voicethread.com/share/1258846/

Internet access and data projector, overhead, or interactive whiteboard, or document camera if available

Collaboration

Educators demonstrate the importance of connecting with sensory images as a way to reach deeper comprehension of vocabulary and concepts as well as enrich their own writing. They model determining a topic and a personification metaphor, brainstorming, and categorizing sensory images. Educators monitor students' personification extended metaphor compositions, guide them in digital storytelling projects, and jointly assess students' final products.

Assessments

The personification extended metaphor creative writing piece, digital storytelling presentations, and rubrics show the process and results of students' learning. Students self-assess their projects as well as each other's work.

Standards

English-language arts keywords: Determine the effects of figurative language; employ poetic devices, tropes, and schemes; accurately cite information.

Technology keywords: Select content and a presentation method for a defined audience and purpose; evaluate projects for design, content delivery, purpose, and audience; and seek and respond to feedback from peers and professionals in evaluating the product.

AASL STANDARDS INDICATORS*

- Respect copyright/intellectual property rights of creators and producers. (1.3.1)
- Contribute to the exchange of ideas within the learning community. (1.3.4)
- Use the writing process, media and visual literacy, and technology skills to create products that express new understandings. (2.1.6)
- Use creative and artistic formats to express personal learning. (4.1.8)

PROCESS

This unit focuses on free-choice vocabulary terms to put the emphasis on creating the extended metaphors to meet standards in English-language arts related to figurative language terms. Specific language arts vocabulary such as text genres or figurative language terms could provide topics. Vocabulary words in any content area can be used as prompts for a similar reading comprehension, writing, and media production sensory images lesson.

DAYS 1 AND 2

MOTIVATION

Educators take turns reading a selection of metaphors on the same topic from *I Never Metaphor I Didn't Like: A Comprehensive Compilation of History's Greatest Analogies, Metaphors, and Similes* (Grothe). Define a

---

metaphor as an example of figurative language that compares two seemingly unlike terms without using "like" or "as." Vote for favorites. Discuss how speakers and writers use metaphors in their daily speech and writing in order to help listeners and readers understand abstract concepts. Cite some examples such as "I've got your back" and "She's skating on thin ice."

Define personification. While one educator reads an example from *The Book of Qualities* (Gendler), the other closes her eyes. "The Wind," "Joy," and "Anger" give a range of emotional responses. After each reading, educators use think-alouds to share sensory responses to each passage.

Ask students to close their eyes. Read additional examples. What kinds of mental images and sensory experiences does this writing elicit? Think-pair-share after reading each example.

Perceiving or consciously creating sensory images are ways people deepen their experiences with texts. Visualization can and should include all five senses. Students deconstruct the sensory images and figurative language used in a personification extended metaphor as a model for their own creative, multisensory writing.

STUDENT-FRIENDLY OBJECTIVES
1. Define literary devices, tropes, and schemes.
2. Identify sensory images by sense type.

PRESENTATION
Play through the VoiceThread example one time while projecting the text. Students think-pair-share their initial responses to the writing with a focus on the sensory images presented in the text and illustrations.

Using the web resource literary devices, tropes, and schemes, review figurative language terms. With students working in small groups, ask them to provide additional examples of each device or term by using the "Numbered Heads Together" instructional strategy.

STUDENT PARTICIPATION PROCEDURES
1. Listen to the definition.
2. Discuss the term and develop examples in the small group.
3. Be prepared to provide an example if number is called.

Continue until students have a beginning understanding of all of the literary terms. Project the 4.3 Sample Personification Extended Metaphor. One educator reads the first paragraph expressively. The other educator shares a sensory image or an example of figurative language.

STUDENT PARTICIPATION PROCEDURES
1. Discuss the paragraph in the small group.
2. Jot down notes.
3. Be prepared to provide an example if number is called.

Using "Numbered Heads Together," involve the groups in providing additional examples. Educators take turns reading. Stop at the end of each paragraph for students to identify sensory images and figurative language.

PRESENTATION, PART 2

Project the 4.3 Teacher Resource—Completed Category Web. Discuss how to complete the category web as prewriting for composing a personification extended metaphor. Note literary devices, tropes, and schemes examples on the matrix.

Brainstorm possible topics for compositions, such as revenge, boredom, fear, greed, determination, narcissism, lucky, ego, innocence, faith, snob, and hypocrisy. Students choose a topic as an individual, with a partner, or in a small group. Brainstorm ideas for ways to "personify" this term. Brainstorm, record, and categorize ideas on the 4.3 Category Web.

STUDENT PRACTICE PROCEDURES

1. Determine a word.
2. Complete the category web.
3. Include examples of literary devices, tropes, and schemes under sensory categories.

GUIDED PRACTICE

Educators monitor for understanding of literary devices, tropes, and schemes.

CLOSURE

Ask for volunteers to share examples of figurative language from their category webs. Ask other students to identify the dominant sense and share a mental image.

DAYS 3, 4, AND 5

MOTIVATION

Share the final product, the VoiceThread example. Note how the narration and images selected heighten the sensory experience of the presentation. Notice that some images represent the words literally while others represent them figuratively. Review the 4.3 Teacher Resource—Completed Category Web. Educators use think-alouds to demonstrate how to visualize aspects of the prewriting on the category web to inform the final product.

PRESENTATION—DAY 3

If organizing this assignment as partner or small group work, demonstrate creating a wiki or Google doc for collaborative work.

Project and review the 4.3 Personification Extended Metaphor Assignment Sheet and Rubric. Discuss strategies for composing the piece.

PRESENTATION—DAY 4 OR 5

Show the sample storyboard for the presentation. Discuss Web 2.0 tool and software options for the presentation and where to find copyright-free images, music, and sound (see storyboarding and tool possibilities at www.storytrail.com/impact12/web2.0_tools.htm). Note how the original images were cited on the VoiceThread example. Demonstrate how to cite an image that is not original. As a class, assess the VoiceThread with the 4.3 Group Work and Multimedia Product Rubric.

STUDENT PRACTICE PROCEDURES
1. Complete category web.
2. Compose a personification extended metaphor and assess it with the rubric.
3. Use a storyboarding tool to plan a Web 2.0 presentation that includes original or copyright-free images, sounds, or music.
4. Determine who will narrate or how the narration will be recorded.
5. Cite sources.
6. Self-assess with the 4.3 Group Work and Multimedia Product Rubric.
7. Link the presentation to a central location.

GUIDED PRACTICE
Educators monitor for satisfying the various rubric criteria. Support students in linking the presentation to a shared URL. (For students or groups that need more time to complete their projects, allow them to do so over a weekend as homework.)

DAY 5 OR 6

CLOSURE
Volunteers share their work. (If students created individual pieces, divide the class in half.) Ask classmates to close their eyes and visualize as a volunteer reads the personification extended metaphor expressively. Share the most effective imagery from listeners' point of view. Show the multimedia presentation. Think-pair-share comparisons between listeners' visualizations and digital storytelling presentations. Continue to share on day 7 if needed.

REFLECTION
How do writers use sensory images and figurative language to draw the reader into the text? How do readers use sensory imagery to deepen their engagement with texts? How can print and images work together to create meaning?

EXTENSIONS
Share students' digital storytelling presentations more widely in the library and classroom. Invite other classes or students' families to view and respond to the presentations.

Encourage students to continue collecting vivid sensory images and figurative language passages from texts they read and to incorporate sensory imagery into their writing. Use vocabulary prompts in other content areas to create personification extended metaphor pieces. Continue to use sensory imagery to support comprehension in all genres and disciplines.

5

Reading Comprehension Strategy Three

Questioning

It is our belief that questioning is at the very core of understanding. Every nugget of learning germinates from an investigation of some kind.

—Carol Koechlin and Sandi Zwaan

In *Empowering Learners: Guidelines for School Library Media Programs,* AASL charges school librarians with modeling "an inquiry-based approach to learning and the information search process" (2009a, 25). Inquiry and questioning go hand in hand. The questioning reading comprehension strategy can be described as maintaining an inquiry focus with the text—before, during, and after reading. Educators can integrate the questioning strategy into the inquiry process to maximize the impact of both. This approach can help students understand that developing inquiry questions and questioning while reading are connected. Classroom teachers and school librarians are natural partners to design and implement instruction that brings together these important skills for 21st-century learners.

In the same way that reading comprehension strategies involve students in the active process of making meaning from texts, "inquiry shifts the focus of learning from a right or wrong answer to the process of learning and investigation" (Kulthau, cited in AASL 2009a, 25). Learning to initiate the inquiry process with thoughtful, well-formulated questions is a critical component of this learning method, and questioning before reading is an important aspect of this reading comprehension strategy. But questioning in both inquiry and reading comprehension does not end there. Just as effective inquirers continue to ask questions, revisit, and reevaluate their questions throughout the inquiry process, strategic readers also use questioning to propel meaning making during and after reading.

Modeling curiosity is one way that educators influence students' ideas about what it means to be a learner. What are the benefits of being inquisitive? Is there a relationship between being curious and intelligence? If educators and students believe in the growth mind-set as described by Dweck (2006), then pursuing the answers to questions and engaging in questioning to deepen comprehension can be important contributors to intelligence. Questioning keeps people engaged in life and readers engaged with texts. Questions awaken the mind.

The analogy of a driver using the steering wheel to guide the way reminds readers to use questions to be active participants rather than passive observers in the meaning making process. Asking and answering questions before, during, and after reading helps readers establish, develop, and maintain an internal conversation while engaging with texts or pursuing an inquiry process. One of the most obvious purposes for reading is to answer questions. The questions students ask are based on their purpose for reading, their reading proficiency level, and their individual application of comprehension strategies. A driver maps a route for his trip and uses the steering wheel to follow that route. So can readers use questions to guide their reading and learning journeys.

QUESTIONING IN THE CLASSROOM AND IN THE LIBRARY

Traditionally, the common discourse pattern in U.S. classrooms has been "IRE," in which the teacher *initiates* a question, one student *responds,* and the teacher *evaluates* the answer (Wells 1986). Teacher-determined questions are also a feature of traditional research projects. These questions are frequently at a factual level and do not require students to engage higher-order thinking skills as they interact with ideas and information during the information-seeking

process. On the other hand, with educators guiding the inquiry process students can learn to activate or build background knowledge and discover personally meaningful questions. Students' commitment to the learning process and investment in the final product are both likely to be stronger when they have been active in planning and charting the inquiry focus. Becoming strategic readers helps students become independent readers, and a student-centered inquiry process helps them develop skills for lifelong, independent learning.

As we approach this investigation into using questioning strategies to teach reading comprehension, educators must remember that all questions are not alike. It is essential to support students' thinking by modeling questioning that does not end at the knowledge level. Educators must model questioning that stretches readers beyond the facts found "on the line" to think between the lines, to think through and beyond the text. Higher-level questions require that students analyze, synthesize, or evaluate information. School librarians will find that many indicators from the *Standards for the 21st-Century Learner* are effectively supported through higher-order questioning.

McKenzie (1997) identified eighteen different kinds of questions, including a category called "strategic questions," that raise the reader's awareness of his own thinking. When educators model with think-aloud strategies, they reveal their own metacognition and use it as a tool for students to emulate. In this process, students learn that *how* one learns is as important as *what* one learns. When students have learned all of the comprehension strategies put forth in this book, they might ask this strategic question: "Which reading strategy would help me best solve this comprehension problem?"

Strategic questions can be posed before and during the reading and inquiry processes. In every lesson plan offered in this book, questions are used for reflection at the end of a literacy or inquiry experience to help learners bring their focus on what they learned and how they learned it. For excellent resources about stimulating curiosity and understanding through questioning across the curriculum, see Koechlin and Zwaan (2006) and Abilock and Bush (2009). Questions can frame the reader's exploration. Questioning helps establish and reestablish the purpose for reading.

THE QUALITIES OF QUESTIONS

Researchers have found that *cueing* and *questioning* account for as much as 80 percent of what happens every day in a classroom. If this is true, then educators who are conscious of how they use cues and questions can improve their instructional practices as they teach this strategy. After carefully selecting texts, educators can offer cues and questions as previews to what will be important in the literacy engagement. A preview establishes a purpose for reading and helps students focus and prepare for the literacy event. This information is used to frame the listening, viewing, or reading experience. Often these introductions help students remember and connect with what they already know about a topic, theme, author, or illustrator. These cues and questions provide a direct link to the background knowledge strategy discussed in chapter 3.

The *quality* of the questions educators model often determines the depth of learners' interactions with texts and the types of questions they learn to pose. Questions can be divided into three levels of thinking: literal, inferential, and evaluative. Answers to literal questions are defined or explained in the text. Responses to inferential questions are inferred; they are not explicitly stated in the text but are implied by the author between the lines. Evaluative, or applied, questions require thinkers to evaluate information in order to develop a response. These questions are answered beyond the text. As a way to evaluate quality, educators can tally the types of questions they ask. Coteachers can keep tallies for one another and support each other in varying and deepening the quality of their questions.

Introductory questioning provides cues. Through think-alouds, educators share the types of questions that strategic readers ask themselves before they venture into a text. Following are some possible introductory questions:

- What is my purpose for reading this text?
- What genre is this text and what is it about?
- What do I want to learn from this text?
- Am I reading for general or specific information, or am I reading to respond to the theme or point of view of this text?

Asking questions during reading is less common and perhaps more challenging to teach and to learn. Engaging in questioning while reading helps youth learn to think about narrative, text information, or illustrations in ways proficient readers think about them. Cultivating the thinking that follows "I wonder" is one sure way to teach this strategy. The following list gives examples of additional question starters that can guide educators as they model questioning and prompt students:

- I wonder . . .
- Who? What? Where? When? Why?
- How?
- What does it mean?
- What does it remind me of in my own life experience, from another text, in the real world?
- Does this question make me think of another question? What is that question?

Lists like these can be used to create a classroom and library poster for readers' reference during individual and group engagements with texts. Educators and students can add their own question starters to expand or to focus these possibilities.

In addition to "I wonder," educators often ask students to question by using the "five Ws"—who, what, where, when, and why. "How" is often added to the list. At the knowledge level, these clarifying questions immediately situate the reader in the story or informational text and form the basis for comprehension. Creating a category matrix to note questions that are raised before, during, and after reading may serve as a guide for readers to emulate when they are reading and posing their own questions. Questioning is a skill that must be practiced continually with all kinds of texts so that students feel confident to pose literal, inferential, and evaluative questions in all content areas.

INQUIRY IN THE CONTENT AREAS

Because the quality of students' questions sets a course for their inquiry, it is educators' responsibility to help learners develop meaningful questions to guide their process. Questions developed "off the top of their heads" are rarely deep enough to justify instructional time. Framing inquiry in terms of essential questions is one strategy many educators use. These big-picture questions address overarching themes and can be developed in terms of students' personal experience, background knowledge, and concepts and ideas related to required curricular content (Wiggins and McTighe 2005). When educators frame inquiry projects in terms of essential questions, students can generate numerous related questions within an open-ended context and develop their own perspectives through inquiry.

A more student-centered approach may evolve after giving learners adequate time to connect and wonder about an idea, topic, or problem. This can help students question beyond the superficial level and embark on inquiries that offer opportunities to think critically, solve real-world problems, or resolve personally meaningful mysteries. There are numerous instructional strategies that can help learners develop significant questions. Educators can provide students with text sets to activate their background knowledge and help them confirm what they know, identify misconceptions, or collect quick facts that can support question development. K-W-L charts that require students to articulate what they already know about a topic can also help this process. Primary source documents and realia can stimulate initial questions that with educator facilitation can lead to significant inquiry questions. Webbing questions, another strategy, can help students establish relationships and identify patterns in order to deepen their

questioning and, as a result, their inquiry process (McKenzie 2009).

The quality of students' questions guides their inquiry process; the quality of their continuous questioning while reading facilitates their comprehension. The recursive inquiry model described by Stripling (2008) begins with building or connecting with background knowledge, followed by wondering about the topic, idea, or problem. In the wondering stage, students ask questions, make predictions, and develop hypotheses. As they continue, they regularly revisit their original wonderings and continue to revise and ask questions about both content and process throughout the inquiry cycle. This inquiry model is about connecting thinking skills and content. Similarly, using reading comprehension skills, in this case through questioning, is also about connecting thinking skills and content. By facilitating a nonlinear inquiry process model, educators can help students maximize the benefits of questioning as they inquire, read, and interact with all types of texts.

There are discipline-specific questioning strategies that can support readers as they engage with texts in the content areas. Although discipline-focused educators may be familiar with these, school librarians may not be. Also, educators in the disciplines may not be aware of how questions in the content area they teach are similar to and different from those that frame inquiry in other disciplines. Helping students and educators make connections and comparisons across content areas is an important contribution of school librarians who have an interdisciplinary view of students' learning. Figure 5-1 provides a framework for thinking about discipline-specific and cross-discipline questioning.

HOW TO TEACH THE STRATEGY

It is essential that educators help students generate "think-type" questions as compared with "locate-type" questions. We often think of "locate" questions as those for which there is one correct answer or for which critics, essayists, and others have written

---

Fig. 5-1   Cross-Discipline and Discipline-Specific Questioning Matrix

Discipline	Types of Questions
All Disciplines	• How is this text organized? • What are the text features? • Is my background knowledge reliable? • How do these ideas or information relate to my life or apply to the real world?
Arts and Language Arts	• What genre is this text? • How do cultural, historical, and political factors influence this text? • What strategies can I use to comprehend this text?
Mathematics	• What is the problem being presented? • Do I understand the numbers, symbols, graphs, tables, and charts presented? • Can I define all of the vocabulary in terms of mathematical concepts? • What patterns do I detect in this information?
Science	• What is the hypothesis? • Does this data make sense? • Can I define all of the vocabulary in terms of scientific concepts? • How does this process work or happen? • Is this information accurate, logical, reliable, replicable, and clear?
Social Studies	• From whose perspective is this text written? • On what assumptions is this text based? • Is this information factual or is it an opinion? • Is this information comprehensive, authoritative, well organized, and supported by reliable references? • Do I understand the illustrations, maps, realia, and language used in the primary source documents, time lines, and charts presented? • After this event, what changed and what remained the same? Who made it happen and who benefited and who did not?
Technology	• Who made this tool or device and for whose benefit? • How does this tool or device impact access and communication? • Are there laws or rules governing the production, distribution, or use of this tool or device? • Why is this tool, device, or information important?

Developed from Stripling (2003).

---

definitive responses. "Think" questions are those that can be uniquely answered by the questioner. They can also be related to the learning process rather than to specific content. Questions such as the following are reflection questions that promote metacognition: Have I determined the main ideas in this text? How does this information connect with what I learned yesterday? What question could I ask that will help me better understand this concept? With educator modeling and support, readers can learn to question both content and process throughout the inquiry.

Ouzts (1998) notes that studying question-answer relationships (QARs) can help students distinguish between locate-type questions and answers and think-type questions and answers. In this model, students are asked to classify questions by the source of their answers: Is the question literal? Is the answer found "on the line"? The answers to these questions may be found on a specific page in the text, or they may require that readers synthesize information found at various points in the text. Is the question inferential? (See chapter 6.) Is the answer found "between the lines" by combining information in the text with the reader's background knowledge? Do readers have to infer the answer? Or is the question evaluative? Does it require readers to make a judgment or state an opinion? If the question isn't answered in the text, how can an answer be found? Or is there an answer to this question? Is this question simply one for the reader to ponder? Categorizing questions by type and answers by source helps students understand the ways questions support comprehension. Becoming proficient at identifying QARs can also help students negotiate standardized test questions and answers. The category matrix in figure 5-2 shows one way to organize and code QARs.

Educators can provide category matrix graphic organizers such as this one for students' use as they read texts and practice questioning strategies in small groups, with partners, or in individual learning situations. Graphic organizers can prompt students to

remember to ask questions throughout the reading process.

Figure 5-3 illustrates educators' use of think-alouds to model questioning that begins with the cueing strategy framed by the illustrations in an editorial cartoon, continues throughout the reading of the text, and extends beyond the text to reflecting on the cartoon after it has been read. This cartoon is the mentor text for the advanced lesson plan in this chapter; QARs provide a framework for that lesson.

Questioning propels the reader through the text, creating a dialogue between the author, the text, and the reader. The act of asking and answering questions motivates the reader to read on in order to ask and answer more questions. This level of engagement with texts helps the reader achieve comprehension and offers a window into the deeper meanings associated with accessing the author's and illustrator's message or theme and point of view or bias, and the personal meanings made by the reader.

Another strategy, reciprocal questioning or "ReQuest" (Manzo 1969), involves the class reading the text silently before the educator gives a prompt question such as, When did the research take

---

Fig. 5-2   Question-Answer Relationship (QAR) Matrix

	Before Reading	During Reading	After Reading
Who?			
What?			
Where?			
When?			
Why?			
How?			

*Answered "on the line" (in the text in one passage or by connecting information from various parts of the text)

**Answered "between the lines" (by connecting information with own background knowledge)

***Unanswered questions (may require evaluation or further research)

Fig. 5-3   Questioning Before, During, and After Reading

"Asterisk," An Editorial Cartoon, by David Fitzsimmons

Before Reading: Questions Related to the Genre, Title, and Illustrations

Both educators make comments and connections to the genre while reading the illustrations.

A: I know this is an editorial cartoon. Editorial cartoons are published on the opinion page in newspapers. I don't see a date so my first question is when was the cartoon first published? What is the cartoonist's political perspective? The title of this cartoon is "Asterisk." What is does the asterisk represent?

B: When I look at illustrations, I notice there are two men who appear to be dressed as soldiers, but from a time in the past; these are not modern uniforms. One is taller than the other and has a fancier uniform. Is the taller, white-haired soldier George Washington?

  I also notice that in the final panel there is a third man who is dressed in modern-day clothing and carries a briefcase. Who is this man, and how did he get in the same frame with these figures from history?

During Reading: Reading the Print along with the Illustrations

Educators read and stop at the end of each panel. Before resuming reading, the reader asks a question. The listening educator may respond or contribute an additional question.

A: What war are they talking about winning? Where is the shorter soldier's home?

B: The taller white-haired man is holding up a document. Can the bug-eyed shorter soldier read it?

cont.

Fig. 5-3 (cont.)

A: I think the taller man is George Washington because he is telling the soldier the rights afforded to U.S. citizens by the Constitution. Did the common soldiers fully understand what the leaders of the American Revolution were trying to accomplish with the new government?

B: The cartoonist shows a gleeful Washington pointing to the solider as he tells him about his responsibility to vote. Does the cartoonist want to remind citizens of their responsibility to vote?

A: In the final panel, the modern-day man carrying the "$pecial Interests" briefcase reminds Washington about the "asterisk." Is the briefcase full of money? Is the cartoonist saying that the special interest groups with money actually elect or control the government?

After Reading: Further Questions

A: I think the cartoonist wants people to think about whether or not they value the rights afforded by the U.S. Constitution or take them for granted.

B: So few people vote. Is that because people know that their votes don't count for much compared with the influence of special interest groups? Can average voters compete with special interest groups and the money they use to influence elections, politicians, and legislation?

A: Are all special interest groups "bad," or are there special interests that are "good"?

B: Washington's face is crest-fallen. Is the cartoonist saying that the way special interests do business has undermined the original intent of the Founding Fathers and the U.S. Constitution?

Reflections

A: I think the print and illustrations worked together to make readers think about how our government has changed from what the Founding Fathers intended when they wrote the U.S. Constitution. Asking questions before reading by simply reading the title, thinking about the genre, and looking at the illustrations in this cartoon helped me put it in a historical context.

B: Stopping to ask questions while reading this cartoon helped me follow the cartoonist's thinking. He set up the contrast between the past and the present.

A: Continuing to ask questions after reading helps us answer some of the questions we asked before and during reading. Based on this cartoon, I am fairly certain that the cartoonist is speaking out against special interests. I don't know if that makes him a conservative or liberal. Could it make him either one?

B: My lingering question is whether or not most Americans today believe *they* elect the government. Asking questions and thinking about the answers helps me get more meaning out of this cartoon.

place—in the past or present? Students then respond by asking related questions such as, Does the passage begin with "during the Great Depression"? or When was the Great Depression? This process can also include opportunities for students to pose the initial predictions or questions with educators responding with additional questions. Students can also practice this process in small groups and provide questions for one another. The point of this process is to clarify the text through questioning. Focusing on questioning rather than answering is a benefit related to teaching this reading comprehension strategy. Reciprocal questioning technique can also be applied to the four elements of reciprocal teaching process: predicting, questioning, clarifying, and summarizing (Palinscar and Brown 1986).

Questioning the author, or "QtA" (Beck et al. 1997), is another useful framework for teaching the questioning strategy. QtA challenges students to pose questions in order to determine the author's meaning. These questions are targeted to expose the author's assumptions, comment on writing craft, and clarify the intended meaning. Assumption questions, such as why the author would put this character is this predicament or what the author believes about the death penalty, require that students make inferences (see chapter 6). Craft questions can include questions such as how the author could have made this clearer or whether the author could have helped readers understand this concept by including a chart, graph, or diagram. These questions require readers to notice how the text supports or fails to support their comprehension. Clarifying questions might query the author's purpose in writing the piece, his message or theme, or the response he intended to elicit from readers. Questions support an internal dialogue between the reader and the author, the illustrator, or the text and increase readers' understanding of reading as a transaction between the text, author, and reader (Rosenblatt 1995). QtA helps learners become more discerning, critical consumers of texts. Readers who ask these questions can identify gaps in their understanding.

MAKING LITERATURE CONNECTIONS

Matching texts that lend themselves to exploring questioning strategies with the context in which they are used increases their usefulness. Texts that prompt questions for some readers may or may not prompt questions for others. Particular texts that educators choose to teach this strategy are dependent on the purpose for reading, the students' prior knowledge, and their connections to these texts. As a result, it is difficult to make specific recommendations of literature that supports this strategy. Teaching questioning strategies is one of many areas of the curriculum

for which collaboration between classroom teachers and school librarians is critical. Bringing together the teacher's more intimate knowledge of the students and their background knowledge and experiences with the librarian's extensive knowledge of literature and access to resources can yield fertile ground for nurturing readers who become proficient at asking and answering questions while they read.

Textbooks in all content areas can also be used effectively to teach and practice questioning. In the social studies and science curricula, informational texts for which students have incorrect or incomplete background knowledge can also be used to prompt questions. Historical fiction and biographies may lend themselves to practicing questioning strategies. Readers' lack of background knowledge can often prompt them to ask authentic questions before, during, and after reading. Instead of focusing on building a great deal of prior knowledge, educators may better support students in developing questioning strategies by just telling them that questioning is a tool for acquiring background knowledge when confronting challenging texts on unfamiliar topics (see challenging lesson in chapter 9).

Biographies in particular can lead students to uncover how misconceptions can result from in-depth questioning, which can lead to deeper comprehension. For example, in the biography *Claudette Colvin: Twice toward Justice* (Hoose) students can question the reasons behind long-held beliefs about the events leading up to the 1956 Montgomery, Alabama, bus boycott. Why hadn't they previously learned about the teen that refused to give up her seat on a bus nine months before Rosa Parks? With careful reading, learners may question the personal, political, and artistic life of the influential Mexican artist Diego Rivera as presented in *Diego, Bigger Than Life* (Bernier-Grand/Diaz), an illustrated biography portrayed through poems. *Charles and Emma* (Heiligman) brings into focus the tension between Darwin's perspective on the role of God in creation as compared with his deeply religious wife's beliefs. Readers' own understandings, views, and beliefs can be challenged through questioning throughout these texts.

Other tween and young adult informational books share the actual inquiry process with readers. Working alongside forensic scientists, author Sally M. Walker shares their discoveries and hypotheses in her book *Written in Bone: Buried Lives of Jamestown and Colonial Maryland*. In *Ain't Nothing but a Man: My Quest to Find the Real John Henry*, author Scott Reynolds Nelson shares his own inquiry process. Scott includes the questions that launched his thinking about the song "John Henry" or "John Henry, Steel Driving Man," how he revised his questions as he learned more, the sources he used, and even how he dealt with dead ends in his inquiry process. These titles can serve as models for student inquirers.

Fictional texts of all types, both poetry and prose, can also be effective in teaching this strategy. Fantasy or science fiction texts, which by definition present alternate realities, can prompt numerous questions about unfamiliar story elements, such as those presented in the postapocalyptic settings, futuristic characters, and problems in *The Hunger Games* trilogy (Collins). In choosing texts, the primary considerations are students' background knowledge and connections and their interest in the topics, themes, or story elements presented in the texts.

TWEEN, YOUNG ADULT, AND ADULT LITERATURE CITED

The starred title is used in a lesson plan.

Ain't Nothing but a Man: My Quest to Find the Real John Henry, by Scott Reynolds Nelson with Marc Aronson

Charles and Emma, by Deborah Heiligman

Claudette Colvin: Twice Toward Justice, by Phillip Hoose

Diego, Bigger Than Life, by Carmen T. Bernier-Grand, illustrated by David Diaz

The Hunger Games, by Suzanne Collins

Solving Crimes with Trace Evidence, by Gary Jeffrey, illustrated by Peter Richardson

Written in Bone: Buried Lives of Jamestown and Colonial Maryland, by Sally M. Walker

LESSON PLANS

In these how-to strategy lesson plans, classroom teachers and school librarians coteach the lessons. Educators provide think-alouds to demonstrate how to utilize questioning to comprehend texts before, during, and after reading. For these lessons, all of which involve electronic texts, graphic organizers are provided for recording questions. For efficiency, students should access and use these organizers electronically. When using print texts, students can use sticky notes to record their questions and place them on the actual pages of the text where they posed the questions.

Strategic questions that focus on learning how to learn are integrated throughout the lessons. The lessons at the higher levels of development build on the previous one by adding a more sophisticated analysis of questioning strategies. Advanced students may benefit from experiencing the advancing lesson with the same or a different essential question, and challenging-level students may benefit from engaging in all three levels with the resources utilized in the examples or with different texts. All of these lessons can serve as the initial wondering stage for more in-depth inquiry projects.

LESSON PLAN 5.1

Reading Comprehension Strategy Three
Questioning

Reading Development Level: Advancing

Instructional Strategies
Cues, Questions, and Advance Organizers, Categorizing and Comparing

Lesson Length
6 sessions (or facilitate as an ongoing quarter- or semester-long inquiry project)

Purpose
The purpose of this unit is to record questions posed before, during, and after investigating aspects of health and wellness. Students use a category matrix to compare initial questions with questions posed during and after the connecting and wondering stages of inquiry. Throughout the inquiry, students are reminded to question the accuracy of the information they find.

Objectives
At the end of this unit, students will be able to
1. Pose before, during, and after questions using key vocabulary words.
2. Collect and organize questions.
3. Compare initial questions with those asked during and after the inquiry.
4. Extension: Develop a personal health and wellness plan to follow and reevaluate periodically.

Resources, Materials, and Equipment
Artifacts: Various original containers of drinks students enjoy
School or district annual physical examination form
School or district annual preparticipation physical evaluation
Health and Wellness Text Set: Collection of five-minute videos on various topics related to health and wellness (use streaming video if available), databases, trade books, magazines, and more
Health and Wellness Sample Student Wiki: www.storytrail.com/impact12/wellness.htm
Graphic organizers: 5.1 Category Matrix, 5.1 Teacher Resource—Sample Category Matrix, 5.1 Question Comparison Category Matrix, 5.1 Teacher Resource—Sample Question Comparison Category Matrix
Materials: Measuring tapes, scale for weighing and measuring height, eye charts, blood pressure cuffs, jump ropes, or other athletic equipment as needed
Overhead, data projector, or interactive whiteboard

Collaboration

Educators team teach all of the lessons presented. (If continuing this unit as an ongoing inquiry project, they may choose to team teach periodically throughout the project.) Educators facilitate as students develop and categorize questions, create their health and wellness wikis, and complete the question comparison matrix. Collaboration with the school nurse, health or physical education teachers, and athletic coaches is ideal.

Assessment

Educators monitor students' ability to pose questions. The question comparison matrix shows the extent to which students' questions changed or deepened throughout this inquiry process. In addition to the sample student questioning wiki, educators may determine rubric criteria for students' health and wellness plans or design assessments for additional benchmark assignments developed during this initial inquiry or extended beyond the lessons described.

Standards

Reading keywords: Pose or answer questions.
Health education keywords: Analyze healthy and unhealthy diets; explain the importance of a personal dietary and exercise plan; use critical thinking to research and evaluate health information.
Writing keywords: Organize ideas.
Technology keywords: Develop communication products that meet specified needs and address specific audiences.

AASL STANDARDS INDICATORS*

- Develop and refine a range of questions to frame the search for new understanding. (1.1.3)
- Find, evaluate, and select appropriate sources to answer questions. (1.1.4)
- Display initiative and engagement by posing questions and investigating the answers beyond the collection of superficial facts. (1.2.1)
- Organize knowledge so that it is useful. (2.1.2)
- Use technology and other information tools to analyze and organize information. (2.1.4)
- Seek information for personal learning in a variety of formats and genres. (4.1.4)

PROCESS

DAY 1

MOTIVATION

Bring in several original containers of students' favorite drinks, including energy drinks, sodas, juices, coffee, bottled water, and more. Take a quick poll of students' favorite among those presented. Ask: "Do you know if the drinks you consume are healthy for you or not?" "How can you find out?" Lead a brief discussion about reading labels and conducting fast fact searches online.

Cues and questions: Students conduct a brief inquiry into health and wellness and, if participating in the lesson extension, use questioning to develop an individual diet and exercise plan. Project the essential guiding questions for this inquiry project: What are my questions about health and wellness? What is my plan for becoming healthier and maintaining wellness?

---

* Excerpted from *Standards for the 21st-Century Learner* by the American Association of School Librarians, a division of the American Library Association, copyright © 2007 American Library Association. Available for download at www.ala.org/aasl/standards. Used with permission.

STUDENT-FRIENDLY OBJECTIVES
1. Ask before, during, and after questions.
2. Use key health and wellness vocabulary words.

PRESENTATION

Project the school or district's annual physical examination form or annual preparticipation physical evaluation. One educator records on the whiteboard while the other leads the class in skimming and scanning the document for subtopics such as measurements (height, weight, and temperature), vision, organs (eyes, heart, and lungs), and more.

Educators begin a brainstorm by posing possible questions to investigate. While one educator leads the class in a brainstorm of questions related to health and wellness (as prompted by the subtopic list), the other records students' initial questions. Select a subtopic that relates to a video topic from among those selected for the text set.

Announce the topic of a short health video (up to five minutes in length). Each educator uses think-alouds to share before questions. Play the video through one time. Then replay it and pause periodically as educators model asking during viewing questions. Pose after questions following the viewing.

Organize students into teams of two. Distribute the 5.1 Category Matrix to each team. Project the matrix. Note categories and show how to fill it out. Repeat the questioning process with another video. Students follow the participation procedures.

STUDENT PARTICIPATION PROCEDURES
1. Think-pair-share possible before, during, and after questions.
2. Raise hand to pause the video.
3. Raise hand to share a question with the class.
4. Record at least one question per student in each category on the matrix.

GUIDED PRACTICE

Monitor students as they pose questions. Remind students to focus on asking rather than answering questions. Provide additional modeling as needed.

CLOSURE

Groups share the most compelling questions on their category matrices. Review the essential questions. Students conduct a brief inquiry by developing individual health and wellness before, during, and after questions. (If participating in the extension, let students know about the health and wellness plan.)

REFLECTION

How did questioning keep viewers involved with the video? Did all viewers pose the same questions before, during, and after the video?

DAY 2

MOTIVATION

Take a poll. Ask: "How many of you have sought out health and wellness information on the Web?" Conduct a brief discussion about potential benefits and potential harm of using the Web for health information. Project the essential guiding questions.

STUDENT-FRIENDLY OBJECTIVES

1. Ask before, during, and after questions.
2. Record questions in the appropriate cell on a graphic organizer.

PRESENTATION

Project the 5.1 Teacher Resource—Sample Category Matrix. Educators take turns reading and commenting on the before, during, and after questions. Circle questions that ask for more than simple factual responses.

Students can work individually, with partners, or in small groups. Share the text set of resources available to students including databases, trade books, magazines, additional videos, and more. Remind students that the goal is to develop questions that require them to go beyond collecting superficial facts.

STUDENT PRACTICE PROCEDURES

1. Think-pair-share possible before, during, and after questions.
2. Record at least one question per student in each category on the matrix.
3. Evaluate questions for depth.
4. Circle questions that ask for more than simple facts.

GUIDED PRACTICE

Monitor students' questions for depth.

CLOSURE

Students share the most compelling questions on their category matrices. Review the essential questions. Students continue to develop individual health and wellness before, during, and after questions.

DAY 3

Project the sample student wiki. Help students create health and wellness wikis with multiple pages as per the sample. Students record before questions on the wiki home page. Project the 5.1 Teacher Resource—Sample Question Comparison Category Matrix to ensure students know the expected outcome for this inquiry.

DAYS 4 AND 5

Students continue to connect, wonder, and record their questions on their health and wellness wiki. They create a "during" wiki page and record questions on that page as they pursue a line of inquiry. Educators conduct one or more mini-lessons related to the authority and reliability of web-based health information.

On the final day, students record after questions on an "after" wiki page and draft the 5.1 Question Comparison Category Matrix in hard copy and record the information on a "comparison" wiki page. They also record any questions they have about the accuracy of the information they found while searching.

Educators share additional resources and continue to monitor students for using reliable sources for health information. Educators provide database or free-range web searching mini-lessons as needed. Remind students to pose questions about the accuracy of the health information found on the Web.

DAY 6

PRESENTATION

Divide the class into small groups of four to six. Educators model sharing the sample student wiki by following the participation procedures below. Students share their health and wellness wikis with small groups gathered around a computer.

STUDENT PARTICIPATION PROCEDURES
1. Link to individual health and wellness wiki.
2. Report the topic used for comparing before, during, and after questions.
3. Share one question on that topic from the before, during, and after pages of the wiki.
4. Share how one unanswered after question can guide an inquiry related to developing an individual health and wellness plan.

GUIDED PRACTICE

Educators divide responsibilities for monitoring the small groups. They monitor students' presentations and ask clarifying and probing questions as needed.

CLOSURE

Bring the class back together and conduct the reflection orally.

REFLECTION

How did questioning keep readers and viewers involved in reading and throughout the inquiry process? Were there topics that prompted more questions than others? Were there resources that prompted more questions than others?

EXTENSIONS

Students may conduct an ongoing inquiry into health and wellness. They may collect and analyze data regarding their diet, exercise, or other health-related topics. Educators may design additional lessons and develop assessments to measure student learning. This extension can culminate with students creating individual health and wellness plans.

Students may also choose to take action by writing to or dialoguing with school or district food service decision makers, physical education requirement decision makers, or the press and community through authoring articles, letters to the editor, or public service announcements using a variety of Web 2.0 tools. Educators provide learners with checklists and rubrics to guide this work.

Continue to prompt students to ask questions as they interact with texts in all formats in all content areas. Use the strategies in chapter 6 to prompt students to make inferences and the strategies in chapter 7 to prompt students to question the currency, relevance, authority, accuracy, and bias of information.

LESSON PLAN 5.2

Reading Comprehension Strategy Three
Questioning

Reading Development Level: Advanced

Instructional Strategies
Cues, Classifying, Cooperative Learning, Metaphors

Lesson Length
2 sessions

Purpose
The purpose of this lesson plan is to record questions before, during, and after reading to prompt readers to think more deeply about editorial cartoons. Students record questions on a graphic organizer and note QARs. Students evaluate questions to determine which were most helpful and use metaphors to describe the process of asking questions while interacting with text.

Objectives
At the end of these lessons, students will be able to
1. Pose and record before, during, and after questions on a category matrix.
2. Categorize questions based on the possible location of the answer: on the line, between the lines, or unanswered in the text.
3. Evaluate questions and determine their relative importance in comprehending the text.

Resources, Materials, and Equipment
Mentor text: 5.2 Editorial Cartoon "Asterisk," by David Fitzsimmons
Web resource: The Editorial Cartoons of Clay Bennett: www.claybennett.com/archives.html
Graphic organizers: 5.2 Category Matrix, 5.2 Teacher Resource—Completed Category Matrix, 5.2 Question Evaluation Graphic Organizer, 5.2 Teacher Resource—Completed Question Evaluation Graphic Organizer
Materials: Highlighters in three colors for educators and fine highlighters in the same three colors for students (if not working electronically)
Overhead, data projector, or interactive whiteboard

Collaboration
Educators demonstrate collaborative learning and model applying the questioning strategy to understanding an editorial cartoon. Both educators monitor as students work in small groups to question a second cartoon.

Assessment

The students' questioning matrices assess their ability to pose questions before, during, and after reading and to determine QARs. Educators must establish criteria for the quality of completed matrices. Students complete a question evaluation graphic organizer for the second cartoon and compose a one-paragraph reflection in which they develop a metaphor for questioning.

Standards

Reading keywords: Ask relevant questions in order to comprehend text; generate clarifying questions to comprehend text; describe the historical and cultural aspects of a text.

Social studies keywords: Apply knowledge to analyze current issues and events and to analyze choices and decisions in contemporary U.S. society.

AASL STANDARDS INDICATORS*

- Display initiative and engagement by posing questions and investigating the answers beyond the collection of superficial facts. (1.2.1)
- Organize knowledge so that it is useful. (2.1.2)
- Use technology and other information tools to analyze and organize information. (2.1.4)
- Consider diverse and global perspectives in drawing conclusions. (2.3.2)
- Interpret new information based on cultural and social context. (4.4.4)

PROCESS

DAY 1

MOTIVATION

Cues: Project the 5.2 Editorial Cartoon "Asterisk," by David Fitzsimmons. Along with students create a working definition of the editorial cartoon genre by explaining the similarities and differences between graphic novels and editorial cartoons. While one educator solicits students' input, the other records responses on a Venn diagram on the board.

Questioning is one important comprehension strategy that can help readers get more out of texts. Educators use think-alouds to question the editorial cartoon and demonstrate cooperative learning. Students and educators pose questions before, during, and after reading. Students work in small groups to question other editorial cartoons.

STUDENT-FRIENDLY OBJECTIVES

1. Ask questions before, during, and after reading.
2. Decide the question category.
3. Determine the QARs.

PRESENTATION

Project the 5.2 Category Matrix. Distribute copies of the cartoon. As each educator shares questions before, during, and after reading the cartoon, the other records questions in the appropriate categories on the matrix (Who? What? Where? When? Why? How?). See the 5.2 Teacher Resource—Completed Category Matrix. Periodically ask students for additional questions about the cartoon.

STUDENT PARTICIPATION PROCEDURES
1. Raise hand to stop reading.
2. Ask question and determine the category.
3. Propose the QAR.

After reading and recording questions, return to each question and determine where the answer to that question might be: in the text, between the lines, or beyond the text. Use asterisks or highlights to note the QARs.

Divide students into pairs or small groups. Distribute the 5.2 Category Matrix to each student or to each group. Link students to web resource: The Editorial Cartoons of Clay Bennett. Students skim topics and select a cartoon to question.

STUDENT PRACTICE PROCEDURES
1. Discuss ideas with partner(s).
2. Pose and record before, during, and after questions.
3. Code the QAR for each question asked.

GUIDED PRACTICE
Monitor students' group work and completion of the category matrix. Students who finish before others can question additional cartoons.

CLOSURE
As a class, students share and discuss some of their questions as well as any challenges they might have faced in determining QARs.

DAY 2

STUDENT-FRIENDLY OBJECTIVES
1. Determine the most useful question posed in each category: before, during, or after reading.
2. Evaluate the relative importance of questions.

PRESENTATION
Distribute the 5.2 Question Evaluation Graphic Organizer to each student. Project the 5.2 Teacher Resource—Completed Category Matrix. Review the questions posed. Working with partners or in small groups, students determine the most helpful question asked in each category. Share with the whole class to determine if all groups picked the same three questions. Note the similarities and differences.

Discuss how metaphors help speakers and writers explain abstract concepts. Brainstorm some possible metaphors for using questioning to make sense of text (see the example on the 5.2 Teacher Resource—Completed Question Evaluation Graphic Organizer).

STUDENT PRACTICE PROCEDURES
1. Determine the most useful before, during, and after questions.
2. Record a metaphor for the questioning strategy.
3. Compose a one-paragraph reflection that develops the metaphor.

GUIDED PRACTICE

Educators monitor students' ability to determine the most useful question and develop a metaphor in their reflective paragraphs.

CLOSURE

Pair students with partners who read different cartoons. Partners tell the topic of the cartoon, share the most helpful question(s), and read their reflections. Volunteers share their reflective paragraphs with the whole class.

REFLECTION

How did questioning help us comprehend the text? What was the most powerful metaphor you heard? When might you use questioning with other kinds of text?

EXTENSIONS

Conduct an inquiry based on the students' unanswered questions about their cartoons. Continue demonstrating questioning texts throughout the inquiry process.

Provide students with lessons that prompt them to engage in asking before, during, and after questions while learning with other media. Films and websites on science and social studies topics may be especially effective. Make connections between the questioning used for comprehension and the questioning used in the inquiry process.

LESSON PLAN 5.3

Reading Comprehension Strategy Three
Questioning

Reading Development Level: Challenging

Instructional Strategies
Cues and Questions, Classifying

Lesson Length
2 sessions

Purpose
The purpose of this lesson plan is to use questioning before, during, and after reading court cases related to forensic science. Rather than concentrating on answering questions per se, this lesson focuses on recording questions and categorizing them before, during, and after reading. Students can use this process to determine their most pressing questions related to the topic of forensic science and pursue an inquiry based on those questions.

Objectives
At the end of these lessons, students will be able to
  1. Pose questions before, during, and after reading a court case.
  2. Categorize and record questions before, during, and after reading a court case.
  3. Determine questions for further study.

Resources, Materials, and Equipment
  Mentor text: *Solving Crimes with Trace Evidence,* by Gary Jeffrey, illustrated by Peter Richardson
  Web resource: The Innocence Project: www.innocenceproject.org
  Optional web resource: *Fun Trivia*: Quizzes: Forensic Science: www.funtrivia.com/quizzes/sci__tech/
      forensic_science.html
  Graphic organizers: 5.3 Category Matrix, 5.3 Teacher Resource—Completed Category Matrix, 5.3
      Exit Slip
  Overhead, data projector, or interactive whiteboard

Collaboration
While one educator reads the introduction and one famous case, the other records before, during, and after reading questions on a category matrix. After recording questions, educators model determining one or more inquiry questions to pursue.

Assessment
The students' category matrices and exit slips show their use of questioning to achieve comprehension. Educators establish criteria for the quality of completed matrices.

Standards

Reading keywords: Ask relevant questions in order to comprehend; locate facts in response to questions about expository text.

Science keywords: Communicate and apply scientific information extracted from various sources; know that scientific hypotheses are tentative and must be tested before they become theories.

AASL STANDARDS INDICATORS*

- Develop and refine a range of questions to frame the search for new understanding. (1.1.3)
- Display initiative and engagement by posing questions and investigating the answers beyond the collection of superficial facts. (1.2.1)
- Organize knowledge so that it is useful. (2.1.2)
- Use technology and other information tools to analyze and organize information. (2.1.4)
- Interpret new information based on cultural and social context. (4.4.4)

Determine additional standards and indicators for extensions.

PROCESS

DAY 1

MOTIVATION

Cues and questions: How many students watch crime shows on TV or on the Web? What are students' favorites? Think-pair-share: Why do you like these shows?

Every person has a unique fingerprint, right? Is this a scientific hypothesis or a scientific theory? Has it ever been proven? What is the difference between a scientific hypothesis and a theory? What is forensic science? Brainstorm students' initial understandings of forensic science. While one educator solicits students' ideas, the other records them. Keep the brainstorm for later reference.

The purpose of this lesson is to ask questions. Readers use questioning to help them make sense of texts. Although questions are not always answered in the text itself, questions help readers remain active during the reading process, motivate them and keep them involved, and lead them to discover what they don't understand.

Each student assumes the role of a forensic scientist who asks questions about the crime scene, the victim and suspects, the evidence, how the evidence was tested, how the evidence was used in court, and more. Students read about a teen or young adult who was wrongly accused of a crime. Before, during, and after reading, they record questions on a graphic organizer. After this process, they share new information and how this information changed their perspective and record unanswered questions about this case or about forensic science in general. If continuing with the extension, unanswered questions become the initial questions for an inquiry project.

Optional homework the night before the lesson: Ask students to take one or more forensic science quizzes found at www.funtrivia.com/quizzes/sci__tech/forensic_science.html. Educators may begin this lesson by asking students to share what they learned or the questions they had after taking these tests.

STUDENT-FRIENDLY OBJECTIVES

1. Raise hand to pose a question before, during, or after reading.
2. Categorize the question on the graphic organizer.
3. If appropriate, suggest where an answer may be found.

* Excerpted from *Standards for the 21st-Century Learner* by the American Association of School Librarians, a division of the American Library Association, copyright © 2007 American Library Association. Available for download at www.ala.org/aasl/standards. Used with permission.

PRESENTATION

Begin by reading and discussing "Finding Evidence" and "The Silent Witness" in the graphic novel *Solving Crimes with Trace Evidence* (Jeffrey/Richardson), or read from general information about forensics from a trade book, textbook, or website. Discuss and record students' questions with the initial forensic science understandings brainstorm.

Project the 5.3 Category Matrix. One educator reads the first three sentences of "Feline Witness," a brief description of a crime found at the end of the book; the other educator records "before" questions in the appropriate cells on the category matrix. Use 5.3 Teacher Resource—Completed Category Matrix for reference. (If not using *Solving Crimes with Trace Evidence*, model using an example from the Innocence Project website: www.innocenceproject.org/fix/947/.)

Using think-alouds, both educators and students pose during and after questions. Identify and note the question topic (see the key on the category matrix). While reading and recording questions, educators model discussing how questioning helps readers become actively involved in understanding the text. If educators feel it is important to record the answer as well, they record the answers in parentheses as notes.

CLOSURE

Review the questions asked and the categories in which they were placed. Students think-pair-share new information, changed perspectives, or unanswered questions. Record one student's ideas on the graphic organizer or use the sample given on the teacher resource.

DAY 2

Organize the class into partners or trios. Provide the 5.3 Category Matrix for each student.

MOTIVATION

Cues: The use of DNA evidence in criminal trials is relatively new. Many people, particularly youth, have been wrongly convicted of crimes and have been unfairly sentenced to prison terms during the prime of their lives. Later, DNA tests exonerated them. The Innocence Project is an organization that seeks to assist prisoners who "could be proven innocent through DNA testing." Read the statement on the home page.

STUDENT-FRIENDLY OBJECTIVES

1. Pose questions before, during, and after reading an informational text.
2. Record questions and categorize them based on the topic.
3. Identify and record new information, changed perspective, or unanswered questions.

PRESENTATION

Link to the Innocence Project website. Show the Marvin Anderson video. As a class, ask questions about Mr. Anderson's case.

Randomly assign students to one of ten other cases: www.innocenceproject.org/fix/947/Their-Stories .php. Students record before reading background knowledge ("what they already know") and their questions after viewing the first slide in the case. Then they view the entire case, pausing when appropriate to record what they know and their questions as the information unfolds. After they have viewed the slide show, they record "after" knowledge and further questions.

STUDENT PRACTICE PROCEDURES
1. View the first slide, stop, and ask before questions.
2. Discuss all aspects of the case with partner before, during, and after reading.
3. Record background knowledge and questions in before, during, and after categories.
4. Categorize and record topics for each question.
5. Identify and record new information, changed perspective, or unanswered questions.

GUIDED PRACTICE
Educators monitor students' discussions, questioning, and categorizing.

CLOSURE
After reading, review the questions posed before, during, and after reading. Ask students to count up the number of questions about specific topics. In which topic area did students ask the most questions? Ask students to volunteer to share their new learning, changed perspectives, or new questions with the class. (For more participation, do this in half-class groups each facilitated by one of the educators.)

Post students' original brainstorm. Discuss possible misconceptions and new understandings. Distribute the 5.3 Exit Slip. Students fill them out in class or for homework. Allow time for students to discuss reflections with partners, in small or half-class groups, or with the entire class.

REFLECTION
How did asking questions before, during, and after reading keep us engaged with the text? How did questions help us get a deeper meaning of these texts? What can readers do with unanswered questions?

EXTENSIONS
Educators notice if students wrote e-mails to the person whose case they studied. Students may be motivated to learn more about the Innocence Project or get involved in the effort in some way. They may choose to write articles for the school newspaper or submit letters to the editor to the local newspaper or advocate in some other way for the use of DNA testing in criminal cases.

Students' unanswered questions can be used as initial questions to begin individual or small group inquiry projects. Integrate the questioning reading comprehension strategy any time students are engaged in inquiry.

6

Reading Comprehension Strategy Four

Making Predictions and Drawing Inferences

To push beyond the literal text, to make it personal and three-dimensional,
to weave it into our own stories—that is to infer.

—Ellin Oliver Keene and Susan Zimmermann

As learners read and pose questions, they often find themselves answering their own questions with predictions about what will happen next or with inferences drawn from the author's or illustrator's creations. The "on the line" strategy of predicting and the "between the lines" strategy of inferring prompt readers to turn the page to find out if their hypotheses are correct or plausible. Predictions are educated guesses about what will happen next based on what is known from reading the text, but prediction can also involve readers' background knowledge. Inferences require that readers go beyond literal meaning. They use the print and illustrations plus their prior knowledge and experience to make reasonable interpretations of the text. As they do so, readers find clues or connecting points, make predictions or inferences, and draw conclusions. These conclusions or interpretations are a critical part of reading comprehension. Readers who make predictions and inferences before, during, and after they read are actively engaged in the meaning making process.

Accomplished authors and illustrators of well-constructed picture books, novels, and some informational books, particularly those that have a narrative frame, respect the knowledge readers bring to the literary experience. They leave clues for readers to lead them on throughout the reading journey. They rely on readers to flesh out their texts by making connections between clues and readers' own background knowledge, values, and beliefs. For fast-paced lessons, there are many sophisticated picture books that can engage teens' thinking because the themes are relevant to young adults' lives.

For a predictions example, set up the lesson with a conversation about prejudice by reading *Guess What?* (Fox/Goodman), a picture book about prejudging a woman who looks like a witch that may be most appropriate for teen readers. Follow that with an interactive reading of *The Little Bit Scary People* (Jenkins/Boiger). In this book, a young girl sees scary people everywhere. One is a "big boy with thick eyebrows," a Mohawk haircut, and a skull drawn on the bottom of his skateboard. The girl suggests that he really is a nice kid who "kisses his cat on the head and scratches her neck until she purrs." Once students see the pattern in the book, they can have fun predicting the sweet ways the narrator imagines scary people, some of whom are members of her own family. For an inference lesson, read *Rose Blanche* (Gallaz and Innocenti), a picture book in which the fate of a German girl who secretly feeds imprisoned Jewish children during the Holocaust must be inferred at the end of the story. Although reading on confirms or disconfirms the correctness of predictions, inferences are never answered directly in the text (see the example in figure 6-1).

The importance of prediction and inference in reading comprehension stems from the transactional nature of the reading event. If we understand reading as a transaction between a reader, the text, an author's intentions, and the context in which the work is experienced, then the literal denotation of the words on the page and the content of the illustrations are only part of the story. For the transaction to occur, the reader must interpret the text. Each reader's unique interpretation is then an essential component of comprehension.

This perspective honors the role of the reader in making meaning. It suggests that unique interpretations are valued and invaluable. When designing literature engagements, educators foster personalized interpretations by using a reading transaction framework that allows for multiple interpretations. Educators model this through think-alouds while they are coteaching. They demonstrate that different

interpretations of the same text are possible based on readers' background knowledge, beliefs, and values. As students immerse themselves in the deeper between the lines meanings of texts, they come to think of reading as a lived-through experience (Rosenblatt 1995). Just like a trip to a theme park or museum, reading a text is an event to be experienced, an event on which one can reflect and learn.

By sharing their unique responses to what they read, students who discuss their reading with partners or within literature circles learn that there are multiple perspectives that can mirror and enrich or contradict or contrast with their own interpretations of a work. A collaborative social context for talking about books gives readers a place for engaging in discussions and sharing interpretations. Book discussions can become a central part of life in the classroom and in the library (on facilitating literature circles, see Daniels 2002).

Teaching the inference strategy can be quite personally rewarding for both students and educators. Readers are often asked to interact with literal meanings, but inference requires that each reader consider her own beliefs, values, and experiences before drawing conclusions. Readers must take the information provided by the author or illustrator and pass it through their own worldviews in order to determine what makes sense for them. By definition, inference requires that each reader construct a meaning that makes the text a reflection of her experience. In this way, the text becomes integrated into a reader's schema or background knowledge and holds the potential to change that schema. Readers who excel at inference may actually experience a sense of rewriting the text as they read. What better way could there be to feel co-ownership along with the author and illustrator? "To push beyond the literal text, to make it personal and three-dimensional, to weave it into our own stories—that is to infer" (Keene and Zimmermann 1997, 152). Through this deep comprehension process, a reader's newly made meanings are more personal, more personally valued, and longer remembered.

All genres of fiction, including fantasy, science fiction, historical fiction, and realistic fiction but

Fig. 6-1   Predicting and Inferring Before, During, and After Reading

Text: *The Rabbits*, by John Marsden, illustrated by Shaun Tan

Before Reading: Predictions and Inferences Related to the Front and Back Covers

One educator (A) reads the title of the book and the author's and illustrator's names. She also reads the print on the back cover and makes an inference.

> A: The writer describes this book as "a rich and haunting allegory for all ages, all cultures." I'm thinking about the word *allegory*. An allegory uses symbolism to express a message. It is like an extended metaphor in which one thing represents another. The writer says this allegory is "haunting." I associate that word with events that are scary so I infer that this will not be a happy story that ends on an upbeat note.

The other educator (B) makes inferences and predictions based on the cover opened as a double-page spread.

> B: I'm thinking about the title of the book, *The Rabbits*. Although I can't see the faces of the characters wearing hats, I am making an inference that they are "the Rabbits." I know from my background knowledge that book jackets often include an image of the main character or characters. I'm also looking at the huge sailing ship that dominates the scene. There are smaller boats that seem to indicate that the figures, or Rabbits, have come ashore from the ship. My background knowledge tells me that they could be explorers, or to build on the inference about the word *haunting*, maybe they are up to no good. Maybe they are invaders.

During Reading: Predictions and Inferences from the First Few Pages

> A: On the first page, the print tells when the Rabbits came. The illustration on the double-page spread includes petroglyphs, or rock art, and a pile of snakes. I associate snakes with evil. This page seems to confirm my feeling that this is not a pleasant story.

> B: On the second double-page spread, the narrators say the Rabbits looked a bit like them, but I notice that the original inhabitants of this place seem to have simple tools or weapons while the Rabbits have better technology, a machine that seems to be spewing smoke. I predict that the characters with the best technology will "win."

> A: On the third double-page spread, the print says the "old people warned us." My background knowledge tells me the old people, or elders, in a society are thought to be wise. They are also the keepers of the "right ways." Many times younger generations do not listen to their elders or follow traditional ways (the "right ways"). This page also says that more Rabbits came. I predict that the original people will be overrun by Rabbits.

> B: The next page is the cover art. With the information I gleaned from the first few pages of the book, I can infer from this page that these figures are "invaders" rather than explorers.

Ending and After Reading: Confirming Predictions and Testing Inferences

> A: The Rabbits' culture was at first interesting and helpful in some ways to the original inhabitants. But there were too many Rabbits, and there was fighting. From my background knowledge, I know that when there isn't enough land or resources for people, they fight to control resources. They also fight simply to have power. I am making an inference that the creators of this book are using this allegory to comment on how imperialist countries take over weaker countries.

cont.

Fig. 6-1 (cont.)

B: I predicted the Rabbits would "win" because they had better technology, and they did. On the final page of the book, the author and illustrator seem to be saying that the environmental destruction brought on by the Rabbits' invasion has turned out bad for both the original inhabitants and for the invaders. They seem to be saying that no one wins when the earth has been destroyed.

A: For me, this book is about how technology can create problems that must be solved. I think that we have many challenges today in dealing with the environmental impact of technological "advances." Some of those challenges are oil spills, global warming, and plant and animal species extinction, to name a few.

B: For me, this book is about the consequences of imperialism. I made connections to European colonists who came to North America and the impact they had on the indigenous people, the American Indians, and their way of life. In a few short years, these Rabbits overran the original inhabitants. I read the back book jacket information about the author and illustrator; they are both from Australia. I can infer that they knew the impact of British colonization on the aboriginal people of their own country when they were creating the book. I don't know very much about the history of Australia so I would have to do research to find out about that.

Reflections

A: When we were making predictions and inferences as we read, we were more engaged with the print and illustrations in this book. We read on to see if our predictions were correct. We used our background knowledge and evidence in the text to make inferences about the message of this allegory.

B: In the end, our inferences were different, but both are plausible based on the evidence in the text. Making predictions and drawing inferences helped us try to figure out the author's and illustrator's message. We read more deeply by anticipating the events in the story through making predictions. By drawing inferences, we were reading between the lines. The reading experience was more engaging, and I have an idea to conduct some research about Australian history.

mysteries in particular, can be selected to support teaching and learning prediction and inference. Fiction, which allows for a wide variety of interpretations, provides rich fodder for exploring and practicing this strategy. Figure 6-1 uses a sophisticated picture book to show educators demonstrating how to make predictions and draw inferences that engage and propel readers through the text. *The Rabbits* (Marsden/Tan) is an allegory that is most appropriate for a teen readership. This book can prompt students to generate themes related to social science and environmental science topics such as colonization and environmentalism to moral concepts such as fairness or human desires such as power and domination, among others.

As we teach the prediction and inference strategy, we first model and then invite readers to connect profoundly rather than superficially with texts. When we make predictions and inferences, we ask readers to use all of their mental faculties to think between the lines and through the images offered on the page or screen. Before they can make predictions or inferences, readers must bring together the text and their relevant prior knowledge. Then, to continue the analogy of the driver, they can accelerate forward in the text to determine if their predictions are borne out and if their inferences make sense. They can take control of the meaning they apply to the text and can deepen their comprehension.

HOW TO TEACH THE STRATEGY

We can think of making predictions and drawing inferences as specific types of questioning strategies. Predicting and inferring can be practiced at the word level or at the sentence, paragraph, page, or chapter levels or can be accomplished through reflection at the end of a text. A variety of statements and questions can be used to prompt readers' explorations with prediction and inference:

- I predict that . . .
- My guess is that . . .
- I suspect that . . .
- I think this clue means that . . .
- I knew this would happen next because . . .
- I conclude that . . .
- What clues did the author or illustrator give me?
- What do I see in my mind's eye that's not on the page?
- Why did that happen?
- What will happen next? Was I correct?
- What makes sense in this situation?
- What was the author trying to say in this text?
- What was the illustrator trying to show?

Educators can support students' practice of this strategy through the use of graphic organizers that require students to record their thinking. By providing evidence from the print or illustrations, students can "see" their own and their classmates' thought processes on paper. In figure 6-2 a category matrix specifies the evidence from the words and illustrations, the connecting background knowledge, and the resulting prediction or inference.

One way to help youth understand the meaning of the words *predict* and *infer* is to use three- or four-panel cartoons. Visual images with a few or no words can help readers gain experience with logical sequences of thought and plot that characterize much of the reading they will do in their lives. Educators can share the first two panels in each of the highly predictable cartoons in figure 6-3 and ask students to predict the third panel. They can also show all three panels in each cartoon and ask students to infer the fourth panel. Educators can help readers identify the evidence in the image, words, or their background knowledge that leads to predicting or inferring the next frame. Students can also be invited to create

their own cartoons to test their ability to convey plot logically and to leave sufficient evidence from which others can make predictions or draw inferences.

The smaller student-teacher ratio afforded by co-teaching greatly supports teaching and learning this strategy. Modeling for a whole group followed by small group mini-lessons and small group guided practice provides educators with insight into students' thinking or struggles with making inferences. Lessons 6.1 and 6.2 include small group practice facilitated by the school librarian and classroom teacher who can help students know when to stop and infer.

MAKING LITERATURE CONNECTIONS

PREDICTING

Predictable texts are a logical choice to build students' confidence in their ability to predict individual words or story elements. Rhyming poetry and rhyming song lyrics offer readers opportunities to predict the word at the end of the next rhyming line. Educators can share texts students have not previously read or heard to show them how the poet or lyricist has constructed a predictable pattern through the use of rhyme. This can be fun for students, whether or not their hypotheses agree with the rhymes in the text. Educators can share their thinking as they model this important cognitive process. Perennial favorite poets Jack Prelutsky and Shel Silverstein and rhyming songs from many musical eras offer youth fun and useful experiences. To find rhyming fiction titles or rhyming poetry, conduct library catalog searches for "stories in rhyme" or "rhyming poems."

Texts in which the illustrations provide clues to help readers predict the plot sequence offer critical support for this strategy. In classics such as picture books by Chris Van Allsburg and more recent titles such as those by Shaun Tan (see figure 6-4), illustrations supply visual story lines that parallel or extend the authors' words. These texts simply cannot be understood without interpreting the images as well as the print.

Fig. 6-2   Locating Evidence in the Text for Predictions and Connecting
Evidence and Background Knowledge for Inferences

Text: *The Big Elephant in the Room*, by Lane Smith

Text Prompt	Evidence (E) or Background Knowledge (BK)	Prediction (P) or Inference (I)
Cover	Two donkeys are worried about elephant. (E) Donkeys and elephants represent U.S. major political parties. (BK)	The book may be about politics. (I)
Verso of title page	The definition for "big elephant in the room": it's the thing people don't talk about. (E) Religion and politics are two things some people say you shouldn't talk about. (BK)	This could be about politics. (I)
Nut allergy	This friendship is in trouble. (E) They are going to fight about anything and everything. The donkeys are male; they are wearing boy clothes. (BK)	The donkey without the glasses (Donkey B) will have to defend his actions throughout the story. (P)
"Interesting" clothes	People use the word *interesting* when they want to be nice or can't think of anything else to say. (BK) Other characters are laughing. (E)	The donkey with glasses (Donkey A) will not accept his friend's explanations. (P)
Laughed so hard	It is embarrassing when you laugh so hard you wet your pants. (BK) Donkey B told someone else. (E)	Donkey A is even more humiliated because his "friend" told someone else. (I)
Picking for sports teams	This is one of the most competitive situations at school or in the neighborhood. (BK) Donkey B didn't even pick his friend for tiddlywinks. (E)	Donkey A will want to get even with Donkey B. (P)
All the embarrassing incidents	The illustration shows Donkey A messing up over and over again. (E) It's difficult to have a friend that's such a nerd. (BK)	This friendship is in trouble. (P)
Big elephant in the room	The illustration shows an actual elephant. (E) These two were not communicating at all. (BK)	Donkey A is really angry because he now knows more bad things have happened in their relationship than he knew before they started talking about the "elephant." (P) Their friendship is over. (I)

Reflection

This story wasn't about politics. It also wasn't intended to be about Donkey B's unkind treatment of his friend. On the surface, it was supposed to be about an actual elephant in the room. (E) But I think it was really about how low this "friendship" has sunk, and I think my inference that their friendship is over is justified. (I) When communication breaks down in a friendship, the relationship is in trouble. (BK)

Young children will enjoy the funny illustrations and situations in this book, but I don't think they will "get it" because they haven't had a great deal of experience with friendships. (P) I also think my original prediction that this book is about the Democratic and Republican Parties could be inferred at the ending. Politicians today, even within the same party, do not treat each other with respect. Our current political culture could be the "big elephant in the room." Author-illustrator Lane Smith could be suggesting that with this book. (I) As with all inferences about the author's meaning, the only way to find out is to ask him directly.

Fig. 6-3 Using Comics to Make Predictions or Draw Inferences

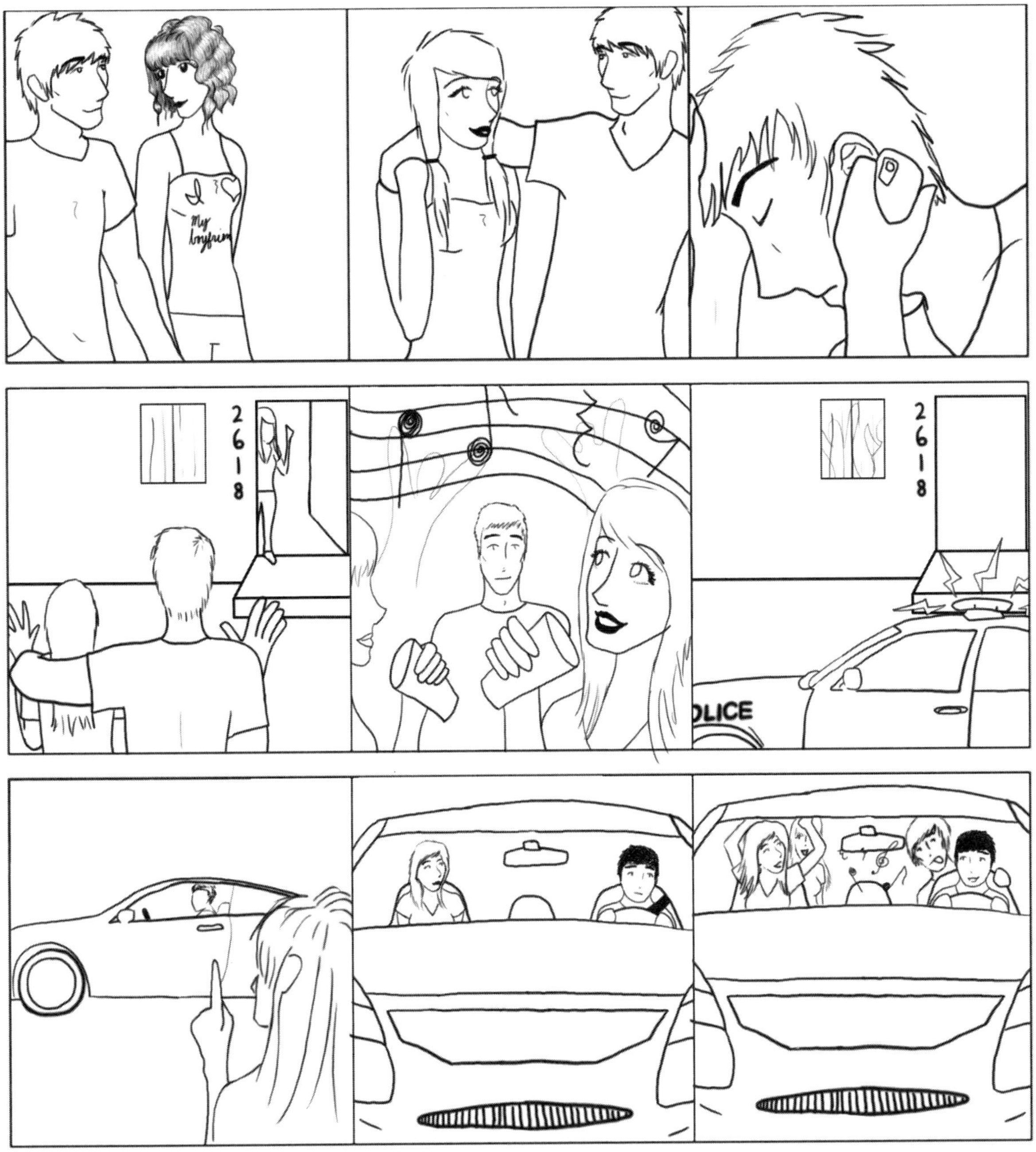

Illustrations by Amy Stewart

Fig. 6-4 Themes in Illustrator Shaun Tan's Work

Title	Author	Possible One-Sentence Theme
The Arrival	Shaun Tan	Immigrants face many hardships and fears when they leave their home countries and arrive in a new culture.
The Lost Thing	Shaun Tan	Bureaucracies and technological culture can be alienating, especially for people who are caring.
Memorial	Gary Crew	When war memories are no longer fresh, citizens do not always respect veterans who gave their lives for their country.
The Rabbits	John Marsden	Technologically advanced people can use their power to invade, dominate, and oppress indigenous people.
The Red Tree	Shaun Tan	When life appears dark, depressing, and scary, a thing of surprising beauty can give one hope.
Tales from Outer Suburbia	Shaun Tan	Life in suburbia can be frightening and alienating and is not what it appears to be on the surface.
The Viewer	Gary Crew	When we look closely at history we often see violence, destruction, and collapse.

INFERRING

Inference, which allows readers to make their own meanings based on limited clues in the text, requires more sophistication than prediction does. Inferring meaning at the word level requires a significant amount of language experience. A picture book about words such as *The Boy Who Loved Words* (Schotter/Potter) may provide challenges for advancing readers to use visual and semantic cues to discover the meanings in Selig's rich word choices: "Selig stayed on the outskirts, always on the *periphery*—listening and collecting delicious words." Unlike inferences beyond the word level that cannot be verified, students can use the glossary in *The Boy Who Loved Words* to check to see if their inferences about Selig's words were correct.

For students who are English speakers, books that include terms in other languages offer practice at inferring word meaning. Students who are proficient speakers or readers of other languages can also furnish definitions after their English-dominant classmates have made their inferences. For example, many young adult novels, such as *Confetti Girl* (López) and *Red Glass* (Resau), include Spanish words and Latino culture references about which non–Spanish speakers

and cultural outsiders may need to draw inferences. Educators can model and encourage readers to seek the expertise of linguistic and cultural insiders to confirm or disconfirm the validity of their inferences.

Comics are another format that supports readers' use of prediction and inference to achieve comprehension. With the rise of graphic novels, this genre is ever more widely available in middle school, high school, and public libraries. Like the examples in figure 6-3, educators can use published comics to support students in making predictions and drawing inferences. Conduct a word search for "cartoons and comics" or "graphic novels" in the online catalog.

Using Picture Storybooks to Teach Literary Devices (Hall 2007) provides an annotated list of books that stretch readers with their use of foreshadowing and inference. One example is *The Mysteries of Harris Burdick* (Van Allsburg), a sophisticated picture book that students can use to practice drawing inferences. Each double-page spread provides readers with a title, a couple lines of print, and an illustration that all beg to be interpreted. Readers can write entire stories based on the clues in the text. They can also be asked to justify their stories by identifying evidence or "clues" in the print and illustrations plus the background knowledge that led them to their unique interpretations. Instead of or in addition to writing, students can be invited to draw the next picture or sequence of pictures in the story as they imagine them.

Identifying the theme of a story is arguably the ultimate inference. Unless specifically stated, readers must infer the author's or illustrator's intended message; Hall (2007) also provides annotated examples for the study of theme. A theme is an overall meaning that is left with the reader, and as such, themes can be uniquely expressed. Sometimes themes are described as morals or lessons, but many times the theme of a story is much more elusive. Asking students to flesh out these topics and to express themes in one complete sentence helps them specify the emotional impact of a particular text. Conversations around theme present readers with ideas for rich discussions. Figure 6-4 shows possible one-sentence themes for picture books created by or with Australian illustrator Shaun Tan. Tween and young adult readers have the necessary knowledge to interpret the metaphors expressed in both the print and images in these texts.

TWEEN, YOUNG ADULT, AND ADULT LITERATURE CITED

Starred titles are used in the lesson plans.

The Arrival, by Shaun Tan

The Big Elephant in the Room, by Lane Smith

The Boy Who Loved Words, by Roni Schotter, illustrated by Giselle Potter

Confetti Girl, by Diana López

*Goin' Someplace Special, by Patricia McKissack, illustrated by Jerry Pinkney

Guess What? by Mem Fox, illustrated by Vivienne Goodman

*Lincoln Shot! A President's Life Remembered, by Barry Denenburg

The Little Bit Scary People, by Emily Jenkins, illustrated by Alexandra Boiger

The Lost Thing, by Shaun Tan

Memorial, by Gary Crew, illustrated by Shaun Tan

The Mysteries of Harris Burdick, by Chris Van Allsburg

The Rabbits, by John Marsden, illustrated by Shaun Tan

Red Glass, by Laura Resau

The Red Tree, by Shaun Tan

Rose Blanche, by Christophe Gallaz and Roberto Innocenti, illustrated by Roberto Innocenti

Tales from Outer Suburbia, by Shaun Tan

The Viewer, by Gary Crew, illustrated by Shaun Tan

LESSON PLANS

Predicting and inferring are similar to questioning in that students must be given opportunities to explore fully their individual thinking and connections. The lesson plans offered focus on drawing inferences, because this strategy is more sophisticated than making predictions and presents greater challenges for middle and high school readers. In these lessons, a smaller student-to-teacher ratio allows educators to maximize interaction before, during, and after reading. Educators provide think-aloud strategies to demonstrate how to utilize these strategies to improve their own comprehension of text. Although graphic organizers are provided for recording inferences, students can also use large sticky notes when using print materials to record their ideas and place them on book covers or pages of text where they found evidence, made connections, and drew inferences.

Using a picture book as the mentor text, the advancing lesson is based on making inferences about the impact of the setting on the mood and tone of the text. The advanced lesson focuses on inferring how non–U.S. art has become part of U.S. popular culture. In the challenging lesson, readers collect facts, draw inferences, and cite sources in a study of historical figures. All three lessons suggest Web 2.0 products as tools for students to demonstrate their ability to draw inferences.

LESSON PLAN 6.1

Reading Comprehension Strategy Four
Drawing Inferences

Reading Development Level: Advancing

Instructional Strategies
Advance Organizers, Categorizing, and Notemaking

Lesson Length
1 session (additional sessions for application and extension)

Purpose
The purpose of this lesson is to draw inferences about the impact of setting on the mood and tone of a story before, during, and after reading a historical fiction text. Inferences are made by combining evidence in the text with readers' background knowledge and research. Note: Any picture book or short story in which the setting has a strong impact on the story can be used for modeling. For the application, picture books, short stories, historical fiction, and classic literary novels such as *The Old Man and the Sea* by Ernest Hemingway are appropriate selections. This lesson can also provide background knowledge for a study of U.S. history and culture immediately after World War II.

Objectives
At the end of this lesson, students will be able to
1. Determine when to pause the reading to draw an inference.
2. Combine specific evidence from the text with background knowledge and research to draw inferences.
3. Record evidence, background knowledge, research, and inferences in preparation for crafting an overarching inference that shows the impact of setting on the mood and tone of the piece.
4. Use notemaking formats.
5. Application: Craft an essay or other product to demonstrate drawing inferences.

Resources, Materials, and Equipment
Mentor text: *Goin' Someplace Special,* by Patricia C. McKissack, illustrated by Jerry Pinkney
Application: Picture books, historical fiction novels, or classic literary works
Graphic organizers: 6.1 Anticipation Guide, 6.1 Category Matrix, 6.1 Teacher Resource—Completed Category Matrix. For the application: Notemaking Chart, Notemaking Graphic Organizer, Works Cited Graphic Organizer, Notemaking and Works Cited Graphic Organizers Rubric. For the extension: the Group Work and Multimedia Product Rubric
Overhead, data projector, or interactive whiteboard, or optional Elmo projector

Collaboration

While one educator reads the mentor picture book, both educators provide think-alouds to share ideas about the impact of the setting on the story. After reading and reviewing the evidence in the text, activating background knowledge, and conducting research using the author's note, each educator draws an inference related to the impact of the setting on the mood and tone. Both educators jointly monitor students' partner or small group guided practice with the mentor picture book or short story.

Assessment

The students' category matrices show their use of evidence, background knowledge, and research to construct inferences that indicate deep comprehension. Educators set criteria for assessing the completeness of the category matrix.

Standards

Reading keywords: Draw inferences; analyze for story elements (setting).

Social studies keywords: Understand the influence of historical events on contemporary culture; recognize how history and geography contribute to a sense of time and place.

Educational technology keywords (for the extension): Plan, design, and present multimedia academic products and collaborative communication activities to share products with audiences inside and outside the classroom.

AASL STANDARDS INDICATORS*

- Use prior and background knowledge as context for new learning. (1.1.2)
- Organize knowledge so that it is useful. (2.1.2)
- Show social responsibility by participating actively with others in learning situations and by contributing questions and ideas during group discussions. (3.2.2)

Determine additional standards and indicators for the application and extensions.

PROCESS

DAY 1 ··

MOTIVATION

Make a connection to a school setting such as the cafeteria, library, or classroom on test day. Tell a brief story about an event in that setting using the third-person point of view. An embarrassing moment in a full school cafeteria reported by a school newspaper reporter could make an interesting plot.

What is a setting in a piece of literature? It includes the place, time of year or day, and historical context of the piece of literature, film, or play. What is the mood or tone? The mood is the feeling the reader or viewer gets when reading a piece of literature or watching a film or play. The tone of a piece is reflected in the emotional state of the narrative voice. If the author does not tell the reader the impact of the setting on the mood and tone of the piece, then the reader must infer it.

---

* Excerpted from *Standards for the 21st-Century Learner* by the American Association of School Librarians, a division of the American Library Association, copyright © 2007 American Library Association. Available for download at www.ala.org/aasl/standards. Used with permission.

Ask the listeners: How is your experience of the event affected by the place it occurred? How does the time of day (or year) affect the story? Describe the mood of the story. (How does it make you feel?) Describe the tone of the story. (How does the narrator's emotional state affect the story?)

Distribute the 6.1 Anticipation Guide. Ask students to read the statements about determining the impact of the setting on the mood and tone. Under the "before reading" column, circle whether they agree or disagree with each statement. Students read a text and reassess these statements after reading.

STUDENT-FRIENDLY OBJECTIVES

1. Decide when to pause to think about the setting and draw an inference.
2. Combine specific evidence from the text with background knowledge or research to draw inferences.
3. Record evidence, background knowledge, and research as notes.
4. Respond to the anticipation guide and state inferences at the end of the reading.

PRESENTATION

Project the 6.1 Category Matrix. Define each category. Evidence is "on the line" information that is actually stated in the text; inferences are "between the lines" ideas. Discuss how inferences are constructed from evidence in the text plus background knowledge or research. Students draw inferences to determine the impact of the setting on the mood and tone of this story.

Note: If multiple copies of the mentor picture book are available, students work in pairs or small groups to read and complete the 6.1 Category Matrix after educators model for the first half of the book. Otherwise, project the book and conduct a whole class lesson.

One educator reads the mentor picture book *Goin' Someplace Special* while the other records evidence, background knowledge, and research from the author's note. Pause the reading to ask a question about the setting. Ask: "When do readers pause to reflect and draw inferences?" Readers pause to draw inferences when they are unclear about the meaning of a word, phrase, or idea. Readers also pause when they think the author or illustrator has given them a clue to understanding the meaning of the story. Educators think aloud to share why they paused the reading. They make notes on the matrix to record evidence in the text, their background knowledge, and research from the author's note and ultimately their inferences.

At the end of the reading, each educator shares how she used the evidence in the text and her own background or the author's note to draw an inference about the impact of the setting on the mood or tone of the story. The other educator records the process on the matrix.

Ask the students to revisit the 6.1 Anticipation Guide. Reread it. Did seeing the process of making an inference about setting increase their confidence in these areas? Circle *agree* or *disagree* in the "after reading" column.

STUDENT PRACTICE PROCEDURES

1. Select a piece of evidence related to the setting from the text and record it on the graphic organizer.
2. Connect the evidence with background knowledge or information from the author's note (research) and record a note about it.
3. Compose an inference based on evidence and background knowledge or research.

GUIDED PRACTICE

Educators monitor students' inferences and group work.

CLOSURE

Students share inferences in small groups or with the entire class. Review the process of making inferences.

REFLECTION

How do readers know when to pause the reading to draw an inference? What do readers do who lack the necessary background knowledge to draw an inference? Why do strategic readers draw inferences?

APPLICATION

Divide the class into small group literature circles. Educators cofacilitate students' guided practice in the classroom or library, or half the groups work in the library while the other half work in the classroom.

STUDENT-FRIENDLY OBJECTIVES

1. Draw inferences.
2. Record evidence, background knowledge, and research as notes on the Notemaking Graphic Organizer.
3. Keep a bibliographic record for resources other than the picture book, short story, or novel.

SUMMARY

Distribute texts and provide an individual 6.1 Category Matrix to each student. Educators teach a bibliographic record strategy. Repeat the student practice procedures, guided practice, closure, and reflection.

EXTENSIONS

Students compose an essay or create a product that demonstrates their understanding of the impact of the setting on the mood and tone of the story. Use a 6+1 Trait® rubric (Education Northwest 2011) or other writing scoring guide to assess students' essays. If students have the choice of a multimedia format for their final product, use the Group Work and Multimedia Product Rubric to guide students' product production. Animoto, Glogster, VoiceThread, and more may be appropriate Web 2.0 tools for these learning objectives.

Continue to guide students in drawing inferences as they read texts in all formats in all content areas.

LESSON PLAN 6.2

Reading Comprehension Strategy Four
Drawing Inferences

Reading Development Level: Advanced

Instructional Strategies
Categorizing and Notemaking

Lesson Length
3 or 4 sessions

Purpose
The purpose of this unit is to draw inferences about the influence of the arts from other cultures and previous decades on today's U.S. popular culture. Inferences are made by combining evidence in the text with readers' background knowledge and research. Note: Any artifact or icon that enters into popular culture can be used for modeling or for students' guided practice. These lessons can also provide background knowledge for a study of the fine arts, literature, history, or culture.

Objectives
At the end of this unit, students will be able to

1. Combine specific evidence from the text with background knowledge and research to draw inferences.
2. Record evidence, background knowledge, research, and inferences in preparation for crafting expository paragraphs for why a particular icon enters into popular culture.
3. Use notemaking formats.
4. Alternate product: Create a multimedia product that demonstrates making inferences about why a particular icon reoccurs in U.S. popular culture and other cultures around the world.

Resources, Materials, and Equipment
Mentor text: *The Scream* (painting), by Edvard Munch

Scream (film), by Wes Craven

"The Scream Video," Animoto: http://animoto.com/play/xMcbn5iXxztXkRE0VcutbQ

Guided practice: *The Thinker,* by Auguste Rodin; *Mona Lisa,* by Leonardo da Vinci; *William Tell Overture,* by Gioachino Rossini; *Romeo and Juliet,* by William Shakespeare (Act 4, Scene 3); *Dracula,* by Bram Stoker (Chapter 8: "Mina Murray's Journal, 11 August, 3 A.M."); and Capoeira (Brazilian dance form)

Additional print and electronic resources to support guided practice, such as *Dracula,* by Bram Stoker, illustrated by Tudor Humphries, or YouTube Capoeira videos.

Graphic Organizers: 6.2 Category Matrix, 6.2 Teacher Resource—Completed Category Matrix, 6.2 Teacher Resource—Research Topics and Notes, 6.2 Teacher Resource—Works Cited for Video
Internet access and overhead, data projector, or interactive whiteboard, or optional Elmo projector

Collaboration

Educators provide think-alouds to draw inferences about the mood and messages of a piece of artwork and model researching this piece. Educators divide the class in half or jointly monitor students' partner or small group guided practice with other pieces of artwork and other art forms.

Assessment

The students' category matrices show their use of evidence, background knowledge, and research to construct inferences that indicate deep comprehension. Educators set criteria for assessing the completeness of students' category matrices. Educators determine a final product or multiple products for this lesson and determine the sequence in which the final products are produced. Students and educators use a 6+1 Trait® or other writing rubric to assess expository paragraphs or the Group Work and Multimedia Product Rubric to assess multimedia products.

Standards

Reading keywords: Draw inferences and conclusions; analyze and provide evidence from the text; consider cultural, historical, and contemporary contexts.

Media literacy keywords: Analyze how words, images, graphics, and sounds work together in various forms to impact meaning.

Social studies keywords: Understand the relationship between the arts and the times during which they were created; identify the impact of popular American culture on the rest of the world; identify examples of art, music, and literature that transcend the cultures and convey universal themes.

For the Alternate Product

Educational technology keywords: Plan, design, and present multimedia academic products; participate in collaborative communication activities to share products with audiences inside and outside the classroom.

AASL STANDARDS INDICATORS*

- Use prior and background knowledge as context for new learning. (1.1.2)
- Find, evaluate, and select appropriate sources to answer questions. (1.1.4)
- Read, view, and listen for information presented in any format (e.g., textual, visual, media, digital) in order to make inferences and gather meaning. (1.1.6)
- Follow ethical and legal guidelines in gathering and using information. (1.3.3)
- Organize knowledge so that it is useful. (2.1.2)
- Use technology and other information tools to analyze and organize information. (2.1.4)
- Conclude an inquiry-based research process by sharing new understandings and reflecting on the learning. (3.1.1)
- Show social responsibility by participating actively with others in learning situations and by contributing questions and ideas during group discussions. (3.2.2)

Select additional indicators for the alternate product or extensions.

* Excerpted from *Standards for the 21st-Century Learner* by the American Association of School Librarians, a division of the American Library Association, copyright © 2007 American Library Association. Available for download at www.ala.org/aasl/standards. Used with permission.

PROCESS

DAYS 1 AND 2

MOTIVATION

Organize students into small groups based on choice of fine art form. Ask students to brainstorm ideas about popular culture. Create a whole class word cloud for popular culture at http://Wordle.net. These are possible words to include besides pop culture: commercial, cool, hot, language, changing, trendy, art, media, trivial, fun, consumerism, music, sticky, and more.

Post and pose the essential question for this lesson: "Why does art from previous generations and other cultures make its way into U.S. popular (pop) culture?"

Demonstrate a web search for images of the mask from Wes Craven's *Scream* movies. Then search for Edvard Munch's painting *The Scream*. Put them side by side on the screen. Note the dates of each artifact. In order to answer the essential question, students draw inferences by combining evidence in the art piece with their background knowledge and research. They analyze the artifact and use critical thinking.

STUDENT-FRIENDLY OBJECTIVES

1. Decide when to use background information or to conduct research in order to draw an inference.
2. Record evidence, background knowledge, and research as notes.
3. Combine specific evidence from the text with background knowledge or research to draw inferences.
4. Record information sources.

PRESENTATION

Project the 6.2 Category Matrix. Define each category. Evidence is "on the line" descriptive information; inferences are unstated "between the lines" ideas. Discuss how inferences are constructed from evidence in the text plus background knowledge or research. Students draw inferences to determine why specific examples of art from previous generations and other cultures have become present-day U.S. pop culture icons.

One educator describes *The Scream* painting while the other records evidence on the graphic organizer (see the 6.2 Teacher Resource—Completed Category Matrix). Ask "What background knowledge do we have that can help us make meaning from these pieces of evidence?" Educators think aloud to share background information about the character in the foreground. Make notes on the matrix to record background knowledge.

Either continue to model for the whole class or have each small group take a component of the painting and repeat the same process of making connections to background knowledge. Record educators' or student groups' connections on the matrix.

Discuss the role of research in building background knowledge. Determine which categories of evidence need more information. Search the Web and use the information about *The Scream* to complete the top part of the 6.2 Category Matrix. Record additional information for other categories using another color font. Use a web-based citation generator to record a citation for the Works Cited or Consulted.

After completing research, each educator uses think-alouds to share how she combines evidence in the text, her own background, and research to draw an inference about the meaning of each aspect of the painting. Educators can take turns making inferences and recording on the matrix.

STUDENT PRACTICE PROCEDURES
1. Describe the piece and record a description in the "evidence" column on the matrix.
2. Connect the evidence with background knowledge and record it.
3. Determine when to seek additional information through research.
4. Record notes and cite sources.
5. Draw inferences based on evidence, background knowledge, or research about why this art has become an icon in U.S. popular culture.

GUIDED PRACTICE
Educators monitor for comprehensible notes, inferences, complete matrices, and citations. Guide students in conducting research and drawing inferences.

CLOSURE
Student groups share their inferences with another small group or with the entire class. Review the process of making inferences.

REFLECTION
How do readers/listeners/viewers know when to stop, think, and connect to background knowledge or to conduct research to draw an inference? Why do strategic readers/listeners/viewers make inferences?

DAY 3 OR DAYS 3 AND 4

SUMMARY
Note: The order of these lessons is dependent on the educators' selection of a final product or the sequence for completion of multiple products.

Project and review the 6.2 Teacher Resource—Completed Category Matrix. Read the directions for composing expository paragraphs about evidence, background knowledge, research, and inferences. Share *The Scream* sample paragraphs or conduct a shared writing to outline or compose several paragraphs related to making inferences about this piece of art.

Provide students with a writing rubric to self-assess their work. Students may compose paragraphs in small groups, with partners, or individually. If students will be creating an alternate product, share the Animoto Video example "The Scream Video." Evaluate the video using the Group Work and Multimedia Product Rubric. Project the 6.2 Teacher Resource—Works Cited for Video.

ALTERNATE PRODUCT
Students collaboratively create a multimedia product that demonstrates their understanding of the piece of art and why it has become part of U.S. popular culture. Use the Group Work and Multimedia Product Rubric to guide students' multimedia product production. Animoto, Glogster, VoiceThread, and more may be appropriate Web 2.0 tools for these learning objectives.

EXTENSIONS
Challenge students to continue to search for pop culture icons, determine their origin, make connections or conduct research, and draw inferences. Create a display or web page to post or link students' work.

Continue to guide students in making inferences as they read texts in all formats in all content areas.

LESSON PLAN 6.3

Reading Comprehension Strategy Four
Drawing Inferences

Reading Development Level: Challenging

Instructional Strategies
Notemaking and Summarizing, Classifying

Lesson Length
4 sessions

Purpose
The purpose of this unit is to draw inferences about a historical figure. Students pose questions, select resources, seek answers, and learn to combine commonly agreed facts with their background knowledge in order to draw inferences. Students use Web 2.0 tools to share their facts and inferences and cite sources. These lessons can be adapted for a study of key figures in history, science, math, literature, the arts, sports, or other human endeavors.

Objectives
At the end of this unit, students will be able to
1. Draw inferences by combining facts with background knowledge.
2. Find, evaluate, and select appropriate sources to answer questions.
3. Classify information as facts or as inferences.
4. Cite evidence in texts in order to justify inferences.
5. Use Web 2.0 tools to share new knowledge.
6. Self-assess with a checklist.
7. Conclude research process by sharing new understandings.
8. Use an exit slip to reflect on learning.

Resources, Materials, and Equipment
Text set of informational books, including *Lincoln Shot! A President's Life Remembered,* by Barry Denenburg, and biographies of key Civil War figures
Commander-in-Chief Lincoln Legacy Space example: www.storytrail.com/impact12/lincoln.htm
Graphic organizers: 6.3 Planning Sheet, 6.3 Template, 6.3 Checklist, 6.3 Teacher Resource—Sample Completed Checklist, 6.3 Exit Slip
Internet access and data projector, overhead, or interactive whiteboard

Collaboration
The educators coteach the lesson. They use think-alouds to model identifying facts and making inferences. They demonstrate how to construct inferences by combining facts and background knowledge. They

both monitor students' research, inferences, and citations. Educators share responsibility for reviewing students' exit slips and assessing their work by making comments on students' checklists and wiki pages.

Assessment

The students' planning sheet, wiki pages, and checklist show the process and results of their learning. Their questions and comments about each other's pages also show their ability to distinguish facts from inferences. Exit slips show how making inferences impacted their comprehension and what questions they still have about this strategy.

Content Standards

Reading keywords: Extract information and use graphic organizers to comprehend text; connect information and events in text to related text and sources; draw inferences and cite evidence in the text.

Writing keywords: Use relevant information; draw valid inferences.

Research keywords: Ask open-ended questions; develop a plan for finding answers.

Social studies keywords: Use historical inquiry to research, interpret, and use multiple sources of evidence; analyze information by categorizing, summarizing, and drawing inferences and conclusions; support a point of view or an opinion on a historical person, issue, or event.

Educational technology keywords: use technology to conduct research or record information; format a multimedia project according to defined output specifications including target audience and viewing environment.

AASL Standards Indicators*

- Find, evaluate, and select appropriate sources to answer questions. (1.1.4)
- Read, view, and listen for information presented in any format (e.g., textual, visual, media, digital) in order to make inferences and gather meaning. (1.1.6)
- Follow ethical and legal guidelines in gathering and using information. (1.3.3)
- Use information technology responsibly. (1.3.5)
- Organize knowledge so that it is useful. (2.1.2)
- Use technology and other information tools to analyze and organize information. (2.1.4)
- Conclude an inquiry-based research process by sharing new understandings and reflecting on the learning. (3.1.1)
- Assess the quality and effectiveness of the learning product. (3.4.2)

PROCESS

This is an outline rather than a detailed procedure.

DAY 1

MOTIVATION

Pose the questions: "How do historians *know* what happened in the past if they weren't actually present?" "How do they *know* the motivations of people they never met?" Make a connection to an incident or event that happened on the school grounds. Ask students for eyewitness accounts (primary sources).

Ask students for what they read in the school newspaper (secondary source). Ask students for what they heard from their friends (less reliable secondary sources). Ask students about how their understanding of the people involved and of the context of the event has affected their opinion of the incident.

Discuss historical inquiry in terms of values and behavior of human beings in relationship to events. Historians must show integrity when they interpret events. They must document sources, corroborate "facts" from several sources, and explain their interpretations, or inferences, based on combining the facts with their own background knowledge. When they draw an inference, they must be clear about the impact of their own background knowledge and experience on their interpretation.

Students ask questions, research, record facts, and draw inferences about key figures from the U.S. Civil War. Students create a two-page "MySpace" wiki for the person. On the first wiki page, students follow a template and post facts and inferences. On the second page, they note the facts (in one color font) and explain their inferences in terms of evidence from reliable sources and their own background knowledge (in a different font color). Students cite their sources. They reflect on how making inferences deepened their understanding of the person and the historical context. In addition, students view each other's work and comment on other students' inferences.

STUDENT-FRIENDLY OBJECTIVES
1. Make a distinction between facts and inferences.
2. Suggest a variety of resources to answer questions.
3. Make notes.

PRESENTATION

Educators and students brainstorm what they already know about Abraham Lincoln and his presidency. Project and use the 6.3 Planning Sheet or a Web 2.0 brainstorming tool to record these ideas. Brainstorm and record possible research questions about President Lincoln.

Project and share the Commander-in-Chief Lincoln Legacy Space wiki home page. Educators discuss sections of the "MySpace" template using think-alouds. Students are to give one thumb up for a fact or two thumbs up for an inference. Volunteers suggest a resource where that fact could be found. The educator who is not reading keeps a log of possible resources and a record of the entries that the majority of students suspect are inferences (record on the 6.3 Checklist).

STUDENT PARTICIPATION PROCEDURES
1. One thumb up for a fact.
2. Suggest a possible resource where that fact could be located.
3. Two thumbs up for an inference.

Educators share the Commander-in-Chief Lincoln Legacy Space wiki inferences page. They note the "blue" inference sections and along with students compare their predictions about which entries were facts and which were inferences. Use think-alouds and discuss how the background knowledge of the creator of the page influenced the inferences.

Review the types of resources, primary and secondary, and multiple formats. Share the print text set. Review citing sources using an online citation maker and common sense.

Form partners for this work and select Civil War figures for this study.

STUDENT PRACTICE PROCEDURES
1. Brainstorm background knowledge about the person.
2. Record questions for research and possible resources on the planning form.
3. Use print resources to build basic background knowledge.
4. Make notes using the wiki page template as a guide.

GUIDED PRACTICE
Students use the print resources to begin their study. Educators monitor the students' initial background knowledge brainstorms, questions, and notemaking.

CLOSURE
Ask volunteers to share a few of their initial questions, a few possible resources, and/or a few compelling facts about these Civil War figures.

REFLECTION
How do we prepare for research? Why is it important to make a distinction between facts and inferences? (Students may not yet be able to answer this question.)

PREPARATION
All students need wiki accounts and need to be invited to join the class wiki. Ideally, students make their own pages. If that is not possible, educators make pages or have student aides make pages for each Civil War figure under study.

Link all of the students' wiki pages to one central class home page. Include information on the page about the purpose of the assignment and information about facts and inferences. Illustrate it in some way, for example, a Wordle with the last names of the historical figures being studied.

DAYS 2 AND 3

MOTIVATION–DAY 2
Demonstrate how to create two wiki pages and how to copy and paste the wiki page template onto the home page. (Ideally, students will use a wiki tool such as wikispaces or pbworks that offers a discussion or comment feature for others to post feedback to their pages. If not, students can provide feedback using pencil and paper.) Demonstrate how to change font color in order to distinguish between facts and inferences.

MOTIVATION–DAY 3
Demonstrate how to add images to wiki pages, including how to caption them and link them to the original source. Note: Only copyright-free images or images in the public domain should be posted to the wiki pages. Demonstrate other wiki formatting features as needed.

PRESENTATION
Return to the inferences page of the Commander-in-Chief Lincoln example. Examine the Works Cited. Share resources that are in the text set that contain primary source documents. Review definitions for primary and secondary source documents. Remind students that facts found in secondary sources should

be corroborated by at least one additional resource. Review the process for making an inference. Demonstrate how to use the checklist to self-assess progress.

Assuming computer access for each partnership, students record facts directly on wiki pages. They also record ISBN numbers, URLs, or complete citations as they consult various sources. Without computer access, students record their notes and sources as modeled by educators.

STUDENT PRACTICE PROCEDURES
1. Determine resources to fill in facts and draw inferences.
2. Draw valid inferences based on information from a variety of resources.
3. Use the 6.3 Checklist to monitor progress.
4. Publish facts and inferences and distinguish between the two.

GUIDED PRACTICE
Educators monitor students' notemaking, citing sources, and ask students to share their thinking when they are recording facts and inferences.

CLOSURE
Volunteers share inferences. Students will view each other's work the next day and comment on each other's inferences. Students who are not yet finished complete their wikis as homework.

REFLECTION
What contributes to people making different inferences from the same information?

DAY 4

PRESENTATION
Share the class home page. Using the sample wiki pages, review and give examples of appropriate constructive feedback or visit one of the student pages and demonstrate commenting on the inference; for example, "Sign-up Date—Inference Makes Sense: This makes sense in 21st-century terms. President Obama has a Facebook page. In Lincoln's day, however, news traveled very slowly. I think we are lucky to have just-in-time communication with our leaders."

Lead a discussion on appropriate and positive feedback. Enforce netiquette. (If students have not had sufficient experience with netiquette, teach it.)

STUDENT PARTICIPATION PROCEDURES
1. Log in and review the home page and inference page of another team's work.
2. Focus on one of the inferences.
3. Use the discussion or comment feature to make an appropriate comment related to an inference.
4. Make constructive comments on additional students' wiki pages.

GUIDED PRACTICE
Educators monitor students' comments. Make sure students are logged in so they get credit for their participation and no comments are made anonymously. To ensure that every team gets at least one comment, assign students or teams to comment on specific pages as well as post comments to any page.

CLOSURE

Collect each team's checklist. Select one or more exemplary student examples. Ask one of the students on the team to read only the facts. Ask the other student to read only the team's inferences. Ask students to define the difference between facts and inferences.

Distribute the 6.3 Exit Slip. Students complete it in class or for homework.

REFLECTION

Which is more complete—just the facts or the facts plus inferences? Why? How do inferences help readers make sense of ideas and information?

ALTERNATE TOOLS

Students can use Google docs or other read-write tools to conduct this work. They can do this with pencil and paper if sufficient technology tools are not available.

EXTENSIONS

Students use facts and inferences to compose an essay that demonstrates how they were able to draw valid inferences from facts plus background knowledge and research. They can practice applying the process of drawing inferences in other content areas.

Continue to guide students in drawing inferences as they read texts in all formats in all content areas.

7

Reading Comprehension Strategy Five

Determining Main Ideas

Determining importance means picking out the most important information when you read, to highlight essential ideas, to isolate supporting details, and to read for specific information.

—Stephanie Harvey and Anne Goudvis

As information specialists, school librarians are acutely aware of the challenges students face when they are confronted with an excess of information. It isn't easy for proficient adult readers to sift through a daily barrage of data and telecommunications to determine what is important; for many youth it can be truly daunting. Just as fish are unaware of the water in which they swim, 21st-century teens, the Millennials who were born into the Information Age, may not realize the impact of this barrage on their ability to focus, determine importance, and set priorities. Many are not yet aware of the distinctions that can and should be drawn between data, information, knowledge, and wisdom.

To be useful, data must be organized into something accessible as information. Information is only a set of facts until someone determines its importance, internalizes it, and turns it into knowledge through use. And although we may not all agree on the manifestations of wisdom, we do know it requires an accumulation of knowledge and the ability to discern connections and relationships. Sorting out these distinctions is critical for students, workers, and citizens of this century. It is important that educators scaffold students' formal experiences with mining data, using information, and creating knowledge so they can effectively transfer these skills and successfully apply them in their outside-of-school experiences as well.

In school-based learning experiences, educators who clearly establish learning objectives provide a scaffold that supports students in determining main ideas. In teacher-directed lessons, educators give students clear purposes for reading. Educators must also demonstrate that as the purpose for reading changes, the reader's focus changes as well. It is also essential to give students at all grade levels and levels of reading proficiency opportunities to determine and to set their own purposes for reading, a lifelong learning skill.

Main ideas are always dependent on the purpose for reading. If students are reading fictional texts and exploring story elements, then characters, setting, plot, and theme are the main ideas. If someone is reading an informational text for the latest, most unusual scientific discovery to satisfy his own curiosity, he will most likely focus on a different main idea than if he were conducting research for a five-page report or studying for a science exam. If reading to find the main idea in a passage on a standardized test, the reader will look for the best answer from the test maker's perspective. While practicing and applying this strategy, readers have the opportunity to use evaluation, a higher-order thinking skill.

Main ideas can be determined at the whole-text, chapter, page, passage, paragraph, or sentence (word) level. In *Mosaic of Thought*, Keene and Zimmermann (1997) discuss *considerate* and *inconsiderate* texts in the context of readers searching for main ideas. A considerate text is one that provides support or scaffolding for readers' access to the important parts; inconsiderate texts do not. In many fictional texts, clearly presented narrative structures or story elements offer such a framework. On the other hand, most expository texts are built around dominant themes, concepts, or key ideas. Some informational texts for teens are written with a narrative frame that supports readers as they apply their background knowledge about how stories work, which they developed while hearing oral stories and reading fiction (see "Making Literature Connections" in chapter 5). More traditional informational texts include other considerate features that help readers determine the main ideas from the author's (or book designer's) point of view. Text features such as tables of contents, indexes, time lines, and glossaries point the way to main ideas. Graphics, including illustrations, photographs, charts, maps, tables, captions, and more, support readers as they decide what is important. Headings and subheadings, font variations, and other print features signal relationships and relative importance among the pieces of information presented. Figure 7-1 shows text features commonly found in content area textbooks.

Both fictional and informational texts use varying font size or style to alert readers to important ideas and concepts. Some texts of both kinds use predictable text structures such as sequencing, question and answer, cause and effect, or problem and solution to guide readers (for a useful description and a table of graphic organizers to support a focus on various text structures, see Fisher, Frey, and Lapp 2009, 95–99). Signal words often indicate which structure is being used. For example, these are some words that indicate sequencing: *first, next, then,* and *finally*. Once students become aware of these reader supports, they can incorporate them into their own student-authored texts.

As we teach determining main ideas, educators model, then invite readers to make judgments about which ideas are most important and which are less important. Main ideas are the foundation on which the details rest. Just as the tires on a car must bear its significant weight and allow it to move, we ask readers to think of main ideas as the base that defines what's most important, the foundation on which the supporting details rest. Readers must learn how to prioritize information as an essential skill in reading comprehension as well as in information literacy. As readers determine main ideas, they develop their background knowledge or schemas and strengthen their ability to store, recall, and use ideas and information.

HOW TO TEACH THE STRATEGY

School librarians will recognize the connection between determining main ideas and information literacy, the skills needed to "select, evaluate, and use information appropriately and effectively" (AASL 2007, 2). Not only do these skills apply to printed reference texts but they also apply to texts in multiple formats that require learners to bring multiple literacies to bear in making sense of ideas and information. Just as information literacy has become more complex, so has determining main ideas. *Standards for the 21st-Century Learner* indicator 2.1.2 is "Organize knowledge so that it is useful" (AASL 2007, 4), and learning to make effective notes is a critical component of this skill (see chapter 2).

While mining for relevant information, readers must distill the essential from a sentence, an image, a passage, a paragraph, a chapter, or an entire text. With opportunities to practice this strategy at all levels of complexity, students can build their abilities to separate main ideas from supporting details. Determining main ideas requires that readers discard some information. With a clear purpose in mind, a reader

Fig. 7-1   Text Features in Textbooks

Type of Element	Text Features
Elements That Organize	• Chapters • Headings • Lists of figures or lab experiments • Subheadings • Time lines • Titles
Elements for Locating Information	• Indexes • Lists of figures • Page numbers • Tables of contents
Elements for Explanation and Elaboration	• Diagrams • Charts and tables • Figures • Graphs • Glossaries • Maps • Online interactive resources • Sidebars (such as "Did you know?")
Elements That Illustrate	• Drawings and paintings • Photographs • Primary source documents
Elements That Notify	• Bolded words • Italics, font size, and other font changes • Learning objectives
Elements That Check for Understanding	• Alternative assessments • Quizzes • Reviews • Summaries

Adapted from Fisher, Frey, and Lapp (2009)

can decide what information to disregard. Questions such as the following can help students determine main ideas:

- What is or was my purpose for reading?
- What new ideas or facts did I learn?
- What do I want to remember from this text?
- What will I do with this information?
- What was the author's or illustrator's purpose in writing or illustrating this text?

Students who are comfortable with the narrative frame may need extra support when interacting with expository writing. Guidelines for reading informational texts can be posted in the library and in the classroom. Educators can model the following sequence and give students many opportunities to practice these strategies:

- Set a purpose for reading.
- Preview covers and inside book flaps; book-walk to read illustrations.
- Preview text features (main ideas): titles, subtitles, captions, charts, maps, time lines, and graphs.
- Determine text structure such as compare/contrast, cause/effect, or problem/solution and apply features of that text structure to determine main ideas.
- Slow down for new vocabulary or difficult concepts.
- Use the glossary or a dictionary.
- Stop to talk about a passage, make notes, and write about learning.
- Reread or use other fix-up options when the meaning isn't clear (see chapter 8).

A critical part of working with main ideas involves recording significant learning while reading or viewing. Educators can post a chart such as the Notemaking Chart in both the library and classrooms to remind students of the goal of notemaking and the types of notes. The school library literature is rich with models for making notes. The "trash-and-treasure" notemaking method offered by Barbara A. Jansen is one that begins with skimming for keywords to answer researchable questions (search for "trash and treasure" at http://big6.com). The Cornell Notemaking Graphic Organizer offers a variation of a format found in *Tools for Teaching Content Literacy* (Allen 2004). The Notemaking Graphic Organizer combined with the Works Cited Graphic Organizer offers another way to structure notemaking.

In *Classroom Instruction That Works: Research-based Strategies for Increasing Student Achievement* (Marzano, Pickering, and Pollock 2001), notemaking is highlighted and elaborated with different formats: teacher-prepared notes, informal outlines, webbing, and a combination of outline and webbing. A variation of teacher-prepared notes is a skeleton outline, which provides a scaffold for students by leaving blanks for them to fill in as they listen, read, or view. The English Companion website is also an excellent source for a wide variety of notemaking formats (www.english companion.com/Tools/notemaking.html).

Shared notemaking is one way to start students on the path of making effective notes. Educators use think-alouds to demonstrate how they distill the main ideas from a passage and then show students their process for recording notes that clearly reflect what they learned. Students should have many experiences working with partners and in small groups to talk about texts, determine main ideas, and then record notes on group or individual notemaking sheets.

The next step after making notes is to use them to summarize learning. By definition, summaries focus on main ideas. In their meta-analysis of teacher-conducted studies, Haystead and Marzano (2009) found significant increases in students' comprehension after they were taught summarizing strategies such as clarifying what is important, understanding text structures, and creating graphic representations. These strategies can be used by educators at the beginning of a lesson when texts are previewed, for determining notemaking graphic organizers that reflect specific text structures, or as a review before summarizing after notemaking. Figure 7-2 provides ways to apply these strategies as learners prepare to summarize.

Again, educators first model summarizing as they review group notes and then compose whole-class summaries of the main ideas found in the notes. Practice in writing partner and small group summaries helps students prepare to summarize independently. When conducting long-term inquiry or research projects, readers can be asked to summarize their learning at the end of notemaking sessions. These summaries serve as formative assessments for learners as well as educators. Benchmark summaries can help measure students' progress toward understanding the topic under investigation or the inquiry or research process in use.

Using an excerpt from *Ancient Greece* (Morgan), figure 7-3 shows an example of the notemaking and summarizing process. The purpose for reading is clearly stated at the beginning. The learner first reads through the entire excerpt, then reviews the purpose for reading and reads through the excerpt a second time. During the second reading, he deletes information that is already known or facts that don't fit the purpose for reading. Next, he can make substitutions that help explain vocabulary or concepts. In this example, the page number for the map was added. What remains of the excerpt are the main ideas. Students can practice this process on photocopies of texts, deleting unimportant information by striking it through with a pencil, adding substitutions with pen, and using highlighters to flag main ideas.

After engaging in this process, the reader then uses the main ideas to make notes in his own words. From the notes, he can compose a summary of the main ideas in his own words and in complete sentences. Students are also encouraged to record their questions as they make notes or summarize. These questions help guide learners as they read on. Notemaking and summarizing are often referred to as *study skills*, but they are two of the most powerful skills students can develop to identify the main ideas of their learning (Marzano, Pickering, and Pollock 2001, 48). Reading and writing are the two sides of the literacy coin; one cannot and should not be separated from the other.

Fig. 7-2   Strategies to Support Summarizing

Name of Strategy	Examples or Application
Clarifying What Is Important	• Reviewing purpose for reading • Determining genre and organization of text
Essential Terminology	• Checking for understanding of subject-specific vocabulary
Determining and Using Features of Text Structures and Signal Words	• Argumentative (opinion followed by reasoning) • Cause/effect (event and results) • Chronological (sequential as in a time line) • Compare/contrast (similarities and differences) • Descriptive (definitions) • Generalizations (followed by examples) • Narrative (story grammar) • Problem/solution (statement of problem followed by one or more possible solutions and outcome)
Text Layers	• Multiple text structures (within a longer expository text)
Learners' Graphic Representations	• Flowcharts • Graphic organizers (that show patterns) • Maps • Matrices • Time lines • Venn diagrams • Webs

Text excerpt from *Ancient Greece*, by Nicola Morgan

Purpose for Reading: To learn general information about influential ancient Greeks and choose one for further research

Excerpt: "The ancient Greeks created a powerful and exciting civilization more than 2,000 years ago. Ancient Greek civilization started in about 800 B.C. and flourished until the Romans conquered it in 146 B.C., but its importance lasted for much longer.

"At its height, ancient Greece covered most of the map below. Yet the importance of ancient Greece is not about how much land it covered but about what was achieved in knowledge, science, art, literature, architecture, technology, and politics.

"One way of understanding a civilization is to look at the individuals who made important discoveries or affected the lives of ordinary people. These men and women might have been politicians, architects, scientists, poets, or playwrights. For some of these people, we have only a few reliable details about their personal lives but it is what they achieved that is so interesting and important.

"We have a great deal of information about the ancient Greeks, which has been pieced together from various sources. Archaeologists have dug up buildings and found items used by the people of that time. Archaeologists have also discovered pottery and vases on which ancient Greeks began writing from about 800 B.C. onward" (4–5).

Deletions and [Substitutions]: "~~The ancient Greeks created a powerful and exciting civilization more than 2,000 years ago. Ancient Greek civilization started in about~~ 800 B.C. ~~and flourished~~ until ~~the~~ Romans conquered ~~it~~ in 146 B.C., ~~but its importance lasted for much longer.~~

"~~At its height, ancient Greece covered most of the map below. Yet the importance of ancient Greece is not about how much land it covered but about what was achieved in knowledge, science, art, literature, architecture, technology, and politics.~~

"~~One way of understanding a civilization is to look at the~~ individuals ~~who made~~ important discoveries or affected the lives of ordinary people. [superstars] ~~These men and women might have been~~ politicians, architects, scientists, poets, or playwrights. ~~For some of these people, we have only a~~ few reliable details about their personal lives ~~but it is what they achieved that is so interesting and important~~" [achievements].

~~We have a great deal of~~ information ~~about the ancient Greeks, which has been~~ pieced together ~~from various sources.~~ Archaeologists ~~have dug up~~ buildings and found items used ~~by the people of that time. Archaeologists have also discovered~~ pottery and vases ~~on which ancient Greeks began writing from about~~ 800 B.C. ~~onward~~" (4–5).

Notes
Ancient Greece—800 B.C.–146 B.C.
Map—page 4
politicians, architects, scientists, poets, or playwrights = great achievements (little known about personal lives)
archaeologists—buildings—pottery/vases include writing (since 800 B.C.)

Main Ideas
There were superstars in ancient Greece. Archaeologists have found information about their achievements in buildings and other artifacts and in writing on pottery and vases. Learning about their achievements can help me understand ancient Greek civilization.

New Questions
Who was a famous poet in ancient Greece?
How were his or her poems recorded?
How do we know he or she was famous?
Do we know anything about his or her personal life?

MAKING LITERATURE CONNECTIONS

Any text related to students' interests or the curriculum can be useful in teaching main ideas: magazine and newspaper articles, pamphlets and brochures, all forms of digital media, and textbooks. Whenever possible, text sets created to support learning this strategy should include as many formats as possible. Textbooks in particular can and should be used to teach determining main ideas. These texts are often written above students' proficient reading levels and do not always take readers' background knowledge into consideration. Many readers find it difficult to create a personal context and relevance for information as presented in textbooks, which results in decreased motivation.

To provide scaffolds for reading textbooks, educators can construct graphic organizers that help readers focus on the main ideas found in keywords, headings, subheadings, captions, and other supports before, during, and after reading. School librarians should consider their role in helping teachers teach and students learn to read content area textbooks effectively and fluently. A textbook is, in fact, a reference book and can be integrated into research and inquiry projects along with other reference resources.

When students are searching for main ideas to answer questions posed by educators or questions of their own making, the structural support found in high-quality informational books offers them a scaffold for locating and determining main ideas. Educators can design graphic organizers to assist readers as they notice which features of a particular informational book best support their learning. School librarians should be aware of the text features offered in expository texts as they build their collections. Many publishers offer informational texts as volumes in a series, which means that students can develop schemas for a particular text format and anticipate where and how to locate main ideas in all the titles of a particular series. Opposing Viewpoints (Greenhaven), At Issue (Gale), The Human Body and How It Works (Chelsea House), and Careers in Focus (Infodase) are some of the many considerate texts in

series format available for middle and high school libraries and classrooms.

School librarians must cast a wide net to collect and integrate informational resources from across the Dewey spectrum to support teaching curriculum. Some effective informational texts make use of the more familiar narrative frame. Susan Campbell Bartoletti and Jim Murphy are two informational book authors who excel at combining well-researched, informative narratives with primary source documents and compelling illustrations. For some readers, informational books with narrative frames may provide a bridge between fiction and more traditional nonfiction books.

Poetry and poetic prose embedded with science, social studies, or cultural studies information such as biographies like *Carver: A Life in Poems* (Nelson), *Diego, Bigger Than Life* (Bernier-Grand/Diaz), and *Your Own, Sylvia: A Verse Portrait of Sylvia Plath* (Hemphill) can challenge students to determine main ideas. Authors' notes, appendices, and embedded expository passages in well-researched and documented historical fiction titles such as *Chains* (Anderson) or *Good Masters! Sweet Ladies! Voices from a Medieval Village* (Schlitz/Byrd) and innovative fiction that contain primary source documents such as *Countdown* (Wiles) can be excellent resources of factual information and determining main ideas lessons.

ONLINE READING COMPREHENSION AND DETERMINING MAIN IDEAS

What are the "new literacies"? Although various scholars and researchers define the "new literacies" differently, we can think of them as literacies that have been made possible by digital technologies, such as Internet searching, blogging, collaborating with wikis, communicating via instant and text messaging, telecomputing projects, and more. These literacies are also known as ICTs, or information and communication technologies. As Coiro et al. note, digital literacies have been "adopted by so many, in so many different places, in such a short period, and with such profound consequences. No previous technology for literacy permits the dissemination of even newer technologies of literacy to every person on the Internet… [or provides] access to so much information that is so useful, to so many people" (2008, 2–3).

As a result of the ever-evolving nature of technological advances in information and communication resources and tools, readers and writers, students and adults alike must develop their ability to learn, unlearn, and relearn in order to effectively comprehend, use, and create these texts. Leu et al. delineate five major functions of the "new literacies," which parallel the way librarians have long conceived of the information search process (2007, 45):

1. Identifying important questions

2. Locating information

3. Analyzing information

4. Synthesizing information

5. Communicating information

From identifying inquiry questions that are worth pursuing to communicating and sharing information and new knowledge, these are precisely the skills and strategies on which effective secondary school librarians have focused their teaching. In fact, school librarians have taught these skills with printed texts for decades. And in doing so, they have taught students to use informational books in a nonlinear way that although slower and with fewer distractions parallels the way online searchers use hypertext. With the publication of AASL's *Standards for the 21st-Century Learner,* the imperative to coteach these skills and strategies with classroom teacher colleagues is clearer than ever before.

Although there is little research in the area of online reading comprehension (Coiro et al. 2008), one frequently cited study of seventh-grade science students conducted by the New Literacies Team found that students' off-line reading proficiency is not correlated with their online reading proficiency and vice versa (Leu et al. 2005). The interventions in this study used a learning and teaching model in which teachers provided guided demonstrations, think-alouds, and scaffolded strategy practice in locating, evaluating,

synthesizing, and communicating information while using the Internet. (Note: These are the precise instructional methods recommended for off-line reading comprehension strategy instruction and the methods used in the lessons in this book.) The study found that students who had the best comprehension and recall of the content knowledge were those who experienced intensive integration of technology in the context of this learning and teaching model.

Because a great deal of instructional time in secondary libraries is dedicated to interacting with electronic texts, it is natural for school librarians to coteach online reading comprehension with classroom teachers. There are, however, many challenges for students in the area of determining main ideas within digital texts. When students conduct search engine or database searches, they are confronted with decisions related to the relative importance of the hits they receive. Which hits will lead them to find the main ideas related to their inquiry? Which will take them on an unproductive tangent? Once readers have found a website they wish to explore, they often have a difficult time determining the author of the site and if the author has authority on the topic. Learners must also determine if the site is current, when it was last updated, and whether or not the information is accurate. To complicate this situation further, many electronic texts do not have the text features of printed materials such as those found in textbooks, particularly elements for locating information and elements that notify (see figure 7-1). These challenges present opportunities for coteaching essential main ideas of web-based texts in discipline-specific and interdisciplinary lessons and units of instruction.

Educators are acutely aware that a large percentage of students are engaged in reading and writing electronic texts daily. One unique and critical contribution school librarians can make to the professional conversation about online reading comprehension is taking a leadership role in measuring and advancing students' actual abilities to read and solve problems with information they locate and interact with on the Web. Librarians can codesign pre- and posttests and formative assessments with classroom teacher colleagues and use tools such as Trails9 (www.trails9.org).

Although school librarians may have been addressing this strategy with digital texts for many years, they may not have done so with the intention of teaching determining main ideas as a reading comprehension strategy. They may not have used think-alouds to reinforce the metacognitive processes involved in the information search process. As coteaching reading online texts and online reading comprehension strategies becomes increasingly important for students and educators, classroom-library collaborative lessons can center on locating, reading, and evaluating information and thinking about the processes used to comprehend digital formats, main ideas essential to the new literacies.

TWEEN, YOUNG ADULT, AND ADULT LITERATURE CITED

Ancient Greece, by Nicola Morgan

Carver: A Life in Poems, by Marilyn Nelson

Chains, by Laurie Halse Anderson

Countdown, by Deborah Wiles

Diego, Bigger Than Life, by Carmen Bernier-Grand, illustrated by David Diaz

Good Masters! Sweet Ladies! Voices from a Medieval Village, by Laura Amy Schlitz, illustrated by Robert Byrd

Your Own, Sylvia: A Verse Portrait of Sylvia Plath, by Stephanie Hemphill

LESSON PLANS

In their tool kits, every secondary librarian should have several well-honed database lessons in several content areas. The lesson plans offered in this chapter focus on main ideas related to web searching, or open web searching compared with database searching. Although educators hope students will always select resources that have been vetted by publishers, librarians, or other authorities, we know that youth regularly use search engines to access information. Therefore, these lessons offer students practice in applying open web searching "main ideas" at three levels of sophistication. These foundational skills are important for all readers in the 21st century.

The advancing lesson focuses on determining currency and relevance in a science topic from analyzing search hits. The advanced lesson focuses on determining accuracy through authorship, author's credentials, and sources cited using the research question from the advancing lesson. At the conclusion of this lesson, readers compare a web search to a database search and discover the need for critical thinking regardless of the search tool. The challenging lesson uses reciprocal teaching (Palinscar and Brown 1986) applied to determining bias. Using this strategy can help learners internalize questions that strengthen metacognition. At the conclusion of this lesson, students are asked how bias impacts their understandings and opinions. All lessons can easily be adapted for online learning experiences in any content area.

Reading Comprehension Strategy Five
Determining Main Ideas

Reading Development Level: Advancing

Instructional Strategies
Categorizing, Notemaking and Summarizing

Lesson Length
2 or 3 sessions

Purpose
The purpose of this lesson plan is to learn how to determine currency and relevance, digital literacy main ideas, while conducting an advanced search on two different search engines. Students identify keywords, domains, and currency, rank hits according to relevance to the search question, and compose a summary of their findings.

Objectives
At the end of these lessons, students will be able to
1. Compare searches on two different search engines.
2. Record URL roots, domains, and dates.
3. Rank hits based on relevance to the search question.
4. Compose a summary of the process and results.

Resources, Materials, and Equipment
Graphic organizers: 7.1 Category Matrix, 7.1 Teacher Resource—Completed Category Matrix, 7.1
Summary Checklist, 7.1 Teacher Resource—Sample Summary
Overhead, data projector, or interactive whiteboard

Collaboration
Educators model conducting an advanced search on one search engine, recording URL roots and domains, keywords, dates, and ranking hits by relevance using notemaking formats. Educators monitor students' guided practice as they search another search engine and compare results.

Assessment
The students' completed category matrices, checklists, and summaries show their ability to conduct, analyze, and summarize a search for the purpose of determining currency and relevance.

Standards

Reading keywords: Identify the main ideas and supporting details; record data in order to see the relationships between ideas and information; evaluate the relevance of sources; use notes to compose summaries.

Writing keywords: Use graphic organizers as prewriting tools; write a summary that includes main ideas and relevant details.

Science keywords: Investigate a research question.

AASL STANDARDS INDICATORS*

- Find, evaluate, and select appropriate sources to answer questions. (1.1.4)
- Monitor gathered information, and assess for gaps or weaknesses. (1.4.3)
- Organize knowledge so that it is useful. (2.1.2)
- Reflect on systematic process, and assess for completeness of investigation. (2.4.2)
- Develop directions for future investigations. (2.4.4)

PROCESS

DAY 1

MOTIVATION

Pose the questions and poll the class: "Do raisins contribute to tooth decay?" "How do you know the answer to this question?" Share ideas. Ask: "How could you find out or check to make sure your answer is correct?"

Conducting a web search is one relatively quick way to learn answers to seemingly straightforward questions, but there are some main ideas that searchers need to keep in mind as they determine the currency and relevance of the hits they get from a search. Readers should ask these questions *before* linking: On what type of domain is the information hosted: .com, .org, .edu, .net, or other domain? What are the keywords in the hit information? When was the information published? How relevant is the hit to the question posed?

Currency and relevance are two main ideas related to web searching. The essential questions for these two main ideas are: Is this information current enough to answer my question (currency)? Does this information answer my question (relevance)?

STUDENT-FRIENDLY OBJECTIVES

1. Conduct advanced searches on two different search engines.
2. Use keywords to collect data regarding currency and relevance.
3. Determine the relevance of hits to the question posed before linking.

Presentation

Project the 7.1 Category Matrix. Educators use think-alouds while reviewing the criteria for evaluating web hits using this graphic organizer. Students work as a whole class to collect data about main ideas related to search engine results. Then they work individually or with a partner to collect data from another search engine.

* Excerpted from *Standards for the 21st-Century Learner* by the American Association of School Librarians, a division of the American Library Association, copyright © 2007 American Library Association. Available for download at www.ala.org/aasl/standards. Used with permission.

Conduct an advanced Google search. Use "raisins" and the exact phrase "tooth decay." Use think-alouds as one educator facilitates student participation and the other records information on the category matrix (see the 7.1 Teacher Resource—Completed Category Matrix for reference). Also note the "sponsored" links and discuss those briefly.

STUDENT PARTICIPATION PROCEDURES
1. Raise hand to contribute information.
2. Indicate where information should be added to the category matrix.
3. Suggest a note.

When the category matrix is complete, educators communicate expectations regarding the completeness of the category matrix. Ask: "From the descriptions of the hits, can we determine a definitive answer to this question?"

Distribute the 7.1 Category Matrix electronically. List possible search engines. Students work individually or with a partner to search a different search engine and record their findings on individual category matrices.

GUIDED PRACTICE
Educators monitor students' searches, completeness of the matrices, and notemaking.

CLOSURE
Think-pair-share ideas about why currency and relevance are two important main ideas for web searching. If students complete their searches on the first day, discuss the results in terms of answering the research question.

DAY 2 OR 3

After students have completed their category matrices, discuss the next step. Note: Category matrices or the summary can be completed as homework. Peer review should be done in class.

STUDENT-FRIENDLY OBJECTIVES
1. Determine which categories of data should go in each paragraph.
2. Compose a five-paragraph summary.
3. Self-assess with the checklist.
4. Exchange summaries with a classmate and peer review.

PRESENTATION
The category matrix helps organize data so it is useful. Scientists often present a summary of the process in which they engaged to collect data, their analysis of the data, and the meaning they ascribe to the data. Distribute the 7.1 Summary Checklist. Project the 7.1 Teacher Resource—Completed Category Matrix. Review the checklist and the additional self-assessment and peer review questions. Highlight sections of the data that can be integrated into each of five paragraphs. Compose a sample paragraph from the data. If appropriate, project the entire teacher resource and assess it with the checklist. Educators demonstrate how to conduct a peer review.

GUIDED PRACTICE
Educators monitor students' composition of summaries and peer reviews.

CLOSURE

Form groups of four or five students who analyzed the results from different search engines. Students share their results and compare the data they collected. Conduct the reflection orally or in writing.

REFLECTION

How did focusing on currency and relevance as main ideas in web searching influence reading the search results? Why should information, scientific information in particular, be current? What makes a hit relevant? What was missing from these results? What's next?

EXTENSIONS

Students can repeat this lesson multiple times in different content areas asking different questions. They can engage with the 7.2 advanced lesson and continue this process by adding two additional web searching main ideas to their repertoires: authority and accuracy.

In their research and inquiry projects, continue to reinforce the importance of currency and relevance of information.

Reading Comprehension Strategy Five
Determining Main Ideas

Reading Development Level: Advanced

Instructional Strategies
Advance Organizers, Categorizing, Notemaking, and Comparing

Lesson Length
3 sessions

Purpose
The purpose of this lesson plan is to learn how to determine authority and infer accuracy, digital literacy main ideas, while conducting an advanced search on two different search engines. Students identify authors, authors' credentials, currency, and sources. After collecting information from articles that lack authors or authority and unverifiable information, educators demonstrate a database search that further complicates the need for authority and accuracy. Students compare the results of database and web searches.

Objectives
At the end of these lessons, students will be able to
1. Limit a search by domain.
2. Record URL roots, domains, and dates.
3. Determine and record authors and authors' authority.
4. Locate contact information and infer accuracy.
5. Compare and contrast a database search with a web search.
6. Suggest next steps for searching based on the need for authority and accuracy.

Resources, Materials, and Equipment
Graphic organizers: 7.2 Anticipation Guide, 7.2 Category Matrix, 7.2 Teacher Resource—Completed Category Matrix, 7.2 Teacher Resource—Sample Database Search, 7.2 Venn Diagram, 7.2 Teacher Resource—Completed Venn Diagram
Overhead, data projector, or interactive whiteboard

Collaboration
Educators model conducting an advanced search on one search engine, recording URL roots and domains, dates, authors, authors' authority, and accuracy of the information. Both educators monitor students' guided practice as they search another search engine and compare results. Educators model a database search and guide students in comparing the results between the database and one of the web searches.

Assessment
The students' completed anticipation guides, category matrices, and Venn diagrams show their ability to conduct and analyze searches for the purpose of determining authority and accuracy.

Standards
Reading keywords: Identify the main ideas and supporting details; skim and scan; record data in order to see the relationships between ideas and information; determine the reliability, validity, and accuracy of sources. For extension, use notes to compose summaries.

Writing keywords: Use graphic organizers as prewriting tools. For extension, write a summary that includes main ideas and relevant details.

Science keywords: Investigate a research question; understand that scientific hypotheses must be supported by evidence and tested before they are incorporated into theories.

AASL STANDARDS INDICATORS*
- Find, evaluate, and select appropriate sources to answer questions. (1.1.4)
- Monitor gathered information, and assess for gaps or weaknesses. (1.4.3)
- Organize knowledge so that it is useful. (2.1.2)
- Reflect on systematic process, and assess for completeness of investigation. (2.4.2)
- Develop directions for future investigations. (2.4.4)

PROCESS
DAY 1

MOTIVATION
Distribute the 7.2 Anticipation Guide and newspaper pages to students working with partners. (Be sure that students have all the necessary pages for articles that begin on one page and end on another.) Ask students to circle the author's name and author's credentials or contact information on as many articles as possible. Tell students to put a box (rather than a circle) around another category called "corporate authors." These articles were "authored" by news agencies or other groups rather than by individuals. Ask students to complete the table at the top of the 7.2 Anticipation Guide and count the total number of articles on their pages and establish a percentage for the number with identifiable individual authors with credentials or contact information. Share the percentages.

Do students think they can determine authorship on web pages as easily as they did in newspaper articles? Students complete the anticipation guide by reading each statement and circling "agree" or "disagree" in the left-hand column. Students jot down some initial thoughts about the importance of authorship and the relationship between authorship and accuracy on their anticipation guides.

STUDENT-FRIENDLY OBJECTIVES
1. Conduct advanced searches limited to .edu sites on two different search engines.
2. Collect data focused on authorship, authors' credentials, or contact information as an indicator of accuracy of information.

* Excerpted from *Standards for the 21st-Century Learner* by the American Association of School Librarians, a division of the American Library Association, copyright © 2007 American Library Association. Available for download at www.ala.org/aasl/standards. Used with permission.

PRESENTATION

Provide a scenario: In a previous web search to answer the question whether raisins promote tooth decay, researchers who conducted advanced web searches using a number of different search engines were unable to establish a definitive answer to the question. In the first five results, their web hit domains were one .org and four .com sites. The researchers hypothesized that an .edu search would provide better results and a definitive answer to the question under investigation.

Project the 7.2 Category Matrix. Educators use think-alouds while reviewing the criteria for evaluating web hits using this graphic organizer. What does authority mean? What does accuracy mean? What is the relationship between authority and accuracy? Students work together as a whole class to collect data about authority and accuracy, main ideas related to search engine results. Then they work individually or with a partner to collect data from another search engine.

Distribute the 7.2 Category Matrix electronically. Along with students determine the keywords for a search. Conduct an advanced Google search. Use "raisins," the exact phrase "tooth decay," and limit the results to .edu sites. Use think-alouds as one educator facilitates student participation and the other records information on the category matrix. Note the lack of "sponsored" links in the hits.

Link to each article. Post and state the essential questions: Does this author have appropriate credentials (authority)? Can I verify this information with another reliable source (accuracy)? Skim and scan to confirm a positive or negative response to the question under investigation. While educators guide students and make notes on the projected matrix, students jot down notes on their own matrices. Use the 7.2 Teacher Resource—Completed Category Matrix for reference.

STUDENT PARTICIPATION PROCEDURES

1. Raise hand to contribute information.
2. Indicate where information should be added to the category matrix.
3. Suggest a note.
4. Jot down a note on the graphic organizer.

When the category matrix is complete, educators communicate expectations regarding the completeness of the category matrix. Ask: "From these articles, can we determine a definitive answer to this question?" Note the lack of authorship, authors' credentials, and references in these sources. Students work individually or with a partner to use the same keywords to search a different search engine and record their findings on individual category matrices. They also limit their searches to .edu domain sites.

GUIDED PRACTICE

Educators monitor students' searches, completeness of the matrices, and notemaking.

CLOSURE

Think-pair-share: Why are authority and accuracy two important main ideas for web searching? What is the importance of a bibliography or Works Cited? Note: If students are doing this work individually, category matrices can be completed as homework.

DAY 2 OR 3

After students have completed their category matrices, discuss the results in terms of answering the research question.

STUDENT-FRIENDLY OBJECTIVES
1. Compare a database search with a web search.
2. Record similarities and differences on a Venn diagram.
3. Suggest a next step.

PRESENTATION
Project the 7.2 Teacher Resource—Completed Category Matrix. Review the data. For these search engine examples, total the positive and negative responses to the research question. Ask: "Are researchers satisfied with the authority and accuracy of this information? Why or why not?"

Lead students in a database search for an answer to this research question (see the 7.2 Teacher Resource—Sample Database Search). Working with partners or in small groups, students duplicate this search so they have the search results on the computer screen in front of them. Collectively review the first five hits for authority and accuracy.

Distribute and project the 7.2 Venn Diagram. Review how to use a Venn diagram to compare and contrast. If students need to record notes before comparing, educators can distribute additional copies of the 7.2 Category Matrix. Students compare and contrast the database search with the web search of .edu sites in the areas of determining authorship, authors' credentials, authors' contact information, citations or references, and their own inferences related to the accuracy of information.

GUIDED PRACTICE
Educators monitor students' completion of Venn diagrams.

CLOSURE
Form groups of four or five students who analyzed the results from different search engines. Students share their Venn diagram comparisons. What were the similarities or differences?

Discuss possible next steps in the process to seek a definitive answer to this research question. Leave room for the possibility that the scientific hypotheses related to raisins actually preventing tooth decay must be tested in a wide variety of conditions before it can be incorporated into a theory. Perhaps it is too soon to seek a definitive answer to this question.

REFLECTION
How did focusing on authority and accuracy as main ideas in web searching influence the usefulness of the search results? What makes information authoritative? What contributes to the reader's ability to infer accuracy? What questions remain related to authority and accuracy?

EXTENSIONS
Educators guide students as they use these Venn diagrams as prewriting for composing a summary on the topic of authority and accuracy (see lesson plan 7.1). Students repeat this lesson multiple times in different content areas asking different search questions.

Educators reinforce the need for searchers to slow the pace of their searches in order to assess search results for specific criteria. They reinforce that using a database is not the cure-all for every search question. Critical thinking is necessary regardless of the search tool.

LESSON PLAN 7.3

Reading Comprehension Strategy Five
Determining Main Ideas

Reading Development Level: Challenging

Instructional Strategies
Advance Organizers, Categorizing, Notemaking and Summarizing

Lesson Length
3 sessions

Purpose
The purpose of this lesson plan is to learn how to determine bias and how bias shapes information, digital and media literacy main ideas. Students gather data and analyze two websites about Dr. Martin Luther King, Jr. They identify website authors' authority and bias, currency of information, navigation as an indicator of currency, citations, and site content. After answering four reciprocal teaching questions, students synthesize their findings from three websites, cite examples, and provide their own analysis and interpretation in a synthesis essay.

Objectives
At the end of these lessons, students will be able to
1. Collect data on website content.
2. Analyze three websites for authority, bias, and currency.
3. Compose a synthesis essay about the impact of bias in the media.
4. Cite evidence as part of their analysis.
5. Cite sources.

Resources, Materials, and Equipment
Resource: "Sunday Morning Fact-Checking—Jake Tapper & Bill Adair | April 14, 2010—David Shields | ColbertNation.com." *Colbert Nation | The Colbert Report* | Comedy Central. Web. www.colbertnation.com/the-colbert-report-videos/270738/april-14-2010/sunday-morning-fact-checking---jake-tapper---bill-adair.

Graphic organizers: 7.3 Admit Slip, 7.3 Category Matrix, 7.3 Teacher Resource—Example Category Matrix, 7.3 Teacher Resource—Completed Category Matrix, 7.3 Teacher Resource—Sample Synthesis Essay and Works Cited, 7.3 Synthesis Essay Rubric

Overhead, data projector, or interactive whiteboard

Collaboration

Educators model the components of reciprocal teaching and record data related to author's authority, bias, and website content. Educators monitor students' guided practice as they record data in order to analyze two additional websites and conduct writing conferences while students compose five-paragraph synthesis essays.

Assessment

The students' completed category matrices, essays, and rubrics show their ability to analyze websites for bias and apply the components of reciprocal teaching for the purpose of determining the impact of bias on people's opinions.

Standards

Reading keywords: Identify the main ideas and supporting details; record data in order to see the relationships between ideas and information; evaluate the authority and objectivity of sources.

Writing keywords: Provide evidence from text to support analysis; structure ideas in a persuasive way; paraphrase, summarize, quote, and accurately cite all researched information using a standard format.

Social studies keywords: Identify bias in written, oral, and visual material; analyze current events.

Media literacy keywords: Analyze how one issue or event is represented across various media to understand the bias.

AASL STANDARDS INDICATORS*

- Find, evaluate, and select appropriate sources to answer questions. (1.1.4)
- Respect copyright/intellectual property rights of creators and producers. (1.3.1)
- Monitor gathered information, and assess for gaps or weaknesses. (1.4.3)
- Organize knowledge so that it is useful. (2.1.2)
- Assess the quality and effectiveness of the learning product. (3.4.2)

PROCESS

DAY 1

MOTIVATION

Students evaluate websites for bias. Define and discuss bias if necessary. Distribute the 7.3 Admit Slip to all students. If appropriate, students read it silently and circle ideas that are especially important to this topic. Reread "Check the Facts" chorally in a whisper. When readers come to ideas they circled, they read those portions at regular volume. After rereading, ask students to respond in writing to the questions at the end of the admit slip. Discuss with partners or the whole class before presenting the lesson. Pose the essential questions: "Is this author's bias clear?" "How does bias shape information?"

STUDENT-FRIENDLY OBJECTIVES
1. Use website navigation to determine authority and bias.
2. Collect data focused on authors' credentials or contact information, bias, and objectivity of information.

PRESENTATION
Post the reciprocal teaching components and these questions on the board:
1. Predict—Do you think the author of this site will make his or her bias evident? Why?
2. Question—How do you know the author's bias?
3. Clarify—How can you go about confirming the author's bias?
4. Summarize—How does the bias impact your understanding of the information presented?
5. Synthesize—How does this author's bias influence your opinion on the topic?

Read through the steps and questions. Project the 7.3 Category Matrix and review the criteria on the graphic organizer. Link to http://factcheck.org.

Students ask educators to predict by posing the question: Do you think the author of this site will make his or her bias evident? Why? A possible rationale is these authors will be transparent about their bias because they are attempting to hold others accountable for their biases and for representing information accurately.

Project and complete the 7.3 Category Matrix for this site. Use the 7.3 Teacher Resource—Completed Category Matrix for reference. Students ask the question: How do you know the author's bias? Using think-alouds, educators use navigation to locate information about the authors.

Students ask the clarifying question: How can you go about confirming the author's bias? Educators guide students in gleaning information from the "about" page and conduct a web search for more information about this site and its authors. Discuss authority, bias, citations, navigation, updates, and site content while making notes.

STUDENT PARTICIPATION PROCEDURES
1. Raise hand to contribute information.
2. Indicate where information should be added to the category matrix.
3. Suggest a note.

When the category matrix is complete, educators communicate the expectations regarding the completeness of the category matrix.

CLOSURE
Students ask educators to summarize: How does the bias impact your understanding of the information presented? Educators share their ideas. Students think-pair-share. Record students' ideas on the board. Educators ask students: Is this site bias-free? Cite the related links as evidence of a "progressive" perspective. Discuss.

Students use these reciprocal teaching questions while they analyze bias on two additional websites. They write a five-paragraph synthesis essay to answer the questions: How do you determine bias on a website? Why should you do so?

If engaging in the alternative product, students compose a Web 2.0 presentation to share relating their understanding of bias in the media. For the extension, students conduct an in-depth inquiry on the topic of bias in the media and compose a persuasive essay or multimedia product to synthesize their understanding of the impact of bias on information.

If appropriate, preview and share the *Colbert Nation* video listed in the resources. Discuss bias in the video.

REFLECTION
Why is bias a main idea when interacting with media? Does bias affect books as well as websites and other media? How do you confirm the author's bias?

DAY 2

PRESENTATION
Distribute the 7.3 Category Matrix electronically. Project the 7.3 Teacher Resource—Example Category Matrix. Review the categories and the reciprocal teaching questions.

Students work with a partner to analyze two websites for bias and record their findings on individual or shared category matrices. Students take turns asking one another the reciprocal teaching questions.

STUDENT PRACTICE PROCEDURES
1. Use reciprocal teaching questions to guide your work.
2. Use the site navigation or conduct web searches to investigate bias.
3. Make notes on the category matrix.
4. Respond in writing to the reciprocal teaching questions.

GUIDED PRACTICE
Educators monitor students' use of the reciprocal teaching questions, data collection, completeness of the matrices, and use of notemaking formats. Use questions to probe students' thinking.

CLOSURE
Clarify by asking: How did you determine bias on the sites you investigated? Think-pair-share. Why is bias a main idea when interacting with media?

REFLECTION
Which strategy—predict, question, clarify, or summarize—helped you the most with determining the impact of the author's bias on the information presented?

DAY 3

STUDENT-FRIENDLY OBJECTIVES
1. Respond to the reciprocal teaching questions in writing.
2. Compose a five-paragraph synthesis essay with information from all three websites.
3. Use the rubric to guide your work.

PRESENTATION
If necessary, educators model composing a five-paragraph synthesis essay. Define synthesis as:

INFORMATION + INTERPRETATION = SYNTHESIS

The synthesis essay can be written in class or as homework. Syntheses can also be presented with alternative products. Individual or small group presentations using VoiceThread, Animoto, Glogster, or other Web 2.0 tools would be effective. Use or adapt the Group Work and Multimedia Product Rubric from chapter 6 for this purpose.

GUIDED PRACTICE

Educators conduct writing conferences if the synthesis essays are written in class.

CLOSURE

Form groups of four or five students who did not work together as partners. Educators facilitate students sharing their synthesis essays or multimedia presentations. Take a poll to determine which reciprocal teaching question helped students the most when reading, writing, and thinking about bias.

REFLECTION

How did thinking about bias as a main idea influence your understanding of the information you read? In the future, what questions related to bias will you ask yourself as you interact with media? What kinds of information will you look for in determining bias?

EXTENSIONS

Students continue this line of thinking as an inquiry project. They analyze additional websites and other media to conduct a more extensive investigation related to bias in the media.

Educators guide students as they use these reciprocal teaching questions in other contexts and other content areas. Educators reinforce the need for searchers to slow the pace of their inquiry in order to determine the bias of a website or other text. Critical thinking is necessary regardless of the media or topic under investigation.

8

Reading Comprehension Strategy Six

Using Fix-up Options

The difference between proficient and striving readers is their awareness of when they lose comprehension and how they respond to it when they do.

—Elaine McEwan

How does a reader know when she has lost comprehension? Monitoring her own meaning making and getting back on the road when she has lost her way may be one of the most difficult tasks for any reader. The fix-up options strategy offers readers processes they can use to recover meaning, such as rereading, reading ahead, or figuring out unknown words. The tricky part is knowing when to use which of these options.

In *Paper Towns* (Green), high school senior Quentin Jacobsen is desperately searching for his best childhood friend and potential romantic partner, Margo. He believes she has left him clues in highlighted sections of Walt Whitman's poem "Song of Myself." "I sat alone with 'Song of Myself' for a long time, and for about the tenth time I tried to read the entire poem starting at the beginning, but the problem was that it's like eighty pages long and weird and repetitive, and although I understand each word of it, I couldn't understand anything about it as a whole. Even though I knew the highlighted parts were probably the only important parts, I wanted to know whether it was a suicide-note kind of poem. But I couldn't make sense of it" (150).

Effective readers like Green's character Quentin monitor their comprehension; they realize when the text is not making sense. Instead of giving up in frustration, they learn and use "fix-up options" when they have lost comprehension. Striving or struggling readers are less likely to realize when they have lost the thread of meaning and therefore less likely to engage in the most basic option, rereading the text (Johnston 2004). This is especially true for readers who have not yet fully grasped the concept of reading as making meaning rather than reading as word calling. As educators teach this strategy, it is critical to use think-alouds to share the point at which comprehension is lost or to share the clues that lead the reader to suspect there is more to the text than appears on the surface.

The first five reading comprehension strategies presented in this book—activating or building background knowledge, using sensory images, questioning, predicting and inferring, and determining main ideas—can be used both in the recognition of a loss of comprehension and in the effort to recover it. When the reader is no longer making connections as she reads, she should begin to suspect that she has lost the thread of meaning. Texts quickly become boring when the reader fails to make text-to-self, text-to-text, or text-to-world connections. Without bringing her background knowledge and prior experience to bear, the distance between the author, the text, and the reader grows wider and can become a gap too wide to cross. A reader who strives to make meaning notices when the communication offered by connections is interrupted: the voice in her head becomes silent and the movie in her head pauses or the screen goes blank.

The reader who can no longer visualize the story or information presented in the text has lost comprehension. With her senses turned off, the reader's imagination can no longer access the meaning behind the print on the page or screen. Reading that does not engage the imagination does not touch the mind or the heart, and the lived-through experience or information is not stored in memory. The significance of the text is nowhere to be found.

Questioning, predicting, and inferring are activities that express curiosity. When the reader is not questioning the author or the text, when she is not seeking to ask and answer her own questions, she already has lost interest and may have lost comprehension as well. Readers who predict what will come next are actively following a trail that leads them to information that may confirm or disprove their educated guesses. If the reader's interest wanes and she is no longer engaged in reading on to find out more, chances are she is no longer finding significance in the reading. Making inferences also shows a commitment to teasing out the meaning in the text. When the thrill is gone, comprehension is often the victim.

Losing the ability to determine what is most significant to the thread of the narrative may also be a signal that comprehension is lost. When the reader cannot distinguish between main ideas and supporting details, it can indicate that she is overwhelmed by the text. Without the ability to use her schemas for the narrative framework or text structures in order to put the information presented into a hierarchy of importance, the reader can be quickly buried in meaninglessness. She may have forgotten her purpose for reading. Not knowing what to pay attention to as she reads, she may become frustrated and quickly tune out or be easily distracted.

What should a reader do when she realizes she has lost comprehension? Why, use fix-up options, of course! Educators must teach readers to recognize the symptoms of lost comprehension and then provide them with tools for fixing up their meaning making. In the figure 8-1 excerpt from Emily Dickinson's poem "Part Four: Time and Eternity XXVII," the reader uses several fix-up options to recover comprehension. The complete poem and process are found in lesson plan 8.2 (advanced fix-up strategy) in this chapter.

Here is where the driver applies the brakes to her car. When the reader is unsure where she's headed, she can employ fix-up options to retrace her steps, find where she lost her way, and get back on the road of meaning making once more. Fix-up options are tools that readers can rely upon to find their way home, to make sense of what they read. Learning to self-monitor for comprehension and then to use fix-up options when comprehension is lost gives readers responsibility for their own process, ownership that is critical for the success of lifelong, independent reading and learning. The fix-up strategy empowers readers to succeed.

Fig. 8-1 Sample Fix-up Options

Text: Excerpt from "Part Four: Time and Eternity XXVII" from *The Complete Poems*, by Emily Dickinson

Because I could not stop for Death,
He kindly stopped for me;
The carriage held but just ourselves
And Immortality.

Fix-up Options

Read the entire poem	
Study the illustrations or other text features.	The "D" in Death is capitalized. The poet personifies Death by capitalizing his name.
Make an inference.	The narrator/poet was busy living and couldn't stop her work. So Death stopped for her. The word *kindly* may be used ironically here.
Study the illustrations or other text features.	The "I" in Immortality is also capitalized. The poet is personifying Immortality by capitalizing his name. (**Inference:** I think he is also male. I infer that Death and Immortality are friends.)
Create a visualization.	I imagine a shiny black horse-drawn carriage pulling up in front of the poet's home. Death steps out of the carriage wearing a black suit and top hat. He bows deeply, offers his hand, and ushers the poet into the carriage. Reluctantly, she enters to find Immortality sitting on the seat beside her.
Make a prediction.	I think the poet will be sorry she got into the carriage.

HOW TO TEACH THE STRATEGY

Think-alouds in which educators and more proficient readers model both their loss and their recovery of comprehension are essential in helping less proficient readers grasp the two-part process. Proficient readers must first model how to monitor comprehension and notice when it is lost. Then they choose and use fix-up options to regain it. The questions in figure 8-2 can be posted in the classroom and the library to remind students of the warning signs that they are lost and are not effectively using the active reading strategies they have learned.

When readers lose comprehension, they must "read the signs" and select the appropriate options to get back on the road. To engage students in learning these options, educators can use "Fix-up Options: Read the Signs!" These two Animoto videos are based on the analogy of reading road signs that require drivers to slow down, take stock of their situation (comprehension), and get back on the road (using fix-up options). One video is accompanied by music with a slow tempo (http://animoto.com/play/W1Jb61RviJIcd70IfYY5zA); the other has the exact same content but has fast music (http://animoto.com/play/0z9oyTxo5TJN5nJw12Ct1Q). Educators may

---

Fig. 8-2   Am I Still Actively Reading? Questions to Monitor Comprehension

Am I making connections?
Am I visualizing and using all my senses as I read?
Am I asking questions?
Am I making predictions and inferring as I read?
Am I determining main ideas?
Can I summarize what I'm reading?

If you cannot answer "yes" to these questions, then you may have lost comprehension. What can you do? Slow down, use fix-up options, and get your comprehension back on track!

---

find that one or the other video is more effective for teaching fix-up options or motivating students to learn the fix-up options strategy.

Students can also develop their own metaphors for lost comprehension. Some readers may think of comprehension in terms of the "voice" inside their heads—"Am I lost or confused?" Others may think in terms of a "video" showing the action on a screen inside their minds—"Who shut off the projector?" Others may think about staying on a path and notice as they wander off the trail. It is important to involve students in determining their own signals, because they alone can recognize the moment they lose the thread of a story or the core of an informational text.

In *Strategies That Work: Teaching Comprehension to Enhance Understanding,* Harvey and Goudvis offer a lesson to help readers monitor their own comprehension (2000, 85). This is an adaptation of the process they suggest. Students write a number and "Huh?" on a sticky note and place it on the text where they become confused. As they reread or read ahead, they pay close attention to the point at which their confusion is cleared up. Students can take another sticky note, record the number from the "Huh?" sticky note, draw a lightbulb on it, and place it in the text where they regained comprehension. This way, both students and educators can notice where students lose comprehension and where they get back on track. These are important steps toward eventual independence and accessing fix-up options automatically.

As this strategy lesson suggests, monitoring comprehension must be continuous throughout the reading. Readers who wait until they reach the end of

the text before they realize they have no idea what it means have wasted time and effort by continuing long past their loss of comprehension. There is no simple way for readers to master self-monitoring. Modeling by educators or more proficient peers is a place to begin, but readers surely need a great deal of practice with a wide range of texts that present a variety of comprehension challenges. The three sample lessons at the end of this chapter include specific support for modeling and monitoring meaning making using three different genres of text: a speech, a poem, and an essay.

Loss of comprehension can develop at the word, sentence, paragraph, chapter, or whole-text level. It seems natural for readers to start investigating this phenomenon at the word level. Students often meet challenging words while reading library resources and content area textbooks. School librarians, who are reference resource lovers, may be inclined to guide struggling students toward a print or online dictionary or encyclopedia before encouraging them to use context clues. If classroom teachers are asking students to use context clues before turning to a reference resource, then school librarians should do so as well. Shared classroom and library goals and objectives in the area of vocabulary development and concept attainment are essential. If the school librarian is using the same strategies and terms as the classroom teacher, students benefit. Through curriculum conversations and collaborative planning and coteaching, educators can provide consistent support for students.

These are some of the steps readers take when learning new vocabulary. When attempting to read an unknown word, students learn to skip the word and read to the end of the sentence. They can then guess at the meaning or replace the unknown word with one that makes sense. They should then reread both the sentence before and the sentence in question with the substituted word to determine if it makes sense. Readers are encouraged to use context clues—the words around the unknown word and the images in illustrated texts—to figure out meaning. They can also look for prefixes, suffixes, or roots of the unknown word with which they may already be familiar. If a student knows that *oceanography* is the study of oceans, then she may infer that *topography* may be some kind of field of study. Educators can help readers make these connections and inferences.

After pursuing these primary strategies, readers can choose to check text features such as the glossary or index. If these features are not available, they can consult a secondary source such as a dictionary, thesaurus, or encyclopedia. They can also ask a peer. Educators should balance providing students with answers to their word-level questions with prompting them to discover the word's meaning on their own through one or more of these options. Remember, in teaching reading comprehension strategies the reader's independence is the ultimate goal.

At the sentence, paragraph, chapter, and whole-text levels students can use the sixteen fix-up options recommended by Zimmermann and Hutchins (2003, 163), which have been adapted in figure 8-3. The fix-up options are sequenced according to relative difficulty of application. In this chapter's three lesson plans, fix-up strategy self-monitoring sheets include all sixteen options, which are also listed on the reverse side of the bookmark, available on the web extra site in either black and white or color.

Offering a complete tool kit, these sixteen fix-up options present learners with a review of the reading comprehension strategies addressed in this book. Students at all proficiency levels can be encouraged to use as many options as necessary to regain comprehension. Educators must explain and model the use of each option and of multiple options during how-to strategy lessons. Readers should be clear that

one option alone, such as rereading, may not be sufficient to recover meaning. Keeping a tally sheet is one way to review the various options and to notice which options readers are using most frequently or not at all.

Rereading and reading ahead are the most easily modeled and practiced fix-up options. Stopping to think is likewise easy to model, but students must be clear about what prompted the more proficient reader to reread, read ahead, or pause the reading in the first place. In think-alouds, educators should provide students with a broad range of possibilities, such as an unknown word or phrase or a difficult or new concept, a new character, a change in the speaker or in the point of view, or an inability to summarize what has been read. Visualizing, posing questions, and predicting are options that link directly to the reading comprehension strategies discussed in chapters 4, 5, and 6, respectively. Using an illustration (such as a chart) or a text feature (such as a bold glossary word) are options that readers should connect with the strategy of determining main ideas (chapter 7).

Asking someone for help is another fix-up option. When educators model getting help from someone, they should clearly articulate the kind of help they need. "I don't get it" is not enough. Readers must learn to be more specific about their loss of comprehension and the kind of help they seek. For example, a reader can ask for help understanding why a character acted in a particular way or how a graph illustrates the idea found in the print. Using precise language is an important part of modeling fix-up questions to ask peers and adults.

Figuring out unknown words should be demonstrated using context clues first, as noted above. Sentence structure, or syntax, provides readers with important context clues about the part of speech of the unknown word. These options can be modeled, practiced, and reinforced with *cloze procedures* in which educators think aloud and students fill in the blanks. Students hypothesize the part of speech required and use the context clues to suggest missing words (see the glossary at www.alaeditions.org/web extras/ for an example). Figuring out unknown words by reading between the lines is one type of inference.

Fig. 8-3   Fix-up Options Self-Monitoring Sheet

Options	Option Used	Example(s)
1. Reread.		
2. Read ahead.		
3. Stop to think.		
4. Try to visualize.		
5. Ask a new question.		
6. Make a prediction.		
7. Study the illustrations or other text features.		
8. Ask someone for help.		
9. Figure out unknown words.		
10. Look at the sentence structure.		
11. Make an inference.		
12. Connect to background knowledge.		
13. Read the author's or illustrator's note.		
14. Write about the confusing parts.		
15. Make an effort to think about the message.		
16. Define/Redefine the purpose for reading this text.		

Adapted from Zimmermann and Hutchins (2003)

Students can make inferences about all story elements as well as root causes or resulting effects of information presented in expository texts (chapter 6). To make effective inferences, students must successfully use their background knowledge, which is the next option. The self-recognition that they do not have enough background knowledge is of course necessary before they can remedy it (chapter 3).

The final four options may be the most sophisticated. Some authors and illustrators give readers insight into themes and meanings of texts from the creators' perspective when they explain their motivation for writing or connections to the story or topic. Some readers may be in the habit of skipping over the "author's note" or "note to readers" section of a book. They may also have difficulty comprehending authors' notes, which are sometimes written at a more sophisticated level than the text itself. Writing has been called "thinking on paper." When readers make the time to write about their confusion, they may be able to identify the source of their problem, or they may be able to work through their misunderstanding. Making a conscious effort to think about the message, moral, or theme of the text is a high-level inference (chapter 6). Combining conscious thinking and writing about confusion can be most effective. Students need to be prompted to use writing about their confusion as a fix-up option.

Redefining the purpose for reading in order to make sense of a text is an advanced option for educators to model and one for which students can reach. As students learned when studying main ideas, the purpose for reading determines the reader's focus. The care with which readers pay attention to comprehension has a great deal to do with their purpose for reading and their commitment to meaning making. With a low investment in the text, readers may decide to read on after comprehension is lost if they believe they can piece together what they missed or if what they are reading has little importance to their lives. If, on the other hand, a reader's main goal is to make meaning throughout the reading, then she will most likely slow down, retrace her steps, and apply one or more fix-up options to regain comprehension.

MAKING LITERATURE CONNECTIONS

Texts that support monitoring comprehension and using fix-up options have one thing in common: they are confusing to the reader. Identifying texts to teach this strategy requires educators to be sensitive to the unique background experiences and reading development of the students in their charge. Informational texts in particular, especially if they are long, can present comprehension challenges for striving readers who may struggle with fluency. These texts often contain specialized vocabulary, pronouns that require readers to locate the referent, and appositives that define or explain a word, phrase, or concept. Educators can facilitate engagements with these texts by demonstrating how to chunk texts into manageable parts and monitor comprehension during reading through notemaking or other recall strategies.

A text built around an unfamiliar text structure such as cause and effect or problem and solution can

also be bewildering to the reader. A text in content areas with new or specialized vocabulary or concepts can confound the reader. Texts that use idiomatic expressions, dialect, and jargon can be confusing to students who are not insiders to a particular culture, are new to a particular region, are learning a second language, or are novices in the discipline. Science fiction texts that require readers to follow an alternate reality with all of its imagined characteristics clearly in their minds can be mystifying. Poetic texts that use figurative language can pose challenges to students who lack the background or experience to make the necessary comparisons between literal and figurative meanings. When educators are selecting mentor texts for teaching fix-up options, they can look to every genre for examples.

Ultimately, every text has the potential to leave a reader perplexed. It is up to the reader to recognize the loss of comprehension during the reading process. In addition to using young adult material, educators must model both the loss of comprehension and the use of fix-up strategies with texts written for adults. This helps students realize that using the fix-up strategy is a lifelong learning skill. Recognizing the need for self-monitoring in meaning making is a prerequisite for teaching fix-up options. Monitoring comprehension and using fix-up options are two sides of the same coin.

LESSON PLANS

In these lessons readers are asked to maintain active engagement in the reading process in order to extract as much meaning as possible from the texts. This process involves reading slowly, stopping to use fix-up options, and recording notes about the speaker/narrator/author's message. The three lesson plans use a speech, a poem, and an essay, respectively, to model and give readers opportunities to practice this strategy. These are common text types with which students must interact on standardized tests. The fix-up options graphic organizer for each lesson asks students to respond in ways that may be most appropriate for the type of text under consideration. Educators are encouraged to apply these options to other texts and to modify these graphic organizers as they see fit. Ideally, educators will introduce and reinforce the options at teachable moments when the need for a fix-up occurs spontaneously while reading a text.

Educators determine when to share the Fix-up Options PowerPoint, one or both of the "Fix-up Options" Animoto videos, or the bookmarks. These resources can be shared in the classroom the day before the lesson or can be used before and after the first-day presentation component of this lesson.

In these lessons, educators ask students to brainstorm how they know when they have lost comprehension and no longer understand what they are reading, viewing, or hearing or to discuss the consequences of miscommunication caused by a lack of comprehension. Record and save students' ideas. Use their ideas to create a class and library chart similar to figure 8-2. Although fix-up options can be taught in formal lessons such as these, the most effective way to teach this strategy is at teachable moments with authentic and troublesome texts. In fact, monitoring the loss of comprehension may be the most important component of these lessons.

LESSON PLAN 8.1

Reading Comprehension Strategy Six
Using Fix-up Options

Reading Development Level: Advancing

Instructional Strategies
Categorizing, Notemaking and Summarizing

Lesson Length
2 sessions

Purpose
The purpose of this lesson plan is to use fix-up options to determine the theme of a speech.

Objectives
At the end of these lessons, students will be able to
1. Define all sixteen fix-up options.
2. Determine when they have lost comprehension.
3. Practice metacognition and record when they apply the fix-up options.
4. Interpret the theme of a speech using the information they gained while using fix-up options.
5. Justify their interpretation using examples from the text.
6. Describe the process of using fix-up options.
7. Share their interpretations in half-class groups.

Resources, Materials, and Equipment
The Gettysburg Address read by several actors: www.americanrhetoric.com/speeches/gettysburg address.htm

The Gettysburg Address: www.historyplace.com/speeches/gettysburg.htm

Additional speeches: www.historyplace.com/speeches/previous.htm

Fix-up Options PowerPoint

"Fix-up Options: Read the Signs!" Animoto videos: http://animoto.com/play/W1Jb61RviJIcd70I fYY5zA (the slow side) and http://animoto.com/play/0z9oyTxo5TJN5nJw12Ct1Q (the fast side)

Graphic organizers: 8.1 Fix-up Options Graphic Organizer and Checklist, 8.1 Teacher Resource— Completed Fix-up Options Graphic Organizer (with checklist and sample paragraphs)

Overhead, Internet access, data projector, or interactive whiteboard

Collaboration
Educators role-play losing comprehension. They model using the fix-up options strategy. They monitor students' use of fix-up options and graphic organizer recording. They facilitate half-class group sharing and reflections after students complete graphic organizers and summary paragraphs.

Assessment

The students' completed graphic organizers and their paragraphs show the process and results of their learning. Educators apply writing rubrics to students' summaries.

Standards

Reading keywords: Extract information and use graphic organizers to comprehend text; connect information and events in text with background knowledge.

Writing keywords: Prewriting; interpretation; summarize.

Social studies keywords: Use a variety of rich primary and secondary source material including speeches.

AASL STANDARDS INDICATORS*

- Read, view, and listen for information presented in any format (e.g., textual, visual, media, digital) in order to make inferences and gather meaning. (1.1.6)
- Collaborate with others to broaden and deepen understanding. (1.1.9)
- Monitor gathered information, and assess for gaps or weaknesses. (1.4.3)

PROCESS

DAY 1

MOTIVATION

One educator (A) begins to read an encyclopedia article about the Civil War, the battle at Gettysburg, or President Abraham Lincoln. (Select a particularly dry excerpt.) Almost immediately, the other educator (B) shows symptoms of a loss of comprehension: yawning, looking at the clock, tapping her pen, fidgeting, and more. Educator A asks: "What did you learn from what I've read so far?" Educator B can't respond. Educator A: "Well, then what are your questions?" Educator B can't respond.

Think-pair-share what happened in this scene. Solicit responses from students. Ask: "Could boredom be a symptom of lost comprehension?"

STUDENT-FRIENDLY OBJECTIVES

1. Use fix-up options to explicate the speech line by line.
2. Make notes on a graphic organizer.
3. Record one or two phrases that describe the theme of the speech.

PRESENTATION

Begin with one educator reading the entire Gettysburg Address. Alternately, use one of the media versions listed in the resources section above. Students sit with partners and follow along on a printed copy of the speech.

Distribute and project the 8.1 Fix-up Options Graphic Organizer. Reread the speech. Educators model reading in chunks and provide think-alouds during a line-by-line interpretation of the speech. Check off fix-up options when used and record comprehension process in notemaking format. Use the 8.1 Teacher Resource—Completed Fix-up Options Graphic Organizer for reference. Students record on individual

---

* Excerpted from *Standards for the 21st-Century Learner* by the American Association of School Librarians, a division of the American Library Association, copyright © 2007 American Library Association. Available for download at www.ala.org/aasl/standards. Used with permission.

graphic organizers as well. Educators use questioning to involve students in supplying notes to include on the graphic organizer. Circle portions of the text that may require further exploration.

Educators model using the first two paragraphs of the speech and give student partners the responsibility for using fix-up options for the remainder of the speech. Alternately, educators facilitate a whole-class example and then provide students with additional speeches to interpret with a partner (see resource above).

STUDENT PARTICIPATION PROCEDURES
1. Take turns reading lines of text with a partner, no more than two sentences at a time.
2. Think aloud.
3. Note which fix-up options were used and where they were used.
4. Record notes on graphic organizer.
5. Circle words and phrases that need further exploration.

GUIDED PRACTICE
The educators support partners in thinking aloud, completing the graphic organizer, and discussing the speech.

CLOSURE
Review the process of slowing down or stopping when comprehension is lost. Review the fix-up options. Students and educators assess which options were used most frequently and which were used less often or not at all. Speculate on why each option was or was not used.

DAY 2

STUDENT-FRIENDLY OBJECTIVES
1. Compose a summary using evidence in the text.
2. Compose a second paragraph that describes how fix-up options helped in interpreting the speech.
3. Use the checklist as a guide.
4. Share interpretation and process of using fix-up options with classmates.

PRESENTATION
Project the summary checklist. Review the criteria. If appropriate, share a portion or all of the sample paragraphs on 8.1 Teacher Resource—Completed Fix-up Options Graphic Organizer.

GUIDED PRACTICE (OR SEE THE EXTENSIONS)
Students use the checklist to guide their interpretations and compose individual paragraphs to justify their interpretation and describe their use of fix-up options to make meaning.

CLOSURE
Divide the class into two groups. Each educator facilitates a group sharing their interpretations and fix-up options process. Discuss unanswered questions. Conduct the reflection orally or in writing.

REFLECTION

How do we know when we have lost comprehension? How do we determine when to delve more deeply into a text? Why is this important? How do fix-up options help meaning making?

EXTENSIONS

Repeat this process with students working with partners to interpret different speeches (see resource above for additional speeches). Select speeches based on historic time period under study or a topic such as civil rights.

Use the fix-up options graphic organizer as needed for difficult or dense texts in any content area.

LESSON PLAN 8.2

Reading Comprehension Strategy Six
Using Fix-up Options

Reading Development Level: Advanced

Instructional Strategies
Categorizing, Notemaking and Summarizing

Lesson Length
2 sessions

Purpose
The purpose of this lesson plan is to use fix-up options to interpret the tone (narrator's feeling) of a poem.

Objectives
At the end of these lessons, students will be able to
1. Define all sixteen fix-up options.
2. Determine when they have lost comprehension.
3. Practice metacognition and record when they apply the fix-up options.
4. Interpret the tone of a poem using the information they gained while using fix-up options.
5. Justify their interpretation using examples from the text.
6. Describe the process of using fix-up options.
7. Share their interpretations in half-class groups.

Resources, Materials, and Equipment
Mentor text: Emily Dickinson poem "Part Four: Time and Eternity XXVII" from *The Complete Poems* (1924): www.bartleby.com/113/4027.html

Fix-up Options PowerPoint

"Fix-up Options: Read the Signs!" Animoto videos: http://animoto.com/play/W1Jb61RviJIcd70I fYY5zA (the slow side) and http://animoto.com/play/0z9oyTxo5TJN5nJw12Ct1Q (the fast side)

Graphic organizers: 8.2 Fix-up Options Graphic Organizer, 8.2 Teacher Resource—Completed Fix-up Options Graphic Organizer, Checklist, and Sample Paragraph (with checklist and sample paragraphs)

Overhead, Internet access, data projector, or interactive whiteboard

Collaboration
Educators role-play losing comprehension. They model using the fix-up options strategy. They monitor students' use of fix-up options and graphic organizer recording. They facilitate half-class group sharing and reflections after students complete graphic organizers and summary paragraphs.

Assessment

The students' completed graphic organizers and their paragraphs show the process and results of their learning. Educators may apply other writing rubrics to students' summaries.

Standards

Reading keywords: Extract information and use graphic organizers to comprehend text; connect information and events in text with background knowledge.

Writing keywords: prewriting, interpret, summarize.

AASL STANDARDS INDICATORS*

- Read, view, and listen for information presented in any format (e.g., textual, visual, media, digital) in order to make inferences and gather meaning. (1.1.6)
- Collaborate with others to broaden and deepen understanding. (1.1.9)
- Monitor gathered information, and assess for gaps or weaknesses. (1.4.3)

PROCESS

DAY 1

MOTIVATION

Give an example of a teen who has a rudimentary knowledge of the local language meeting a blind date. Demonstrate how a failure to comprehend can result in miscommunication. For instance, in France the expression "*C'est terrible!*" can mean that something is either "terrible" or "awesome" depending on the context and the speaker's facial expressions and gestures. A shallow interpretation of this expression could lead the teen to have the opposite impression of the native speaker's communication. Role-play this couple meeting on a blind date.

The purpose of this lesson is to read deeply in order to extract as much meaning as possible from a poem. The goal is to understand the poet's intended meaning for this work. This involves reading slowly, stopping to use fix-up options, and recording notes about the meaning of the poem and the process of interpreting it.

STUDENT-FRIENDLY OBJECTIVES

1. Use fix-up options to explicate the poem line by line.
2. Record interpretations in terms of fix-up options and evidence in the text.

PRESENTATION

Begin with one educator reading the entire Emily Dickinson poem "Part Four: Time and Eternity XXVII" that begins "Because I could not stop for Death." Students sit with partners and follow along on copies of the poem. Educators model reading in chunks. They use think-alouds to share their line-by-line interpretations of the first one or two stanzas of the poem.

Project the 8.2 Fix-up Options Graphic Organizer. Check off fix-up options when used and record comprehension process in notemaking format. Use the 8.2 Teacher Resource—Completed Fix-up Options Graphic Organizer as a reference. It is important that educators demonstrate that there is no single interpretation of a piece of literature. Circle portions of the text that may require further exploration. Record students' contributions.

STUDENT PARTICIPATION PROCEDURES

1. Take turns reading lines of text with a partner, no more than one stanza at a time.
2. Think aloud.
3. Note which fix-up options were used and where they were used.
4. Record notes on graphic organizer.
5. Circle words and phrases that need further exploration.

GUIDED PRACTICE

The educators support partners in thinking aloud, completing the graphic organizer, and discussing the poem.

CLOSURE

Students and educators assess which options were used most frequently and which were used less often or not at all. Speculate on why each option was or was not used.

DAY 2

STUDENT-FRIENDLY OBJECTIVES

1. Compose a summary using evidence in the text.
2. Compose a second paragraph that describes how fix-up options helped in interpreting the poem.
3. Use the checklist as a guide.
4. Share interpretations and process of using fix-up options with classmates.

PRESENTATION

Project the summary checklist. Review the criteria. If appropriate, share a portion or all of the sample paragraphs on the 8.2 Teacher Resource—Completed Fix-up Options Graphic Organizer.

GUIDED PRACTICE

Students use the checklist to guide their interpretations and compose individual paragraphs to justify their interpretation and describe their use of fix-up options to make meaning.

CLOSURE

Divide the class into two groups. Each educator facilitates a group sharing the fix-up options process and interpretations. Discuss unanswered questions. Conduct the reflection orally or in writing.

REFLECTION

How do we determine when to delve more deeply into a text? Why is this important? How do fix-up options help in meaning making?

EXTENSIONS

Repeat this process with students working with partners to interpret additional poems by Dickinson or other poets. Select poems based on literary time periods or some other organizing characteristic. Educators may decide to extend this lesson into an inquiry of Emily Dickinson and her work (see 9.2 advanced lesson).

Use the fix-up options graphic organizer as needed for difficult or dense texts in any content area.

LESSON PLAN 8.3

Reading Comprehension Strategy Six
Using Fix-up Options

Reading Development Level: Challenging

Instructional Strategies
Categorizing, Notemaking and Summarizing, Analogies

Lesson Length
2 sessions

Purpose
The purpose of this lesson plan is to use fix-up options to interpret an essay. If continuing with the 9.3 synthesizing lesson, this essay serves to build background information for that unit of study.

Objectives
At the end of these lessons, students will be able to
1. Define all sixteen fix-up options.
2. Determine when they have lost comprehension.
3. Practice metacognition and record when they apply the fix-up options.
4. Summarize and interpret an essay.
5. Justify interpretation using examples from the text.
6. Identify the most useful fix-up option for this text.
7. Describe the process of using fix-up options by creating an analogy.

Resources, Materials, and Equipment
Mentor text: "Harlem: The Culture Capital"—Excerpts from the essay by James Weldon Johnson, originally published in *The New Negro: An Interpretation,* edited by Alain Locke (1925): http://nationalhumanitiescenter.org/pds/maai3/community/text1/johnsonharlem.pdf

Fix-up Options PowerPoint

"Fix-up Options: Read the Signs!" Animoto videos: http://animoto.com/play/W1Jb61RviJIcd70IfYY5zA (the slow side) and http://animoto.com/play/0z9oyTxo5TJN5nJw12Ct1Q (the fast side)

Graphic organizers: 8.3 Fix-up Options Graphic Organizer, 8.3 Teacher Resource—Completed Fix-up Options Graphic Organizer (with sample paragraphs and analogy)

Overhead, Internet access, data projector, or interactive whiteboard

Collaboration
Educators role-play losing comprehension. They model using the fix-up options strategy. They monitor students' use of fix-up options and graphic organizer recording. Both facilitate small group sharing with the entire class and reflections after students complete graphic organizers, summary paragraphs, and analogies.

Assessment

The students' completed graphic organizers, summary paragraphs, and analogies show the process and results of their learning. Educators may apply writing rubrics to students' summaries.

Standards

Reading keywords: Extract information and use graphic organizers to comprehend text; connect information and events in text with background knowledge.

Writing keywords: Prewriting, interpret, summarize.

Social studies keywords: Describe the impact on American society of cultural movements in art, music, and literature, including the Harlem Renaissance.

AASL STANDARDS INDICATORS*

- Read, view, and listen for information presented in any format (e.g., textual, visual, media, digital) in order to make inferences and gather meaning. (1.1.6)
- Collaborate with others to broaden and deepen understanding. (1.1.9)
- Monitor gathered information, and assess for gaps or weaknesses. (1.4.3)

PROCESS

MOTIVATION

One educator (A) begins to read from an academic journal article. Almost immediately, the other educator (B) shows symptoms of loss of comprehension: yawning, looking at the clock, tapping her pen, fidgeting, and more. Educator A asks: "What did you learn from what I've read so far?" Educator B can't respond. Educator A: "Well, then what are your questions?" Educator B can't respond. Educator A: "This passage is four or more pages long. What strategies can you use when you don't understand a long, difficult text?" Students think-pair-share.

STUDENT-FRIENDLY OBJECTIVES

1. Use fix-up options to explicate the text line by line.
2. Record interpretations in terms of fix-up options and evidence in the text.

PRESENTATION

What are some strategies we can use when a challenging text is lengthy and difficult to understand? Brainstorm some ideas, including dividing it into smaller chunks. After educator modeling, students use fix-up options to support their comprehension of a chunk of an essay by James Weldon Johnson titled "Harlem: The Culture Capital" that was originally published in a book in 1925. They work with a partner or in small groups to read and interpret a chunk of the essay, share their interpretations with students who read different parts of the essay, and compose summaries that justify their interpretations with evidence in the text. Groups also identify fix-up options that were particularly useful and develop an analogy for using fix-up options.

Distribute copies of the essay. One educator reads the entire first paragraph. Sitting with partners or in small groups students follow along. Educators model reading in chunks and think aloud about their line-by-line interpretation of the first one or two paragraphs of the essay.

Project the 8.3 Fix-up Options Graphic Organizer. Reread the first paragraph. Check off fix-up options used and record comprehension process in notemaking format (see the 8.3 Teacher Resource—Completed Fix-up Options Graphic Organizer). Demonstrate that there is no single interpretation of a piece of literature. Circle portions of the text that may require further exploration. Students contribute their thinking. Record students' ideas as well.

Assign individuals, partners, or small groups chunks of the essay to practice this process. They jigsaw and share within another group to interpret the entire essay.

STUDENT PARTICIPATION PROCEDURES
1. Take turns reading lines of text, no more than one or two sentences at a time.
2. Think aloud.
3. Note which fix-up options were used and where they were used.
4. Record notes on graphic organizer.
5. Circle words and phrases that need further exploration.

GUIDED PRACTICE
Educators support individuals, partners, or small groups in thinking aloud and completing the graphic organizer. Educators form expert groups to bring their interpretation from their chunk to a group discussion of the essay.

CLOSURE
Review the reason for using fix-up options and the strategy of chunking texts into smaller, more manageable parts.

DAY 2

STUDENT-FRIENDLY OBJECTIVES
1. Suggest the tone of the piece in one or two phrases.
2. Summarize the essay using evidence in the text.
3. Write about the most useful fix-up option.
4. Develop an analogy for using fix-up options to comprehend text.
5. Share summaries and analogies.

PRESENTATION
Project the fill-in-the-blanks component of the graphic organizer. Review the meaning of "tone" of a piece of literature, the narrator or author's feeling toward the subject matter. Review how to summarize using evidence in the text. Ask students to review the options they used most frequently and to think about how one or more of those options helped them understand the text.

Define an analogy as an extended simile: A is to B as C is to D. Give several examples (see the 8.3 Teacher Resource—Completed Fix-up Options Graphic Organizer).

GUIDED PRACTICE

Educators support individuals, partners, or small groups as students complete the graphic organizer. They may ask students to compose individual responses and analogies. If so, students may complete this work as homework.

CLOSURE

Conduct closure as a whole class or divide the class into two groups. Educators facilitate partner, small group, or half-class sharing of summaries. Discuss unanswered questions. Share the most helpful fix-up options. Speculate on why those options may have helped with this particular piece of writing. Share analogies.

REFLECTION

How do we determine when to delve more deeply into a text? Why is this important? How do fix-up options help in meaning making?

EXTENSIONS

Repeat this process with students working individually, with partners, or in small groups to interpret additional essays or other literary works. Langston Hughes's poem "Theme for English B" makes a compelling segue if studying additional Harlem Renaissance literature. Select work based on literary time periods or another organizing characteristic. Educators may decide to extend this lesson into an inquiry about Harlem Renaissance artists and musicians. If so, continue with the 9.3 synthesizing lesson in this book.

Use the fix-up options graphic organizer as needed for difficult or dense texts in any content area.

9

Reading Comprehension Strategy Seven

Synthesizing

The "information age" places higher-order literacy demands on all of us … these demands include synthesizing and evaluating information from multiple sources. American schools need to enhance the ability of children to search and sort through information, to synthesize and analyze the information they encounter.

—Richard Allington

Synthesizing is putting it all together, being sure that all the working parts of our metaphorical car are functioning and under the control of a strategic driver. Unlike a summary, which is just the facts and only the facts, synthesis goes a step further. True, the summary comprises the main ideas as selected by the reader, but in the selection process the reader analyzes the information he has gathered and filters it through his own interpretations. *Synthesis* sheds light on the significance of texts from the reader's point of view. Although it is possible to synthesize the information found in just one text, the more common practice of this strategy, particularly from a school library perspective, involves bringing together information from several sources. As readers synthesize they sort and evaluate information. They may find agreement among text sources or encounter conflicting "facts." Synthesizing, similar to determining main ideas, requires that readers make value judgments.

Modeling and practicing this comprehension strategy is a natural activity for classroom-library collaboration. With a focus on information literacy, school librarians are perfectly positioned to serve as teacher leaders with expertise in teaching synthesizing. Teaching students to access information efficiently and effectively, to evaluate information critically and competently, and to use information accurately and creatively is part and parcel of the school librarian's instructional role. If "synthesis is the process of ordering, recalling, retelling, and recreating [information] into a coherent whole" (Keene and Zimmermann 1997, 169), then surely the library with its rich array of resources is the perfect location for modeling and practicing this strategy. In fact, physical and virtual libraries of all types may be where students continue to put this lifelong learning skill into practice.

Synthesizing requires that readers use the strategies offered in this book to read, to evaluate, and to use ideas and information. Synthesis requires longer-term, in-depth learning. When students are exploring curriculum-based subjects or independent inquiry topics, the school librarian can offer expertise in teaching information literacy skills and strategies. The library collection, the Web, and interlibrary loan can supply the resources students and classroom teachers need to be successful. Keeping accurate bibliographic records and making notes effectively, which are core information literacy skills, are even more critical when students are synthesizing information from multiple sources. Classroom teachers will appreciate school librarians who can codevelop graphic organizers that help students maintain organization as they gather information.

With a library collection aligned with classroom curricula and the independent reading and research needs of the learning community, the school librarian can support resource-based units of instruction. This is a pivotal professional role for school librarians. Classroom-library collaboration supports educators in assessing the effectiveness of specific resources within a print and electronic text set before, during, and after the lesson. Educators can note which titles generate the most interest among students. They can determine which resources present particular challenges to readers. Through resource evaluation at the point of practice, educators can collaboratively guide the library's collection development and effectively expand the available resources with web-based information and through interlibrary loan.

Units of study that focus on synthesis invite increased opportunities for interdisciplinary teaching and learning. "When we focus only on our own disciplines, we miss opportunities to see the larger picture of student learning on campus and to learn from each other's pedagogical practices and discussions. When we talk only to those who teach what we teach, we run the risk of mistaking our part for the whole or thinking about what we teach in isolation from other forms and forums of teaching and learning" (Jacobs and Jacobs 2009, 72–73).

Including multiple educators in synthesis collaborations can enhance student outcomes and educator engagement. Students can benefit when several content area classroom teachers collaborate with the school librarian to develop interdisciplinary units of study. Students also benefit when specialists such as art or music teachers participate in designing, implementing, and assessing lessons. School librarians and classroom teachers can also increase their own knowledge in these domains as they learn alongside students. Classroom-library collaboration to teach and practice synthesis is not just more effective, it's also more fun. With two or more educators to monitor student learning and adjust instruction, students may experience greater learning success, and educators may find more enjoyment in teaching long-term projects. These broader partnerships have the potential to develop a culture of collaboration throughout the school community.

For students to synthesize information effectively and make it their own, they must develop all of the reading comprehension strategies discussed in this book and use them to make meaning. They must analyze the information found in various resources, interpret it, and put it back together into a transformed and coherent whole. Readers who can synthesize are like the expert drivers who know the interrelationships of all the car parts so well that they are able to drive not only effectively and safely but also with more pure enjoyment. Students who master this strategy are proficient at comprehending the texts they read, combining information from multiple sources, and passing that information through their own interpretations. It is through this process that learners generate knowledge that creates, develops, and revises their schemas.

HOW TO TEACH THE STRATEGY

Synthesizing requires that readers determine main ideas from multiple sources, summarize information, and add their own interpretations. Graphic organizers such as the Informational Text Self-Monitoring Graphic Organizer in figure 9-1 can be developed to help readers record main ideas with a focus on new information as they make connections, use fix-up options, and form responses, interpretations, and questions. Addressing multiple strategies on one graphic organizer helps readers see how comprehension strategies are related. An organizer such as this one helps readers practice metacognition: they can see what they learned and how they learned it.

Although a summary meets the criteria for learning at the comprehension level on Bloom's taxonomy (Bloom et al. 1956), synthesizing is a higher-order thinking skill. Synthesis is the process of learning from others' ideas and transforming those ideas through analysis and interpretation to offer a new meaning. Through synthesis, the learner makes information and ideas his own. Some examples of verbs associated with synthesizing are *construct, design, devise, formulate, imagine, invent,* and *propose.* Each of these actions suggests that the learner goes beyond the facts to suggest his own ideas, to offer his own interpretations.

It should be noted that Anderson et al. (2001) have suggested a revised Bloom's taxonomy. They changed Bloom's nouns to verbs and added "creating" to the top of the taxonomy. While I agree with both of those changes, they also eliminated synthesis from the thinking skills and did not address synthesizing per se in their work. I believe that is a mistake. While verbs such as create, design, generate, and write formerly associated with synthesizing now appear in the "creating" category, others are missing. Where are verbs such as modify, combine, explain, reorganize, and reconstruct that more clearly communicate synthesis? Without synthesis in which readers interpret information from multiple sources based on their purpose for reading, schemas, beliefs, and values, other actions

associated with creating (such as mixing, remixing, publishing, and building mashups) will likely become imitative rather than inventive. In the world of new literacies in which readers interact with multiple literacies even within one text, I believe educators need to model and teach learners to synthesize information in order to maximize their creativity.

In addition to synthesizing the factual aspects of the information they read, hear, or view, students need opportunities to express their responses to texts and integrate their responses into a synthesis. Readers' responses can be described in many ways. They can make text-to-self connections that include their prior knowledge, experiences, and feelings. They can respond to specific story elements such as the setting or theme. They can pose questions about concepts or topics and suggest what-if scenarios. The important thing about a response is that it not be merely a restatement of the story or facts. A response is unique to the reader and demonstrates the central role of the reader in the reading transaction. Combined with information or evidence from texts, readers' responses are the other main ingredient in synthesis.

When middle and high school readers interpret texts, they explain meaning in relation to their own beliefs, judgments, or circumstances. To that end, another way for students to conceive of synthesis is expressed in the following formula:

Information + Interpretation = Synthesis

Unit design is one way to ensure that students incorporate their own interpretations into their synthesis projects. Assignments must require that students do more than cut and paste information and call it a report. Designing instruction so that students are required to think about the ideas and information they read is fundamental. Involving students in asking authentic questions, analyzing information, and transforming what they have read through synthesis means expecting them to do more than regurgitate facts. *Ban Those Bird Units: 15 Models for Teaching and Learning in Information-Rich and Technology-Rich Environments*

Fig. 9-1   Informational Text Self-Monitoring Graphic Organizer

Student's Name: _____

Text Title: _____

Author/Illustrator: _____

1. I reread to better understand information about the following:

2. I made notes about the five Ws and the H.

    Who? _____

    What? _____

    Where? _____

    When? _____

    Why? _____

    How? _____

3. I found this new information the most interesting or surprising to me:

4. I learned this new information by reading

    a. the print?

    b. the illustrations?

    c. the captions?

    d. a graphic such as a map, chart, graph, or photograph?

    e. something else? (Name it.) _____

5. What connections am I making?

    What do I think or feel about this information?

    What does this information mean to me?

6. What are my new or unanswered questions?

(Loertscher, Koechlin, and Zwaan 2004) is an exemplary resource for guiding classroom-library collaboration to help students achieve synthesis.

Still, students must be able to back up their responses and interpretations with evidence in the text. In a 1996 study of students in a tenth-grade advanced-placement American history class, researchers learned that after reading a variety of online documents, students' opinion papers did not include evidence from the texts to support their opinions or perspectives. Nor did their descriptive papers explain conflicting information they had encountered in texts. The researchers concluded that explicit instruction on how to use and evaluate information from multiple sources should begin in elementary school (Stahl 2005). Teaching the reading comprehension strategy of synthesis using multiple texts is a place to begin.

Print and electronic information-seeking skills can be taught during instruction focused on synthesis. Resource location skills and using the text features of informational books are tasks that may be required for students engaged in learning this strategy. Teaching students to use the online catalog efficiently and effectively can be integrated into units of instruction in which students select their own text sets and materials. Skimming, scanning, and notemaking are subskills in the inquiry process and can be taught or reviewed during synthesis lessons. When a savvy school librarian shares expertise in searching web-based and database resources, classroom teachers as well as students can further develop their electronic literacy skills. Teaching students how to evaluate resources, particularly websites, for relevance, currency, authority, accuracy, and bias, which are the main ideas of the new literacies, can be easily integrated into lessons in which learners are expected to synthesize information. For students, practicing synthesis requires them to master a valuable set of subskills and strategies, many of which can be taught most effectively through classroom-library collaboration.

MAKING LITERATURE CONNECTIONS

When choosing texts for the purpose of synthesizing ideas and information, educators can provide students with carefully selected text sets of resources at various reading levels, in multiple genres, and in a variety of formats, including websites and other technology sources. Developing text sets collaboratively can be a valuable learning experience for both classroom teachers and school librarians, who may bring different strengths and perspectives to the table. One educator may be particularly knowledgeable in the area of print resources, while the other may be savvy about web-based resources. One may be more familiar with fiction titles, the other more versed in informational sources. Together, educators can develop engaging text sets for student exploration.

Ultimately, educators must give students the responsibility to develop their own text sets on a particular topic or theme. By collecting and evaluating resources, students can demonstrate what they have learned about the strengths of various genres in supporting research and inquiry projects. They can assess the works of favorite authors, illustrators, and web-based resources for their usefulness in achieving learning objectives. After classroom teachers and school librarians have modeled collecting and using text sets, students are ready to assume responsibility for this aspect of the inquiry process. Educators can then serve in an advisory role.

SYNTHESIS: A 21ST-CENTURY STRATEGY

The persistent information overload of 21st-century life has made synthesis as a strategy more important than ever. Although we cannot predict what new ICT tools and devices will be available to students even five years from now, we can feel certain that their daily lives will include accessing, evaluating, and synthesizing information in multiple formats from multiple sources. As educators, we guide students through the information literacy process and encourage them to apply reading comprehension strategies and develop their own interpretations of the ideas and information they read, hear, and view. In the process we can help them develop the critical thinking skills they will need to maximize their life options and negotiate the challenges of the future.

It is never too late to begin connecting reading with meaning making and meaning making with generating knowledge that can make a difference in the world. At middle school and high school when far too many students may be inclined to opt out of reading or be at risk of dropping out of school, educators can motivate students by teaching them strategies they will need to be successful. Helping students develop reading proficiency can set them on a course of learning that serves them well throughout their lives. Classroom teachers and school librarians who codesign, coteach, and coassess instruction for students to make connections between reading comprehension strategies and information literacy can help them become more strategic readers who will use these skills effectively over their lifetimes. They may even choose to use their knowledge to make the world a more humane and just place for all of us. Now that is maximizing your impact!

LESSON PLANS

These lesson plans for teaching synthesis are units of instruction at three levels of literacy development. They can be used as springboards for deeper inquiry projects. Educators should use the inquiry process of their choice to frame these lessons. Hopefully, this process has been adopted schoolwide or districtwide.

In the advancing unit, students use the background knowledge they developed while reading a historical fiction novel to formulate inquiry questions. They pursue answers to their questions by determining main ideas for a historical newspaper article and advertisement. The advanced synthesis unit extends the 8.2 fix-up options lesson based on an Emily Dickinson poem. This inquiry integrates information-seeking skills and music into an interpretation of her poem. In the challenging unit, students build on the essay they deconstructed in the 8.3 fix-up options lesson and use it as background knowledge to further their study of the Harlem Renaissance. They investigate artists and musicians of the period in order to deepen their understanding of the cultural significance of this period in American life. In all of these units, students apply the synthesis strategy and information literacy skills to comprehend and interpret information from multiple sources in multiple formats.

All three lesson plans can be enriched through engaging students in individual or group work that involves them in further demonstrating their learning using Web 2.0 tools. When students create multimedia products, educators should conduct mini-lessons on the ethical use of information in web-distributed products. Encourage students to create their own media or point students to copyright-free images and sound. Educators may use or adapt the Group Work and Multimedia Product Rubric from chapter 6. For possible Web 2.0 tools, see "Productivity Tools" at www.storytrail.com/impact12/web2.0_tools.htm.

In order to synthesize, students need time to explore and immerse themselves in a topic, to investigate various resources in many formats, and to reorganize information and combine it with their own interpretations. Through classroom-library collaboration, educators are able to help students sustain the motivation and interest required to complete a long-term project. These valuable opportunities to go deeper set the stage for more independent inquiry projects that can be core schooling and lifelong learning experiences for students.

LESSON PLAN 9.1

Reading Comprehension Strategy Seven
Synthesizing

Reading Development Level: Advancing

Instructional Strategies
Advance Organizers, Categorizing, Notemaking and Summarizing

Lesson Length
6 or 7 sessions (or more for the extensions)

Purpose
The purpose of this unit is to conduct an inquiry into a social studies topic. The unit involves students building background knowledge by reading a historical fiction novel, identifying social studies inquiry topics, making notes on a graphic organizer, synthesizing information from multiple sources, demonstrating knowledge using technology tools, and self-assessing using rubrics.

Objectives
At the end of this unit, students will be able to
1. Use background knowledge to guide an inquiry project.
2. Conduct inquiry, make notes, and record sources.
3. Synthesize information from multiple sources to determine main ideas about the topic of the inquiry.
4. Present main ideas using a journalistic writing technique.
5. Present cultural knowledge in the form of a product or service advertisement.
6. Self-assess process and product with a checklist.
7. For extension: Follow the writing process to pursue an extended inquiry on the topic under investigation.

Resources, Materials, and Equipment
Historical Fiction Inquiry Pathfinder (and Historical Fiction Novels Text Set): www.storytrail.com/impact12/historical_fiction_inquiry.htm

Trade, Reference Book, and Electronic Resources Text Set(s) organized by historical time periods

Graphic organizers: Notemaking Graphic Organizer, Works Cited Graphic Organizer, 9.1 Assignment Sheet, 9.1 Admit Slip, 9.1 Teacher Resource—Completed Admit Slip, 9.1 Topic Selection Graphic Organizer, 9.1 Newspaper Article Graphic Organizer, 9.1 Teacher Resource—Completed Notemaking Graphic Organizer, 9.1 Teacher Resource—Completed Bibliography Graphic Organizer, 9.1 Teacher Resource—Completed Newspaper Article Graphic Organizer, 9.1 Teacher Resource—Sample Newspaper Article, 9.1 Notemaking and Bibliography Graphic

Organizers Rubric, 9.1 Newspaper Article Rubric, 9.1 Newspaper Advertisement Rubric, For extensions: 9.1 Teacher Resource—Sample Essay—Event, 9.1 Teacher Resource—Sample Essay—Person

Overhead, Internet access, data projector, or interactive whiteboard

Collaboration

Educators model completing graphic organizers. They also model synthesizing information from a variety of sources. The language arts teacher may take full responsibility for the historical novel, or educators may cofacilitate literature circle discussion groups. Educators monitor students' inquiry process and share responsibility for guiding and assessing students' graphic organizers, articles, and advertisements. They share responsibility for collating students' articles and advertisements by historical time period. This unit is designed to be cotaught with English-language arts and social studies teachers. It can be extended into a more in-depth inquiry.

Assessment

Students' notemaking and bibliography graphic organizers and rubrics, admit slips or topic selection graphic organizers, articles, advertisements, and rubrics show the process and results of their learning. (If educators choose to engage in the extension with students composing essays, they apply 6+1 Traits® or other rubric for these documents.)

Standards

Reading and writing keywords: Synthesize and make logical connections between ideas and details in several texts; synthesize research into a written or an oral presentation; extract information and use graphic organizers to comprehend text; connect information and events in text to related texts and sources.

Social studies keywords: Understand individuals, issues, and events that shaped U.S. history.

Educational technology keywords: Use technology tools to publish and present.

AASL STANDARDS INDICATORS*

- Find, evaluate, and select appropriate sources to answer questions. (1.1.4)
- Respect copyright/intellectual property rights of creators and producers. (1.3.1)
- Organize knowledge so that it is useful. (2.1.2)
- Use technology and other information tools to analyze and organize information. (2.1.4)
- Conclude an inquiry-based research process by sharing new understandings and reflecting on the learning. (3.1.1)
- Assess the quality and effectiveness of the learning product. (3.4.2)

PROCESS

This is an outline rather than a detailed procedure.

* Excerpted from *Standards for the 21st-Century Learner* by the American Association of School Librarians, a division of the American Library Association, copyright © 2007 American Library Association. Available for download at www.ala.org/aasl/standards. Used with permission.

DAY 1

PREPARATION

Educators booktalk historical fiction novels from the time period under study. (This will be different in different states. Select novels from the historical fiction text set as appropriate or identify others that align with social studies curriculum in your district.) Emphasize historical aspects of these stories. How was life different in that time period? What were the big issues and events of the day? Who were the most influential people? Students select and read novels. This can be done as individual reads or conducted in literature circle format.

As students read or as they come to the conclusion of the historical fiction novel reading period, they record ideas on the 9.1 Admit Slip, which they bring to the library at the beginning of the lesson (see the 9.1 Teacher Resource—Completed Admit Slip).

Note: If the language arts teacher is involved in the collaboration, the remainder of the unit is conducted after students read historical fiction novels and complete the 9.1 Admit Slip. If the collaboration is with social studies teachers only and students have not read a historical fiction novel, they complete the 9.1 Topic Selection Graphic Organizer after browsing trade books, reference books, and websites organized by historical time period.

MOTIVATION

Educators share newspaper articles or advertisements from an event that happened in their youth or in a previous historical time period. Emphasize how life was different in that time period, the big issues and events of the day, and the most influential people in the news. Respond to students' questions.

How do historical newspaper articles give modern-day readers a sense of "being there" in a previous time and place? How do advertisements put those events in a cultural context? How do historians use newspapers and other print media?

STUDENT-FRIENDLY OBJECTIVES
1. Respond to information about a historical event or person.
2. Complete a graphic organizer to identify elements in journalistic writing.

PRESENTATION

One or both educators read or tell about an event or person from history. (The teacher resources for this unit are based on the *March of the Mill Children* [Coleman] and *The Story of Mother Jones* [Koestler-Grack]. Educators may use the 9.1 Teacher Resource—Sample Essay—Person or the 9.1 Teacher Resource—Sample Essay—Event for the presentation.)

STUDENT PARTICIPATION PROCEDURES
1. After educator reads the question, think and discuss with a partner.
2. Raise hand to respond and suggest a note.
3. Circle the main ideas on the sample article.

Distribute and project the 9.1 Newspaper Article Graphic Organizer. Use the 9.1 Teacher Resource—Completed Newspaper Article Graphic Organizer for reference. Educators think aloud as they complete the graphic organizer. Involve students as appropriate.

Distribute the 9.1 Teacher Resource—Sample Newspaper Article. Educators use think-alouds as they begin to circle and label the main ideas as outlined on the 9.1 Newspaper Article Graphic Organizer. For example, circle Mother Jones and three children and write a label with the word *who*. Note the contents of three paragraphs written in journalistic style. Students continue on their own or with partners until they have identified all of the main ideas. Remind students that main ideas are based on the purpose for reading or writing. In this case, the main ideas are determined by the journalistic style of the learning product.

GUIDED PRACTICE

Educators support individuals or partners in identifying main ideas.

CLOSURE

Review the components in a journalistic style newspaper article. Ask students to identify the main ideas in the sample article, including a vivid verb.

DAYS 2, 3, AND 4

STUDENT-FRIENDLY OBJECTIVES

1. Clarify questions for inquiry.
2. Use the text set and Internet Pathfinder.
3. Make notes to answer questions.
4. Record bibliographic information.

PRESENTATION

Distribute the 9.1 Assignment Sheet and review the learning outcomes and products. (If students are not participating in the extension, distribute page 1 only.)

Educators lead students in a preview of the Historical Fiction Inquiry Pathfinder, locally accessible databases, and print resource text set. They note that students are not limited to the resources on the pathfinder. Show the sample newspaper clipping and period advertisements linked to the pathfinder.

Educators model using a notemaking and bibliography strategy to record their notes and sources on the category web. Remind students that the goal of this lesson is to follow the inquiry process. Students use their own questions, determine main ideas that align with the journalistic newspaper style, and synthesize information from multiple sources.

Begin day 3 by reviewing the 9.1 Notemaking and Bibliography Graphic Organizers Rubric. Begin day 4 by reviewing the 9.1 Newspaper Article Rubric and the 9.1 Newspaper Advertisement Rubric. Remind students that main ideas are based on the purpose for reading or writing. In this case, the main ideas are determined by the journalistic style of the learning products.

STUDENT PRACTICE PROCEDURES

1. Review inquiry questions.
2. Use the pathfinder and text set as places to begin.
3. Record information as notes.
4. Record bibliographic information.

GUIDED PRACTICE
Educators monitor students' search process, notemaking, and bibliography entries.

CLOSURE
Review the main ideas in journalistic style. Let students know they will be drafting their newspaper articles and designing their newspaper advertisements during the next class period. Students complete notemaking for homework.

DAY 5

PRESENTATION
Educators model synthesizing information. Project the 9.1 Teacher Resource—Completed Notemaking Graphic Organizer. Show how the notes on the organizer are from multiple resources. Highlight with different colors to show how various notes are connected. Show how the notes were synthesized from various sources to compose the 9.1 Teacher Resource—Sample Newspaper Article.

Students review their notes and complete the 9.1 Newspaper Article Graphic Organizer. Students organize the information into a three-paragraph article following journalistic style. They include their own interpretation of the significance of the event or person. Demonstrate how to find the day of the week for a particular date in history.

STUDENT-FRIENDLY OBJECTIVES
1. Review notes.
2. Complete the article graphic organizer.
3. Synthesize notes in order to compose paragraphs to answer questions.
4. Include own interpretation of the significance of the person or event.
5. Self-assess with the rubric.

GUIDED PRACTICE
Educators conference with students and refer to the 9.1 Newspaper Article Rubric as needed.

CLOSURE
Divide students into historical time periods. Students share their paragraphs with a partner or small group. Students brainstorm ideas for newspaper advertisements from that historical period. Students create advertisements for homework or in class the next day.

DAY 6

PRESENTATION
Educators demonstrate how to copy and paste their keyboarded article into the newspaper clipping generator, download, and save it as a .jpg file. (Watch out for apostrophes!) Submit the document or file. Educators compile students' articles in hard copy or electronically using a wiki or other Web 2.0 tool. Review the 9.1 Newspaper Advertisement Rubric.

STUDENT-FRIENDLY OBJECTIVES
1. Create a newspaper clipping, download, save, and submit the file.
2. Design the print portion of historical advertisement.
3. Draw by hand or use technology tools to illustrate the advertisement.
4. Self-assess with the rubric.

GUIDED PRACTICE
Educators conference with students as needed. Review the rubric as needed.

CLOSURE
Divide students into historical time periods. Using the inside-outside circle structure, students share their completed articles and advertisements (or in-progress advertisements) with partners as they rotate around the circle. Students submit their final advertisements the next day. Students respond to the reflection questions orally or in writing.

REFLECTION
How do we determine main ideas and interpret information? What does it mean to synthesize?

EXTENSIONS
Determine the best way to share students' work. Their articles and (scanned) advertisements can be displayed on the Web or in hard copy individually or collected into displays or books organized by historical time period.

Educators may choose to continue this unit. Students can extend their inquiry and compose in-depth essays to demonstrate their ability to synthesize information. They may also create individual or small group multimedia presentations to demonstrate their learning.

Educators continue to guide students as they distinguish between summaries and syntheses with interpretations. These two terms can be applied and reinforced in various projects in all content areas.

Reading Comprehension Strategy Seven
Synthesizing

Reading Development Level: Advanced

Instructional Strategies
Categorizing, Notemaking and Summarizing

Lesson Length
3 or 4 sessions (or more for the extensions)

Purpose
The purpose of this unit is to conduct an extended interpretation of a poem by developing interpretation questions, making notes on a graphic organizer, synthesizing information from multiple sources, and self-assessing using a checklist.

Objectives
At the end of this unit, students will be able to

1. Explicate a poem using fix-up options.
2. Identify areas of incomplete comprehension and develop questions to explore.
3. Conduct inquiry, make notes and record sources, and interpret findings.
4. Synthesize information from multiple sources to determine which piece of music best exemplifies the tone of the poem.

For extension:

1. Follow the writing process to compose an extended interpretation of the poem and music and the connections between the two.
2. Self-assess with a checklist or rubric.

Resources, Materials, and Equipment
Mentor text: Emily Dickinson poem "Part Four: Time and Eternity XXVII" from *The Complete Poems* (1924): www.bartleby.com/113/4027.html

Dickinson Pathfinder: www.storytrail.com/impact12/dickinson.htm

Dickinson and Classical Music Print and Electronic Text Set

Graphic organizers: 8.2 Fix-up Options Graphic Organizer, 8.2 Teacher Resource—Completed Fix-up Options Graphic Organizer, 9.2 Category Web, 9.2 Teacher Resource—Completed Category Web, 9.2 Category Matrix, 9.2 Teacher Resource—Completed Category Matrix, For extension: 9.2 Poem Interpretation Checklist

Overhead, Internet access, data projector, or interactive whiteboard

Collaboration

Educators model using the fix-up options strategy to determine questions for exploration. They also model synthesizing information from a variety of sources. They both monitor students' inquiry and writing processes. Educators share responsibility for guiding and assessing students' graphic organizers and interpretation paragraphs. They may decide to coteach the extension. This unit can be cotaught with English-language arts and/or music teachers.

Assessment

The students' fix-up options graphic organizers, category webs, and interpretation paragraphs show the process and results of their learning. If pursuing the extension, use the poem interpretation checklist, essay or multimedia project, and other rubrics as determined by the educators and demonstrate student learning.

Standards

Reading and writing keywords: Synthesize and make logical connections between ideas and details in several texts; support findings with textual evidence; synthesize research into a written or an oral presentation; extract information and use graphic organizers to comprehend text; connect information and events in text to related texts and sources.

Music keywords: Identify relationships between the content of other fine arts and other subjects and those of music.

AASL STANDARDS INDICATORS*

- Find, evaluate, and select appropriate sources to answer questions. (1.1.4)
- Respect copyright/intellectual property rights of creators and producers. (1.3.1)
- Organize knowledge so that it is useful. (2.1.2)
- Use technology and other information tools to analyze and organize information. (2.1.4)

Determine additional standards and indicators for extensions.

PROCESS

This is an outline rather than a detailed procedure.

DAY 1

MOTIVATION

Search YouTube and play theme songs from classic "scary" TV shows such as *The Addams Family, The Alfred Hitchcock Hour, The Munsters,* and *The Twilight Zone.* Educators share their interpretations of the tone of each piece. Then open up discussion with students. Think-pair-share. Ask: "How do students feel when listening to this music?" "What emotions were the composers trying to convey?" "What emotions are conveyed by the images that accompany the music?"

Sometimes it is easy to interpret music, a poem, or other text written or composed by a person from another generation. However, it can also be difficult, and the meaning of these texts can be misunderstood. One way to achieve deeper meaning is to analyze a piece of literature or music line by line, conduct

* Excerpted from *Standards for the 21st-Century Learner* by the American Association of School Librarians, a division of the American Library Association, copyright © 2007 American Library Association. Available for download at www.ala.org/aasl/standards. Used with permission.

research on the writer or musician, compare these works with other pieces of art, and synthesize and interpret the information.

Students analyze and interpret a poem, conduct an inquiry about the poet, and determine the best classical musical accompaniment for the poem based on further research and an aural interpretation of the music. The goal is to synthesize and interpret information from multiple sources.

Note: If educators have already taught the 8.2 advanced lesson, ask students to refer to the 8.2 Fix-up Options Graphic Organizer and record their initial interpretation and questions on the 9.2 Category Web. Proceed to day 2.

STUDENT-FRIENDLY OBJECTIVES
1. Use fix-up options to explicate the text line by line.
2. Record initial interpretation ideas.
3. Identify questions for exploration.

PRESENTATION
One educator reads Emily Dickinson's entire poem "Because I could not stop for Death." Students follow on individual or partner copies. Project the 9.2 Category Web and distribute individual copies to students. Educators model recording their initial interpretation on the category web in notemaking format, demonstrating that there is no one single interpretation of a piece of literature. Students record their responses.

Distribute and project the 8.2 Fix-up Options Graphic Organizer. In the first two stanzas, educators model using fix-up options to explicate the poem line by line. Use the 8.2 Teacher Resource—Completed Fix-up Options Graphic Organizer for reference. Record the fix-up options used with the example and circle portions of the text that may require further exploration. Record questions on the 9.2 Category Web. Students work with partners to complete the line-by-line explication. (See the 8.2 advanced lesson for a complete description of this portion of the lesson.)

STUDENT PARTICIPATION PROCEDURES
1. Read a line of text.
2. Think-pair-share.
3. Note which fix-up options were used.
4. Record examples on the graphic organizer.
5. Circle words and phrases that need further exploration.
6. Record these on the category matrix.

GUIDED PRACTICE
The educators support partners in explicating the poem on the 8.2 Fix-up Options Graphic Organizer and recording their initial interpretations and questions on the 9.2 Category Web.

CLOSURE
Review the questions posed by the educators from the first two stanzas. Discuss possible sources to answer these questions, build background, and arrive at a deeper understanding of the text. Ask students to volunteer to share some of their unanswered questions as well.

DAYS 2 AND 3

STUDENT-FRIENDLY OBJECTIVES
1. Follow a pathfinder to search for information.
2. Make notes to answer questions.
3. Record bibliographic information.
4. Record personal responses and interpretations of information.

PRESENTATION

Educators lead students in a preview of the Dickinson Pathfinder and the print and electronic text set. They model using a notemaking and bibliography strategy to record their notes and sources on the category web (see the 9.2 Teacher Resource—Completed Category Web).

As students conduct research, play each of the pieces of classical music. Write the name of the piece being played on the board and refer to it several times during the performance. If collaborating with a music teacher, he plays the pieces in music class and poses questions to stimulate students' interpretations.

STUDENT PRACTICE PROCEDURES
1. Review questions from the category matrix.
2. Use the pathfinder as a beginning resource.
3. Record information, personal responses, and interpretations as notes.
4. Record bibliographic information.

GUIDED PRACTICE

Educators monitor students' search process, notemaking, and bibliography entries.

CLOSURE

Review the distinction between information and interpretation. By day 3 ensure that in addition to recording information students are recording ideas, connections, feelings, or questions in their notes. If conducting the extension, distribute the checklist and ask students to use the checklist to assess their own progress.

DAY 4

PRESENTATION

Educators model responding to the question on the 9.2 Category Matrix. Which piece of music best captures the tone of Dickinson's poem and why? Justify response by including evidence from Dickinson's poem, background knowledge, and inferences made while reading the poem and listening to the music (see the 9.2 Teacher Resource—Completed Category Matrix). Offer students the opportunity to select a different piece of music with which to align their interpretation.

Students review their notes and entries on the 8.2 Fix-up Options Graphic Organizer, the 9.2 Category Web, and the 9.2 Category Matrix. They compose a paragraph to answer the question.

STUDENT-FRIENDLY OBJECTIVES
1. Review notes.
2. Complete the category web with key ideas and interpretations.
3. Compose a paragraph to answer the question.

GUIDED PRACTICE
Educators conference with students as needed. Remind students that synthesizing information from multiple sources and personal interpretation are goals for this work.

CLOSURE
Students share their paragraphs with a small group or use the inside-outside circle technique. They compare their interpretations with those of their classmates. Respond to the reflection questions orally or in writing.

REFLECTION
How do we determine when to delve more deeply into a portion of a text? Why is this important? What does it mean to synthesize and interpret information?

EXTENSIONS
Educators may choose to extend this unit into an in-depth inquiry. Students can read other poems by Dickinson, deepen their research about her work and personal life, and expand the musical choices for their interpretation. They can compose essays to show both synthesis and interpretation or create individual or small group multimedia products to demonstrate their understandings.

Educators continue to guide students as they distinguish between summaries and syntheses with interpretations. Students apply these strategies in various projects in all content areas.

LESSON PLAN 9.3

Reading Comprehension Strategy Seven
Synthesizing

Reading Development Level: Challenging

Instructional Strategies
Notemaking and Summarizing, Classifying

Lesson Length
5 or 6 sessions (in school) and homework (for wiki work)

Purpose
The purpose of this unit is to make notes, build, and synthesize background knowledge by using multiple sources in multiple formats, to present learning creatively using Web 2.0 tools, and to self-assess using a rubric and response sheet. These lessons can serve as preparation for engaging in a study of the literary figures of the Harlem Renaissance and their works, or as an introduction to the historical period in the United States immediately following World War I. It can also stand alone.

Objectives
At the end of this unit, students will be able to
1. Identify and describe the artistic, musical, and other cultural aspects of the Harlem Renaissance.
2. Make notes, cite sources, and organize information.
3. Identify and cite copyright-free images.
4. Synthesize and interpret information from multiple sources in multiple formats.
5. Create a wiki and deliver a technology-facilitated presentation.
6. Self-assess with a rubric and a response sheet.

Resources, Materials, and Equipment
Harlem: A Poem, by Walter Dean Myers, illustrated by Christopher Myers
YouTube video: "Harlem Renaissance" (4 minutes) www.youtube.com/
   watch?v=GlPaSgnjuOI&feature=fvw
Optional CD: *The Harlem Renaissance Remembered,* performed by Jonathan Gross and "Mack" Jay
   Jordon (58 minutes)
Optional DVD *Against the Odds: The Artists of the Harlem Renaissance* (based on the Newark Museum
   exhibit) (60 minutes)
Music by Billie Holiday
Harlem Renaissance Artists and Musicians Print and Electronic Text Set
Harlem Renaissance Pathfinder: www.storytrail.com/impact12/harlem.htm
Mentor text and sample wiki presentation: www.storytrail.com/impact12/holiday.htm

Graphic organizers: Notemaking Chart, 9.3 Teacher Resource—List of Artists and Musicians, 9.3 Notemaking Graphic Organizer, 9.3 Teacher Resource—Completed Notemaking Graphic Organizer, 9.3 Project Checklist, 9.3 Wiki Pages and Citations Rubric, 9.3 Presentation Response Sheet

Internet access and data projector, overhead, interactive whiteboard, CD player, or document camera if available

Collaboration

Educators demonstrate the importance of background knowledge in comprehending culture, including art, music, and literary works. They model synthesizing information from a variety of sources in a variety of formats. They monitor students' inquiry process and product making and share responsibility for guiding and assessing students' learning products. This unit can be cotaught with English-language arts or history teachers and lends itself to extending collaboration to include art and music teachers as well.

Assessment

Students' notemaking sheets, wiki presentations, rubrics, and response sheets show the process and results of their learning.

Standards

Reading and writing keywords: Synthesize and make logical connections between ideas and details in several texts; select a range of texts with different viewpoints on the same topic; support findings with textual evidence; synthesize research into a written or an oral presentation; extract information and use graphic organizers to comprehend text; connect information and events in text to related texts and sources.

Listening and speaking keywords: Listen responsively to a speaker; give presentations using informal, formal, and technical language effectively.

Social studies keywords: Use primary source materials (e.g., photos, artifacts, interviews, documents, and maps) and secondary source materials to study people and events from the past.

Educational technology keywords: Demonstrate functional operation of technology devices; design and create a multimedia presentation; publish and present.

AASL STANDARDS INDICATORS*

- Find, evaluate, and select appropriate sources to answer questions. (1.1.4)
- Respect copyright/intellectual property rights of creators and producers. (1.3.1)
- Organize knowledge so that it is useful. (2.1.2)
- Use technology and other information tools to analyze and organize information. (2.1.4)
- Conclude an inquiry-based research process by sharing new understandings and reflecting on the learning. (3.1.1)
- Assess the quality and effectiveness of the learning product. (3.4.2)

PROCESS

This is an outline rather than a detailed procedure. Depending on the time allotted and the level of collaboration between content area educators, this mini-unit can expand or contract as needed.

* Excerpted from *Standards for the 21st-Century Learner* by the American Association of School Librarians, a division of the American Library Association, copyright © 2007 American Library Association. Available for download at www.ala.org/aasl/standards. Used with permission.

DAY 1

MOTIVATION

Play music by Billie Holiday. Ask if students know this singer. Ask students what they know about present-day Harlem (the place). Educators share what they know as well.

Create a B-K-W-L-Q chart electronically or on the board. Involve students in the process of determining what they already know about the Harlem Renaissance or the time period (1917–1935) in U.S. history between World War I and World War II ("K" on the chart). While one educator leads the discussion, the other records what students know.

Define the Harlem Renaissance as a cultural revolution. Define culture as the languages, religions, arts, social life, and customs of a people. Play the YouTube video: "Harlem Renaissance" (www.youtube .com/watch?v=GlPaSgnjuOI&feature=fvw). One or both educators ask: "What's wrong with this video?" Answer: There are few captions and no citations!

One educator reads *Harlem: A Poem* (Myers/Myers). Project with a document camera if one is available. The other educator records what students learned about Harlem from the video and from Myers's book ("B" on the chart). Circle the names of people and places. Challenge students on the names with which they are unfamiliar. Finally, record students' questions about the places and people whose names they do not recognize ("W" on the chart). Use the notemaking formats on the Notemaking Chart.

Students study the artists and musicians of the Harlem Renaissance in order to build their background knowledge about Harlem culture during that time period.

Objectives for Parts 1 and 2

1. Evaluate a wiki presentation using a rubric.
2. Use ready-reference materials to locate brief information.
3. Determine a topic for study.

PART 1

PRESENTATION

In the library, computer lab, or wherever a class has access to five computers with small group work space, divide the class into five groups. Each group is responsible for one criterion on the 9.3 Wiki Pages and Citations Rubric. Play Billie Holiday music while students review their portion of the rubric. Ask again if students know the singer. (Billie Holiday was pictured in the YouTube video.) Present the sample wiki to the class: www.storytrail.com/impact12/holiday.htm. Educators model using the wiki as support for an extemporaneous presentation and take turns sharing information that relates to the questions developed for this study (see the 9.3 Teacher Resource—Completed Notemaking Graphic Organizer).

STUDENT PARTICIPATION PROCEDURES

1. Read assigned rubric criterion.
2. Collaborate as a group to assess the wiki presentation.
3. Circle score and make notes on the reverse side of the graphic organizer to cite evidence and justify the assessment.
4. Share with the entire class.

GUIDED PRACTICE
Educators monitor group work. Question students about the evidence they cite.

CLOSURE
Each group shares the score it was assigned and gives a justification for the score citing evidence from the wiki. Educators share their comments as well and let students know this is how they will self-assess their own projects. Share what they learned about Billie Holiday and the Harlem Renaissance from this wiki presentation. Add to the "B" on the B-K-W-L-Q.

PART 2

PRESENTATION
Review the list of Harlem Renaissance artists and musicians. Educators lead a discussion regarding strategies for locating ready reference. Educators model how to skim and scan for background information *before* choosing a person to study.

MODELING
Link to the Harlem Renaissance Pathfinder and review the names of artists and musicians, website links, databases, and free-range web searching. Create and share a print and electronic text set of books and resources on this topic. (See possible resources linked from the wiki home page.) Educators booktalk a selection of titles or describe the genres in the text set and model using an advanced Google search and Wikipedia to skim and scan for basic background information.

STUDENT PARTICIPATION PROCEDURES
1. Skim and scan for information.
2. Record top three artists or musicians for study.

GUIDED PRACTICE
Educators monitor students skimming and scanning web and print resources and recording their top three choices.

CLOSURE
What are the advantages of ready-reference sources? What are their limitations? Students turn in their topic choices. Educators assign partners based on students' choices and effective collaborative relationships.

Objectives for Parts 3–5
1. Conduct an inquiry guided by a rubric.
2. Locate, record, and interpret information.
3. Create and present a wiki presentation.
4. Respond to classmates' presentations and self-assess.

PART 3

INQUIRY

Announce the partnerships and provide students with graphic organizers and rubrics electronically or in print. Students may also work individually.

MODELING

Educators role-play developing questions through think-alouds. Project the 9.3 Notemaking Graphic Organizer and record questions, notes, and sources. Reinforce the idea that synthesizing is more than summarizing. Indicate interpretations in bold font (see the 9.3 Teacher Resource—Completed Notemaking Graphic Organizer).

Project and review the 9.3 Project Checklist. Review the copyright-free image captions and citations on the Billie Holiday wiki pages. Link to the URLs for the images. Note the copyright information on each. Discuss strategies for locating copyright-free images, including Wikimedia Commons and the Library of Congress. Educators use think-alouds to share the process of selecting an appropriate image.

STUDENT PARTICIPATION PROCEDURES

1. Develop questions about the topic.
2. Record questions, notes, references, and links to person's background information or artistic works on the graphic organizer.
3. Record interpretations with bold font.
4. Locate copyright-free images and record URLs.

GUIDED PRACTICE

Educators conference with students to monitor students' inquiry process.

CLOSURE

Partners share their successes and challenges in small groups or with the whole class. Educators announce a deadline for completing the inquiry. Project and review the 9.3 Wiki Pages and Citations Rubric.

PART 4

PREPARATION

Create wiki presentation spaces. Educators demonstrate how to set up a wiki home page, edit it, add a wiki page, and insert images. Students create wiki pages with educators' guidance or for homework.

PRESENTATION

After students have completed their independent inquiry, educators model synthesizing information. Project the sample wiki and the 9.3 Teacher Resource—Completed Notemaking Graphic Organizer. Discuss how information came from various sources as noted. Emphasize how interpretation of the information is included. Review each of the pages on the sample wiki, including the Works Consulted and Works Cited. Teach or review how to use an online citation maker.

STUDENT PRACTICE PROCEDURES
1. Review the rubric criteria.
2. Create and compose wiki pages including a Works Cited/Works Consulted wiki page.
3. Insert, caption, and link images.
4. Self-assess product with the rubric.

GUIDED PRACTICE
Educators conference with partners, monitor students' work based on the rubric criteria, and reinforce the overarching objectives for this work: synthesizing information from multiple sources, analyzing, and interpreting it to draw conclusions.

CLOSURE
Students e-mail their wiki URL to the educators who link them all from the Harlem Renaissance Virtual Museum, a wiki created by the educators for this purpose. Review the goal of sharing an extemporaneous talk rather than reading wiki pages. Students practice their presentations in class or for homework.

PART 5 ....

PRESENTATIONS
Student partners share their wikis with small groups in a museum format with presentation stations scattered around the library. Each student completes a portion of the 9.3 Presentation Response Sheet after they view/hear each presentation. They also complete a self-reflection on the process and product of learning. Partners self-assess their wikis using the 9.3 Wiki Pages and Citations Rubric. Educators use the same rubric.

REFLECTION
What did you learn about the artists and musicians and Harlem Renaissance culture? Describe the process of synthesizing information from multiple sources. What questions are still unanswered? What can we do about that?

If continuing with the extension: How could this background knowledge help you better understand the literature, people, or events of this time period?

FURTHER COLLABORATION
Involve art and music teachers in spotlighting the visual artists and musicians of the Harlem Renaissance before, during, or after this unit of study.

EXTENSIONS
Continue this study by reading and discussing the work of Harlem Renaissance writers or study U.S. history and culture immediately following World War I. Make connections with background knowledge built during this initial inquiry project. An optional or additional introduction to this lesson is to view, make notes on key ideas, and discuss the DVD *Against the Odds: The Artists of the Harlem Renaissance* (60 minutes). This resource can be shared in the art, language arts, or history classroom.

Continue to use graphic organizers that indicate students' use of multiple resources in inquiry projects. Reinforce that synthesis is more than a summary of information from multiple texts because it includes the inquirer's own interpretations.

References

Abilock, Debbie, ed. 2008. Visual literacy. *Knowledge Quest* 36 (3).

———. 2010. Film in education: Visual literacy with moving images. *Knowledge Quest* 38 (4).

Abilock, Debbie, and Gail Bush, eds. 2009. The issue is questions. *Knowledge Quest* 38 (1).

Achterman, Douglas L. 2008. Haves, halves, and have-nots: School libraries and student achievement in California. Denton, TX. UNT Digital Library. http://digital.library.unt.edu/ark:/67531/metadc9800/m1/.

———. 2010. 21st-century literacy leadership. *School Library Monthly* 26 (10): 41–43.

Alger, Christianna. 2009. Content area reading strategy knowledge transfer from preservice to first-year teaching. *Journal of Adolescent & Adult Literacy* 53 (1): 60–69.

Allen, Janet. 2004. *Tools for teaching content literacy.* Portland, ME: Stenhouse.

Allington, Richard L. 2001. *What really matters for struggling readers.* New York: Addison Wesley Longman.

American Association of School Librarians (AASL). 2007. *Standards for the 21st-century learner.* http://ala.org/aasl/standards/.

———. 2009a. *Empowering learners: Guidelines for school library media programs.* Chicago: American Association of School Librarians.

———. 2009b. *Position statement on the school librarian's role in reading.* http://ala.org/ala/mgrps/divs/aasl/aaslissues/positionstatements/roleinreading.cfm.

Anderson, Lorin W., David R. Krathwohl, Peter W. Airasian, and Kathleen A. Cruikshank. 2001. *Taxonomy for learning, teaching and assessing: A revision of Bloom's taxonomy of educational objectives.* New York: Longman.

Barth, Roland S. 2006. Improving relationships within the schoolhouse. *Educational Leadership* 63 (6): 9–13.

Beck, Isabel L., Margaret G. McKeown, Rebecca L. Hamilton, and Linda Kucan. 1997. *Questioning the author: An approach to enhancing student engagement with text.* Newark, DE: International Reading Association.

Biancarosa, Gina, and Catherine E. Snow. 2006. *Reading next—A vision for action and research in middle and high school literacy: A report to the Carnegie Corporation of New York.* 2nd ed. Washington, DC: Alliance for Excellence in Education.

Bloom, Benjamin S., ed. 1956. *A taxonomy of educational objectives: Handbook I. The cognitive domain.* New York: David McKay.

Brozo, William G., and Michele L. Simpson. 2007. *Content literacy for today's adolescents: Honoring diversity and building competence*. New York: Teachers College Press.

Buehl, Doug. 2009. *Classroom strategies for interactive learning*. Newark, DE: International Reading Association.

Carnegie Council on Advancing Adolescent Literacy. 2010. *Time to act: An agenda for advancing adolescent literacy for college and career success*. New York: Carnegie Corporation of New York. http://carnegie.org/fileadmin/Media/Publications/PDF/tta_Lee.pdf.

Coiro, Julie, Michele Knobel, Collin Lankshear, and Donald J. Leu, eds. 2008. *Handbook of research on new literacies*. New York: Lawrence Erlbaum.

Cope, Bill, and Mary Kalantzis. 1999. Designs for social futures. In *Multiliteracies: Literacy learning and the design of social futures*, ed. B. Cope and M. Kalantzis, 203–34. New York: Routledge.

Daniels, Harvey. 2002. *Literature circles: Voice and choice in book clubs and reading groups*. Portland, ME: Stenhouse.

Dow, Mirah. 2010. Taking the lead: School library leadership at the university level. *School Library Monthly* 27 (3): 36–38.

DuFour, Richard. 2001. In the right context: The effective leader concentrates on a foundation of programs, procedures, beliefs, expectations, and habits. *Journal of Staff Development* 22 (1): 14–17.

Dweck, Carol. 2006. *MindSet: The new psychology of success*. New York: Random House.

Echevarria, Jana, MaryEllen Vogt, and Deborah J. Short. 2008. *Making content comprehensible for English language learners: The SIOP model*. 3rd ed. Boston: Allyn and Bacon.

Education Northwest. 2011. 6+1 Trait® Rubrics. http://educationnorthwest.org/resource/464.

Fisher, Douglas, and Nancy Frey. 2009. *Background knowledge: The missing piece of the comprehension puzzle*. Portsmouth, NH: Heinemann.

Fisher, Douglas, Nancy Frey, and Diane Lapp. 2009. *In a reading state of mind: Brain research, teacher modeling, and comprehension instruction*. Newark, DE: International Reading Association.

Foer, Joshua. 2006. How to win the world memory championship. *Discover: Science, Technology and the Future* 27 (4): 62–67.

Fontichiaro, Kristin, Judi Moreillon, and Debbie Abilock. 2009. The school librarian's bill of responsibilities. *Knowledge Quest* 38 (2): 61.

Fresch, Mary Jo, and Peggy Harkins. 2009. *The power of picture books: Using content area literature in middle school*. Urbana, IL: NCTE.

Friend, Marilyn, and Lynne Cook. 2010. *Interactions: Collaboration skills for school professionals*. 6th ed. Boston: Pearson.

Fullan, Michael. 2003. *Change forces with a vengeance*. London: Routledge Farmer.

Gardner, Howard. 1993. *Multiple intelligences: The theory in practice*. New York: Basic Books.

Graham, Steve, and Michael Hebert. 2010. *Writing to read: Evidence for how writing can improve reading*. New York: Carnegie Corporation of New York. http://www.all4ed.org/files/WritingToRead.pdf.

Guthrie, John T., and Allan Wigfield. 2000. Engagement and motivation in reading. In *Handbook of Reading Research*, volume 3, ed. M. L. Kamil and P. B. Mosenthal, 403–22. Mahwah, NJ: Lawrence Erlbaum.

Hall, Susan. 2007. *Using picture books to teach literary devices*, volume 4. Westport, CT: Libraries Unlimited.

Harada, Violet H., and Joan M. Yoshina. 2005. *Assessing learning: Librarians and teachers as partners*. Westport, CT: Libraries Unlimited.

Harvey, Stephanie, and Anne Goudvis. 2000. *Strategies that work: Teaching comprehension to enhance understanding*. Portland, ME: Stenhouse.

Haven, Kendall. 2007. *Story proof: The science behind the startling power of story*. Westport, CT: Libraries Unlimited.

Haystead, Mark W., and Robert J. Marzano. 2009. *Meta-analytic synthesis of studies conducted at Marzano Research Laboratory on instructional strategies*. Englewood, CO: Marzano Research Laboratory.

Hunter, Madeline. 1994. *Mastery teaching*. Thousand Oaks, CA: Corwin Press.

Jacobs, Heidi L. M., and Dale Jacobs. 2009. Transforming the one-shot library session into pedagogical collaboration: Information literacy and the English composition class. *Reference & User Services Quarterly* 49 (1): 72–82.

Johnston, Peter. 2004. *Choice words: How our language affects children's learning*. Portland, ME: Stenhouse.

Keene, Ellin Oliver, and Susan Zimmermann. 1997. *Mosaic of thought: Teaching comprehension in a reader's workshop*. Portsmouth, NH: Heinemann.

Koechlin, Carol, and Sandi Zwaan. 2006. *Q tasks: How to empower students to ask questions and care about answers*. Markham, ON: Pembroke.

Krashen, Stephen D. 2004. *The power of reading: Insights from the research*. Westport, CT: Libraries Unlimited.

Laird, Jennifer, Gregory Kienzl, Matthew DeBell, and Chris Chapman. 2007. *Dropout rates in the United States: 2005*. Washington, DC: National Center for Educational Statistics.

Leu, Donald J., Jill Castek, Douglas Hartman, Julie Coiro, Laurie Henry, Jonna Kulikowich, and Stacy Lyver. 2005. Evaluating the development of scientific knowledge and new forms of reading comprehension during online learning. Research report presented at the North Central Regional Education Laboratory, Chicago. http://www.newliteracies.uconn.edu/ncrel.html.

Leu, Donald J., Lisa Zawilinski, Jill Castek, Manju Banerjee, Brian C. Housand, Yingjie Liu, and Maureen O'Neil. 2007. What is new about the new literacies of online reading comprehension? In *Secondary school literacy: What research reveals for classroom practice*, ed. L. S. Rush, A. J. Eakle, and A. Berger, 37–68. Urbana, IL: National Council of Teachers of English.

Levitov, Deborah D. 2009. *Perspectives of school administrators related to school library media programs after participating in an online course, "School Library Advocacy for Administrators."* Unpublished doctoral dissertation. University of Missouri–Columbia.

Loertscher, David V. 2000. *Taxonomies of the school library media program*. Salt Lake City: Hi Willow.

Loertscher, David V., Carol Koechlin, and Sandi Zwaan. 2004. *Ban those bird units: 15 models for teaching and learning in information-rich and technology-rich environments*. Salt Lake City: Hi Willow.

———. 2008. *The new learning commons: Where learners win*. Salt Lake City: Hi Willow.

Manzo, Anthony V. 1969. The request procedure. *The Journal of Reading* 13 (2): 123–26.

Marzano, Robert J. 2003. *What works in schools: Translating research into action*. Alexandria, VA: Association for Supervision and Curriculum Development.

———. 2004. *Building background knowledge for academic achievement: Research on what works in schools*. Alexandria, VA: Association for Supervision and Curriculum Development.

Marzano, Robert. J., Debra J. Pickering, and Jane E. Pollock. 2001. *Classroom instruction that works: Research-based strategies for increasing student achievement*. Alexandria, VA: Association for Supervision and Curriculum Development.

McEwan, Elaine K. 2007. *40 ways to support struggling readers in content classrooms, grades 6–12*. Thousand Oaks, CA: Corwin Press.

McGee, Lea M., and Donald J. Richgels. 1996. *Literacy's beginnings: Supporting young readers and writers*. 2nd ed. Boston: Allyn and Bacon.

McKenzie, Jamie A. 1997. Questioning toolkit. *From Now On: The Educational Technology Journal* 7 (3). http://fno.org/nov97/toolkit.html.

———. 2009. Connecting the dots. *Knowledge Quest* 38 (1): 32–39.

Moreillon, Judi. 2004. Behind the masks: Exploring culture and self through art and poetry. ReadWriteThink.org. http://www.readwritethink.org/classroom-resources/lesson-plans/behind-masks-exploring-culture-395.html.

———. 2007. *Collaborative strategies for teaching reading comprehension: Maximizing your impact*. Chicago: ALA Editions.

———. 2008. Two heads are better than one: The factors influencing the understanding and practice of classroom-library collaboration. *School Library Media Research* 11, http://ala.org/ala/mgrps/divs/aasl/aaslpubsandjournals/slmrb/slmrcontents/volume11/moreillon.cfm.

National Center for Education Statistics (NCES). 2005. *A first look at the literacy of America's adults in the 21st century*. Washington, DC: U.S. Government Printing Office. http://nces.ed.gov/pubsearch/pubsinfo.asp?pubid=2006470.

National Research Council (NRC). 2000. How people learn: Brain, mind, experience, and school. Committee on Developments in Science of Learning, ed. John D. Bransford, Ann L. Brown, and Rodney R. Cocking. *Commission on Behavior and Social Sciences and Education*. Washington, DC: National Academy Press. http://www.nap.edu/openbook.php?record_id=6160.

Ouzts, Dan T. 1998. Enhancing literacy using the question-answer relationship. *Social Studies and the Young Learner* 10 (4): 26–28.

Palinscar, Annemarie S., and Ann L. Brown. 1986. Interactive teaching to promote independent learning from text. *The Reading Teacher* 39 (8): 771–77.

Partnership for 21st Century Skills (P21). 2006. *Results that matter: 21st century skills in high school reform.* http://www.21stcenturyskills.org.

RAND Reading Study Group. 2002. *Reading for understanding: Toward an R&D program in reading comprehension.* Santa Monica, CA: RAND.

Rosenblatt, Louise M. 1978. *The reader, the text, the poem: The transactional theory of the literary work.* Carbondale: Southern Illinois University Press.

———. 1995. *Literature as exploration.* 5th ed. New York: Modern Language Association of America.

Ryan, Mary. 2008. Engaging middle years students: Literacy projects that matter. *Journal of Adolescent & Adult Literacy* 52 (3): 190–201.

Schmoker, Mike. 2006. *Results now: How we can achieve unprecedented improvements in teaching and learning.* Alexandria, VA: Association for Supervision and Curriculum Development.

———. 2011. *Focus: Elevating the essentials to radically improve student learning.* Alexandria, VA: Association for Supervision and Curriculum Development.

Sipe, Rebecca Bowers. 2009. *Adolescent literacy at risk? The impact of standards.* Urbana, IL: NCTE.

Sousa, David A. 2005. *How the brain learns to read.* Thousand Oaks, CA: Corwin Press.

Sparks, Dennis. 2007. *Leading for results: Transforming teaching, learning, and relationships in schools.* 2nd ed. Thousand Oaks, CA: Corwin Press.

Stahl, Katherine A. Dougherty. 2005. Improving the asphalt of reading instruction: A tribute to the work of Steven A. Stahl. *Reading Teacher* 59 (2): 184–91.

Stripling, Barbara. 2003. Inquiry-based learning. In *Curriculum connections through the library,* ed. B. K. Stripling and S. Hughes-Hassell, 3–39. Westport, CT: Libraries Unlimited.

———. 2008. Inquiry: Inquiring minds want to know. *School Library Media Activities Monthly* 25 (1): 2, 50–51.

Trilling, Bernie, and Charles Fadel. 2009. *21st century skills: Learning for life in our times.* San Francisco: Jossey-Bass.

Wald, Penelope J., and Michael S. Castleberry, eds. 2000. *Educators as learners: Creating a professional learning community in your school.* Alexandria, VA: Association for Supervision and Curriculum Development.

Wells, Gordon. 1986. *The meaning makers: Children learning language and using language to learn.* Portsmouth, NH: Heinemann.

Wiggins, Grant, and Jay McTighe. 2005. *Understanding by design.* 2nd ed. Alexandria, VA: Association for Supervision and Curriculum Development.

Wilhelm, Jeffrey D. 2002. *Action strategies for deepening comprehension: Role plays, text structure tableaux, talking statues, and other enrichment techniques that engage students with text.* New York: Scholastic Professional Books.

Wilhelm, Jeffrey D., Tanya N. Baker, and Julie Dube. 2001. *Strategic reading: Guiding students to lifelong literacy 6–12.* Portsmouth, NH: Heinemann.

Wolfe, Patricia. 2001. *Brain matters: Translating research into classroom practice.* Alexandria, VA: Association for Supervision and Curriculum Development.

Zimmermann, Susan, and Chryse Hutchins. 2003. *7 keys to comprehension: How to help your kids read it and get it!* New York: Three Rivers Press.

Zmuda, Alison, and Violet H. Harada. 2008. *Librarians as learning specialists: Meeting the learning imperative for the 21st century.* Westport, CT: Libraries Unlimited.

Index

You may also be interested in

COLLABORATIVE STRATEGIES FOR TEACHING READING COMPREHENSION
Maximizing Your Impact

Judi Moreillon

"Bravo to Judi Moreillon for emphasizing the teacher part of teacher-librarian, for providing a practical guide for effective collaborative teaching, and for helping teacher-librarians assume a leadership role in their school's literacy efforts." – *Teacher Librarian*

PRINT: 978-0-8389-0929-4
170 PGS / 8.5" X 11"

A YEAR OF PROGRAMS FOR TEENS 2

AMY J. ALESSIO AND KIMBERLY A. PATTON

ISBN-13: 978-0-8389-1051-1

HOMEWORK HELP FROM THE LIBRARY

CAROL F. INTNER

ISBN-13: 978-0-8389-1046-7

TECHNOLOGY AND LITERACY

JENNIFER NELSON AND KEITH BRAAFLADT

ISBN-13: 978-0-8389-1108-2

YOUNG ADULT LITERATURE

MICHAEL CART

ISBN-13: 978-0-8389-1045-0

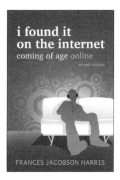

I FOUND IT ON THE INTERNET, 2E

FRANCES JACOBSON HARRIS

ISBN-13: 978-0-8389-1066-5

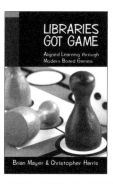

LIBRARIES GOT GAME

BRIAN MAYER AND CHRISTOPHER HARRIS

ISBN-13: 978-0-8389-1009-2

Order today at **alastore.ala.org** or **866-746-7252!**

ALA Store purchases fund advocacy, awareness, and accreditation programs for library professionals worldwide.